John Lewis is a 73-year-old widower who lives in the market town of Somerton, Somerset. He has two sons and six grandchildren. He spends two days a week as a Volunteer Driver transporting patients to and from hospital.

He spends much of his free time walking with his partner and her rescue German shepherd. He is a recent convert to Yoga and loves modern line dancing but doesn't tell anyone because his grandson thinks it's not cool! He also sponsors a charity based in Luhimba, a small village 600 miles south of Dar Salaam, in Tanzania.

Dedicated to my dear late wife, Patricia.

John H J Lewis

AEROPLANES AND AN ANGEL

AUSTIN MACAULEY PUBLISHERS
LONDON * CAMBRIDGE * NEW YORK * SHARJAH

Copyright © John H J Lewis 2025

The right of John H J Lewis to be identified as the author of this work has been asserted by the author in accordance with sections 77 and 78 of the Copyright, Designs and Patents Act 1988.

All rights reserved. No part of this publication may be reproduced, stored in a retrieval system, or transmitted in any form or by any means, electronic, mechanical, photocopying, recording, or otherwise, without the prior permission of the publishers.

Any person who commits any unauthorised act in relation to this publication may be liable to criminal prosecution and civil claims for damages.

All of the events in this memoir are true to the best of author's memory. The views expressed in this memoir are solely those of the author.

A CIP catalogue record for this title is available from the British Library.

ISBN 9781035890705 (Paperback)
ISBN 9781035890712 (ePub e-book)

www.austinmacauley.com

First Published 2025
Austin Macauley Publishers Ltd®
1 Canada Square
Canary Wharf
London
E14 5AA

Table of Contents

Prologue 12

Chapter One: Secondary Technical Schooling 17

Chapter Two: Royal Air Force Station Cosford 21

Chapter Three: Royal Air Force Station Lyneham 34
   An Accidental Flight in a Lightning Jet 44
   Bomb Threat in the Atlantic 46

Chapter Four: Royal Air Force Station Masirah 49
   Cardinal Puff 61
   Rumbo 62
   Fizz Buzz 62

Chapter Five: Back Home 67
   The Near Cross-Channel Disaster 67

Chapter Six: Royal Air Force Station Colerne 72
   Cyprus—A Brief History 76
   Heathrow Plane Spotting 76

Chapter Seven: The Happiest Day of My Life 78

Chapter Eight: Royal Air Force Station Akrotiri 84

Chapter Nine: Royal Air Force Station Wattisham 90

Chapter Ten: Royal Air Force Station Lyneham   **92**

   Our First Home Together   *96*

Chapter Eleven: Search & Rescue Helicopter Cross-Training   **113**

   Royal Air Force Station Cosford   *113*

   HMS Daedalus   *114*

   Westland Helicopters Ltd   *117*

   RNAS Culdrose   *119*

Chapter Twelve: Royal Air Force Station Boulmer   **125**

   A Disaster in the North Sea   *134*

Chapter Thirteen: Royal Air Force Station Laarbruch   **141**

   Ground Defence Training   *154*

   World War Three!   *155*

   West Berlin   *158*

   The Berlin Blockade   *162*

   Checkpoint Charlie   *165*

   The Stasi   *168*

   Holidays   *178*

   The Reichwald Forest War Cemetery   *184*

   Overloon National War and Resistance Museum   *184*

   The Airborne Museum and the War Cemetery at Oosterbeek   *185*

Chapter Fourteen: Royal Air Force Station Cosford   **189**

   Gnat Line   *190*

Chapter Fifteen: Royal Air Force Station Stanley   **200**

   The Gurkhas   *208*

Chapter Sixteen: Back to Cosford   **212**

   Air Radio Techniques Flight   *212*

Chapter Seventeen: Royal Air Force Station Wildenrath   **217**

    Accommodation Challenges, Bauxhof, Erklenz   *221*

    June 1987—The Heron Road Nightmare   *224*

    Deutsche Wanderung   *229*

    A Mad Chase down the Autobahn   *229*

    August 1989—Harrier Way   *230*

    Exercise Red Flag (Nellis AFB, USA)   *231*

    Terrorist Atrocities   *231*

    The Soviet Block Dissolves and the Wall Comes Down   *235*

    Gulf War One—The Invasion of Kuwait   *236*

    11 August 1990   *237*

Chapter Eighteen: Royal Air Force Station Wattisham   **240**

    Number 56 Squadron   *240*

    Number 74 (F) Squadron—The Fighting Tigers   *241*

    My First Fighter Squadron   *241*

    Fred Page   *246*

    The Bevin Boys   *246*

    Squadron Detachments   *248*

Chapter Nineteen: Royal Air Force Station Honington   **255**

Chapter Twenty: Royal Air Force Station Swanton Morley   **258**

Chapter Twenty-One: Royal Air Force Station Wyton   **263**

Chapter Twenty-Two: A New Beginning   **266**

Chapter Twenty-Three: St Athan   **270**

Chapter Twenty-Four: Our Last Move   **275**

Chapter Twenty-Five: The End of My World   **278**

Chapter Twenty-Six: The Saddest Day of My Life   **293**

Goodbye, My Darling	*297*
Chapter Twenty-Seven: And Where to Now?	**306**
Just a Drop	*307*
Chapter Twenty-Eight: Being Widowed	**311**
Chapter Twenty-Nine: A New Beginning?	**316**
Chapter Thirty: Philosophy for Old Age	**317**
The Train	**319**

Dedicated to my darling Patricia.
She fills my dreams like she filled my life; night and day I love her.

Prologue

Following a conversation with my sister Wendy, I commented that I could remember precisely where I was in the world, and what job I was doing in any month or year going right back to my school days. She suggested that I start a diary, which I did. But after a short while, it seemed somewhat pointless because the more I wrote the more events sprang to mind.

I'd often thought about documenting my life as a member of the Royal Air Force. More importantly, since Trisha passed away from Pancreatic Cancer in March 2009, I wanted to put on record my extraordinary time with her; she was the true love of my life. We travelled extensively throughout the UK and Europe both at work and play, not only with Michael and Steven but also once they'd left home and started their own journeys through life.

I thought the first few lines would be the hardest to write. Where do I start? How do I begin to tell you about my life, my feelings and more especially my emotions associated with living with such a beautiful person? Our lives form just the minutest fraction of the blink of an eye in space and time. I feel so privileged and thankful to have been able to spend those 34 years with Trisha. She was gorgeous and I know I'll see her again—but not just yet.

I'm not really sure whether many outside of the family circle will be interested in my life. However, my intention with this chronicle is to leave a legacy of my memories to Michael and Steven and the grandchildren Jacob, Charlotte, Millie, Ellen, Aleix and Elys. In doing so, I've tried to log as much as I can possibly remember. Hopefully, without exaggeration, fibs or misrepresentation and trust, it will give whoever reads it, an idea of the type of work I did before and after meeting my *Guardian Angel*.

Some may say that my recollection of events could possibly be construed as a fabrication and physiologists have suggested that some memories, in our mind's eye, feel like we're watching a film. These memories are then reconstructed from the little bits of information that we've saved, put back together and the brain then fills in the missing parts possibly resulting in the creation of false memories. In my case, I don't believe that to be so.

I firmly believe that some of what I experienced really couldn't have been made up. Some of the explanations, passages and facts may also seem irrelevant. But I've tried to put into context, militarily that is, what went on in a specific geographical area before, during and where appropriate, after my tour of duty.

It will hopefully give a good background to Michael and Steven and maybe trigger memories and kindle some thoughts of their own. It will also help to explain why we moved around as frequently as we did. Also, what it was like to be a member of the armed forces living and working throughout a large part of the Cold War with the Soviet Union and the Warsaw Pact countries.

I trust it will explain, how our nomadic lifestyle affected us as a family, and most of all, I sincerely hope the story doesn't come across as boring!

As members of the military, we were paid to go into harm's way but whilst I never directly took part in any war or conflict, it really was just a case of being in the right place at the right time, the wrong place at the wrong time or any other permutation—whatever is your perspective. The major struggles and conflicts that took place during my service were in Northern Ireland, Cyprus, The Falklands, Bosnia, Oman, Kuwait, Operation Desert Storm (Gulf Wars 1 and 2,) Croatia and Serbia and not forgetting the Cold War.

It's been said that people join the armed forces knowing full well that they may lose their lives in defence of the Queen and country—that's probably always been true and never more so than today. But the thought never entered my mind when first I joined. It was just another job and, in those days, the main thrust of any recruiting advert was to *join the RAF and see the world.*

In some respects, I think it would have been interesting to find out how effective my training had been by being directly involved in a war or skirmish. But there again, what if the training had turned out to be crap and I really didn't learn very much.

My story will also illustrate some of the trials and tribulations associated with living in married quarters and the many constraints imposed on us. I've heard it said that as a member of the armed forces my family and I lived rent-free—not so, we paid the going rate of rent. In total, we lived in 10 service houses and had four homes of our own in the 34 years we were together.

During my 29 years in the RAF, I served on 17 stations and on two occasions I returned to the same unit. Trisha *Followed the Flag* for 22 of those 29 years.

She fully supported me in my job, never questioning or complaining when I was called away on detachments or trips away or indeed when we had to up sticks and move yet again.

I think she actually looked forward to a change of scenery. Even after leaving the RAF, the travelling continued, firstly to South Wales and then to South Somerset—a beautiful county. I hope the boys have some really good memories, I certainly have and I know Trisha did.

I know that all relationships have their ups and downs and don't always meet our expectations. Ours was certainly no different to the norm. However, Trisha and I both tried our very best to bring up the boys in a stable and loving environment. An environment which would help them to achieve their own dreams and aspirations, enabling them to turn out to be decent human beings. I'm pleased to say they genuinely are and make us proud of them and they of us.

Trisha was a truly beautiful mother and wife, who unfortunately, didn't have the best of health for the later part of her life following the eventual realisation that she had developed Myalgic Encephalomyelitis (ME)—more about that later. She was of the old school when it came to cooking. She studied nutrition and cookery, achieved an O-level at school and learnt a lot from her mother; always cooking meals from scratch and not relying on the pre-packed, Convenience rubbish.

The boys were always well clothed, although I must admit, not always with the most expensive or fashionable of items. Trisha was always there for us and she especially made our lives a joy. She had such a very quiet, gentle and placid nature and she really was all things bright and beautiful. On the other hand, she could also, very occasionally, fly off the handle at me or the boys but her annoyance never lasted for very long before returning to her normal tranquil self.

We both believed that a fair amount of discipline was necessary and I sincerely hope that Mike and Steve don't despise us too much for doing what may have appeared at the time to be cruel or heartless. If something specific was wanted then it had to be earned and not just given to keep the peace.

Judging by some of the selfish and spoilt kids we've met, I think that philosophy has rubbed off and helped Michael and Julie do such a good job with Jacob, Charlotte and Millie. I know that as I type this journal, Francesca has, and now Steven and she together are doing just the same with Ellen, Aleix and Elys. I also know Trisha would have absolutely loved Francesca.

If I could have my time over, I'd marry Trisha again, *without hesitation*, and have the same two sons. There would be no pre-conditions, no ifs or buts. However, there is one thing I would do differently and that would be for me to be far more tolerant and patient with her and not to take her for granted as much as I did.

That said, our marriage was one built on trust and honesty. Each and every day one or the other of us would reaffirm their love for each other. Throughout our married life, there were very few days when those three little words weren't spoken. Call me a soppy romantic but Trisha meant the absolute world to me.

It's been said countless times before by people from all walks of life that we tend to hurt those that we really love. All couples argue; it is a natural and healthy expression of needs and wants in a relationship and not necessarily a sign that there is something wrong. That was never more evident than when we lived in South Wales where I said a terribly cruel thing to Trisha.

Whilst I appreciate that it's no defence for being malevolent, I believe it was due to the incredibly rough time that I was going through with my bullying, drunken, alcoholic manager. I'd developed an inguinal hernia which was brought on by my endless coughing due to others smoking in the crew room. My skin cancer had surfaced again and I was in constant pain both day and night. I eventually underwent painful radiotherapy treatment every day for a week.

We were also both extremely concerned for Steven who'd left home two weeks before his seventeenth birthday. Trisha and I bought and insured a small car that would at least give him a certain degree of independence. He'd secured a job with Aire Valley Tree Surgeons in Leeds and went through challenges that would have tried even the most stoic of people.

Apart from the crap pay and working conditions, he witnessed an armed robbery of a post office. He missed a shooting in a pub by a few minutes, was burgled, involved in a road accident, and had his Mini Metro stolen three times, which was eventually trashed by a 13-year-old toerag. He also lived in some quite notorious areas of Leeds (Chapple Town to name but one).

All of that happened before his 19th birthday. Trisha even considered asking him to come home and work locally. But when she mentioned it to him, to his credit, he told us that he wasn't going to be driven away and would stick it out. I'm ashamed to say that due to all of these events, coupled with the debilitating effects Trisha's ME was having on both of us. I told her that I'd had enough and unless things got better, I was off. She cried like I'd never seen anyone cry before.

I know that I would never have carried out the threat and to this day, I bitterly regret even thinking it. I honestly couldn't have loved her any more than I did. We had our normal arguments, disagreements and quarrels, no more or less than any average couple. Believe me, when I say, and it's not just a cliché, but she was my whole life, my very, very best friend. I could never have found anyone who would even slightly compare. I still desperately miss her.

Presumably, God must have considered that Trisha, whilst only 55 years old and just entering the prime of her life, had more than justified her time on earth. He had plans for her next life. Whatever the reason, it must have been a very special one for God to take her from us when he did. And for those of us who are left—I guess we haven't yet fulfilled what is intended for us.

And so on to my story. I could try and be clever and start in the middle of our lives and jump back and forth through the various chapters of our time together. Or I could just start on day one and capture each event that springs to mind. I think the latter option will suffice.

Chapter One
Secondary Technical Schooling

(September 1963 to June 1968)

I began my secondary education at Durrington Secondary Modern School. Having failed the 11 plus exam in 1963, which would have given me access to Salisbury Grammar School, I was given the opportunity to sit what was then classed as a *13 plus* exam.

I'm not really sure why it was so named but I took the exam and passed it which gained me entry to Adcroft Secondary Technical School of Building. The school was located in Trowbridge and specialised in the five building trades which comprised Bricklaying, Plumbing, Plastering, Carpentry and Joinery and Painting and Decorating.

Schooling also covered the standard academic teaching as well as giving a foundation in Technical and Geometrical Drawing, both of which were oriented around the building industry. There were no charges for the school and those who lived in the outer reaches of Wiltshire were allowed to board, again with no charges. There was also a compliment of *Day Boys*.

The overall aim of the three-year schooling was to prepare teenagers for a life in the building industry. The first year was split into three academic terms with each half term giving an insight into one of the five trades. For the second year, we chose three of the five trades, spending one full term on each discipline. Then, for the final year, we concentrated on a trade of our choosing which culminated in an *O*-level being taken in that subject.

Life as a boarder was interesting, to say the least. The academic school day followed the same format as any other state-run school; the main difference was the extracurricular evening activities. There was so much to do that we really were spoilt for choice. For my part, I built my own canoe and during my last year, I spent a great deal of time on the Kennet and Avon Canal.

I was also introduced to beekeeping. The school had three bee hives and I spent many an hour with one of the *live-in* masters learning the intricacies of apiculture. Unfortunately, during one such educational session, he was explaining the roles of the various bees in the hive. He indicated that those bees that were furiously flapping their wings at the entrance were cooling the interior of the hive down by drawing in air.

He then mentioned that there were also one or two *guards* alongside. Their role was to see off any potential intruders such as wasps. I bent down and pointed at one of the guards and it immediately flew straight at the teacher and stung him on the corner of his eye—yep, that was a guard!

The next morning, my name was absolute mud. The teacher walked into the technical drawing class and one side of his face was completely swollen, so much so, that he couldn't see from one eye. He did, however, see the funny side of it.

The sport was big in Adcroft and everyone had to participate. The sports fields were situated approximately three miles from the school and once lunch was finished everyone had to make their way to Wingfield Road. We did have a small minibus that was driven by one of the teachers and for a small sum a seat could be secured, however it was always oversubscribed.

I have endearing memories of running past the Ushers Brewery and if the wind was in the right (or wrong!) direction; the smell of the hops would combine with the whiff of pigs and every other smell associated with pork production that emanated from the Bowyers production facility.

As I remember, we were given no choice as to what sport we played; I enjoyed football but absolutely hated Rugby. I believe it had less to do with not understanding the rules but more about getting almost beaten to death by those who got a thrill out of the physical aspects of the game.

Our game's *strips* were either red or blue tops. On one particularly cold afternoon, I put on both tops to try and stay warm. After my side had scored a try, rather than having to run back to the centre of the pitch, I took off my teams coloured top and stayed behind the goal until the try had been converted hoping to blend in with the opposition—no such luck.

I was spotted and given a severe bollocking for not *entering into the spirit of the game*. I can't remember at what stage we were given the opportunity to select the game we wanted to play, but whenever it was, rugby was not one of my choices. I instead opted to have a go at hockey. I had no idea of the rules but our

PE teacher, Steve Johns, imparted sufficient knowledge so those of us who wanted to learn could do so.

I soon found out that I was a natural. I write using my right hand but played cricket and hockey left-handed or *Cack-Handed* as it was more commonly known. I was later to play for Adcroft's 1st team. The grounding in the sport set me in good stead for later in life.

The Friday morning assembly was always something I looked forward to; the actual get-together was pretty much of a muchness, a sermon from the headmaster, hymns and a diary check. What I really enjoyed was listening to the BBC news for the 15 minutes before the assembly began—the news reader, Alvar Lidell.

He always began the bulletin with his characteristic introduction, "Here is the news and this is Alvar Lidell reading it."

I was fascinated with what was going on in the world. Unfortunately, at the end of my second year, I realised that being a builder wasn't what I really wanted, and instead, planned on joining the RAF. At that time, I had no real idea what trade I would take up and fancied being an airframe fitter. God only knows why! However, rather than wasting my final year, I decided to study plumbing, heating and ventilation.

It must have been during the early spring of 1968 that I picked up some brochures and decided that I would like to join the RAF as an air radar fitter. The reason was that it sounded the most romantic of all the trades, after all, who wanted to be a Rigger or a Bomb Head?

In the '60s, the armed forces were hoovering up the young men and women from Civvy Street in the belief that another world war was imminent. I subsequently attended an interview at the RAF Recruitment office on Colston Avenue, Bristol. Shortly after, I was notified that I was to go to RAF Stafford for a selection interview and undertake a variety of aptitude tests over a three-day period.

I remember very little of the process now but was pleased to learn a few weeks later, that I'd been successful and would begin my apprenticeship in September.

The month of June saw me achieving a pass in two General Certificate of Education examinations (GCE or *O* levels) in plumbing, heating and ventilation (theory and an in-depth practical examination) and geometrical drawing plus seven Certificate of Secondary Education (CSEs). It was not necessarily a sparkling academic achievement but sufficient, nevertheless, to allow me to join the mob.

By the time I finished school, I still had three months before I joined up and rather than kick my heels waiting, I got a job as a *Humper and Dumper* at the Pains Wessex Firework factory near the Highpost Hotel, Salisbury.

There was one benefit above all the others in attending Adcroft as a boarder; it set me in really good stead for the next stage of my life.

Chapter Two
Royal Air Force Station Cosford

(10 September 1968 to 10 February 1971)

RAF Cosford was the No. 2 School of Technical Training located north of Wolverhampton close to the village of Albrighton. The school was primarily responsible for training apprentices and adult trainees (those personnel that had already undergone basic trade training, left Cosford and finally returned to attend a fitter's course, lovingly known as Boggies) in one of the three aircraft electronic trades: Air Radar, Air Communications or Air Navigational Instruments.

There were three craft apprentice entries per year and from the mid-1960s onwards, each entry comprised of at least 100 personnel. There were also technical apprentice courses, a few telegraphy and Woman's Royal Air Force (WRAF) telephonist courses each year. The craft apprenticeship lasted for two years and specialised in one of the three air electronics trades. On completion, the trainee passed out as a Junior Technician whereas the Tech Apps underwent three years of training in all three trades and passed out as Corporals.

I was to join the 213th Craft Apprentice entry, affectionately known as *Crap Apps* and on 9 September 1968, I arrived at Cosford Halt railway station. I and approximately 40 other fellow apprentices had been selected to carry out a six-week lead-in course designed to brush up on Physics, Maths and English before the remainder of the entry arrived in early October.

We'd been arriving throughout the day and as I had travelled from Salisbury via Waterloo, Euston and Wolverhampton, had arrived mid-afternoon. We were taken in a three-ton truck to our accommodation in Fulton Block which housed all of the apprentice wing trainees. I was to live on *H* Flight and was shown to room 25, located on the ground floor, which along with the entries living on five other floors, formed part of 2 Squadron.

It seems a bit of a blur now, but I do remember having tea (or was it dinner?) and then, sitting through various lectures and being told what was going to happen the next day.

Tuesday, 10 September 1968 started very early as there was a lot to do in preparation for what lay ahead. We had breakfast and sat through more lectures and presentations. At 10:00, we were asked if anyone had second thoughts about joining the RAF because once the attestation ceremony was over there would be no backing out unless through exceptional circumstances.

Although the entry wasn't then complete, two people, having spent only one night away from mummy, decided that the RAF wasn't for them! Anyway, those of us who wanted to give it a go, swore our elegance to Queen and country and that was it—I had joined the RAF.

I was still only 16 years old when I joined up and my reckonable service didn't start until my 18th birthday. I initially signed on for nine years of regular service followed by three years as a reservist. That period was to be extended to 12 years of regular service in 1978, extended again to 22 years in 1981, and in 1991, my service was extended for the final time to complete at age 47 years. All personnel retired at age 55—God, that seems so long ago!

We were then paraded and marched to clothing stores where we were issued with a blue canvas holdall, three collar detached shirts, six collars, one set of collar studs, and woollen socks. Also, underwear that went from the waist to just above the knees, two pairs of heavily studded leather boots, a pair of blue Denhams (with rubber buttons), various brushes (clothes, shoe and Blanco) and a button stick (placed behind the uniform brass buttons and designed to stop the Brasso cleaner from staining the fabric).

Also, several items of blue webbing (backpack, 2 side packs and belt all with the associated brasses), two mess tins, a knife, fork and spoon, cup, towels, a Service Dress (SD) Hat, a raincoat and a greatcoat. Along with the all-important blue beret which, when I put it on, it looked a lot like the beret worn by Frank Spencer in the TV comedy 'Some Mothers Do 'Ave 'em'.

Physical fitness was also high on the agenda and we were issued with PE kit comprising of *Plimsolls* (trainers weren't even on the horizon then), shorts and two-coloured tops. I'm sure there were many more items, but that's all that I can remember. We were marched back to the flight, told to put our personal belongings on the bed and follow our new leader, Sergeant Bob Fuller who took us to the Barbers!

I'd actually had quite a close haircut before leaving home—what a waste of money that was. We were also measured for our No. 1 dress uniform, which was made from quite a decent material and also our No. 2 battledress (working) uniform. The battledress was made from a thick, hairy material that during summer was not only hot but incredibly itchy.

However, until those uniforms were tailored or adjusted, we wore Denhams, a webbing belt, boots and a beret. My first payday was a momentous occasion; we paraded in the corridor and had to follow a set procedure before any money passed hands. As we approached the table, behind which sat the Flight Commander and accompanied by a discip Sergeant, we had to stand to attention, salute and recite our service number, rank and name.

If the salute wasn't smart enough you were sent to the back of the queue and the whole performance was repeated. My first wage was £1 and 10 shillings (£1.50), and from that, I had to purchase webbing Blanco, Brasso, dusters and a razor! (I already had all of the necessary washing materials).

I was to receive a pay rise of 10 shillings a week on my 17th birthday and a further rise when I reached 17½ years of age. We were also told that everyone would shave every day even if it wasn't necessary. Smoking was allowed but we had to get permission from the Flight Commander who signed a card endorsing the fact that we were old enough to do so.

The card also showed details concerning our bed-check times and permission to wear civilian clothes, which, in our case, was to be many months away.

The Flight Commander, an ex-Pilot, was very proud of the fact that he'd successfully ejected twice from stricken aircraft. As evidence, he had been awarded two mementoes by the Martin-Baker ejection seat manufacturers; both of which he proudly displayed in his office.

I'd only been on the flight for about a week or so when I started to suffer from major stomach pains. I attended the morning sick parade and was introduced to the sadistic civilian medical officer, Doc Harold. He was a real oddball who would parade everyone in the corridor and walk down the line asking each individual what was wrong.

I remember one lad saying that he was suffering from a headache—the Doc's answer was to hit him on the head with a magazine. For my part when I told him I had stomach pains, he jabbed me in the solar plexus with his finger, and so it went on. Following a more detailed examination, I was admitted to the station medical centre for observation.

Whilst I remember being in a lot of discomfort, it was the first time that I'd come across the true military grandeur and the utter bullshit mentality of the armed forces. There were a couple of other patients in the ward. Between breakfast and before the sadist doctor had visited, we were required to pull the beds away from the wall and dust the window sills and the beds before finally sweeping and polishing the floor.

Apart from that one occasion, I was very seldom ill and didn't report sick many times at all. I don't really remember too much of what went on during the first six weeks. But the time passed very quickly, and before long the remainder of the entry arrived. By then, of course, those of us who had arrived six weeks earlier were, for all intense and purpose—veterans!

It was then that the serious training began. The apprenticeship scheme wasn't just based on learning a trade but also covered such things as general service knowledge, discipline, drill, fitness, personal hygiene and weapon handling. We were not allowed out of the camp for the first six weeks and most evenings were spent cleaning our accommodation and *bulling* our boots.

The boots were covered in small, nobly lumps which needed to be smoothed down. The only way that these lumps could be removed was to apply a thick layer of polish to the leather and set light to it. The trick was to blow the flame out before it burnt through the leather, spit on the polish and, using the index finger inside a duster, carry out small circular motions and polish the entire boot to such an extent that you could see your face in the shine.

Mick Duffel, whom I met at RAF Stafford during the initial selection process, decided that as he had been a member of the Air Training Corps and had reached the exalted rank of Flight Sergeant, he didn't need to listen to advice on how to correctly *Burn your Boots.* He subsequently did his own thing. He successfully burnt a neat hole in the toe of his boot and got a severe bollocking for it.

A full b*ull* night was carried out each Friday evening. After breakfast on Saturday morning, we were subjected to a full inspection which entailed making a square pack out of the bedding (a bed-pack) and laying everything out in a prescribed manner. The inspection was then followed by drill on the parade ground.

As the junior entry, we were also required to attend the Sunday morning church service which we found out much later on wasn't designed to strengthen an individual's religious belief but more to ensure that the station commander didn't have to sit in church on his own!

I joined as an air radar apprentice (the acronym RADAR stands for Radio Aids to Detection and Ranging). In the first year, we learnt basic electricity, basic electronics and fault-finding down to module level on some of the multitude of radar equipment fitted to RAF aircraft. It might be worth remembering at this point that WW2 only drew to a close 22 years earlier and radar systems on aircraft were still pretty basic, analogue systems.

We also learnt some of the skills of hand practices and manufactured various simple electronic circuits in the workshop. Multiple choice (Vote for Joe) progress exams (slip tests) were sat every two weeks and at the end of each quarter, more detailed progress exams were taken. Each training year culminated in a major electronics examination.

The second year concentrated on advanced radar techniques, radar equipment fault-finding down to the component level and more electronic workshops. The final element of the apprenticeship covered the safe maintenance, fault-finding and rectification of aircraft radar systems. I was to train on a multitude of aircraft but my favourite two were the Vulcan and the Avro Shakelton (the latter being based on the Avro Lancaster Bomber). Once again, progress exams were taken on a regular basis.

Some of the officers who took us for the core educational subjects were pilots who were posted in and had to complete a ground tour as academic teachers. One particular Flying Officer, who took us for Physics and Maths, was perpetually messed about by a small Glaswegian lad. The lad was warned on more than one occasion; that he would suffer in the long run if he continued to disrupt the class.

Nobody really understood what was meant by the threat but it soon became clear when we were taken to the airfield for our first Air Experience flight in a Chipmunk aircraft. The pilot turned out to be our Physics instructor! He briefed us as to what sort of manoeuvres we'd be carrying out and as this was the first time anyone had flown; we were assured that the flight would be quite gentle.

We were told that after taking off and having reached about 10,000 (above which, we probably would require oxygen) we would be given the chance to fly the aircraft and carry out some basic turns, climbs and banks. There was one manoeuvre that he was especially proud of which entailed cruising at a steady altitude, and then, asking the student to close his eyes. Then, very gently inverting the aircraft, asking if the student had felt the movement and then, telling him to open his eyes.

My first flight was one of the highlights of my apprenticeship; however, for the Glaswegian, it was a totally different experience. He was strapped into the rear of the aircraft and was gone for quite a while; certainly, a lot longer than the rest of the class had been away. When the aircraft eventually returned, he climbed out of the Chipmunk and whilst not being particularly tall, coupled with the weight of the parachute, he walked with quite a stoop.

He was also carrying a sick bag which looked to be quite full. It transpires the pilot hadn't taken him on a gentle spin around the Shropshire skies as expected. The pilot had carried out some *seat of the pants* flying—he'd got his own back on Eric and I don't think he caused any more trouble!

Our Glaswegian friend was not only a pain in the classroom but almost everywhere he went. He had a unique way of waking up another of his countrymen in the morning. Every now and then, he would quietly get out of bed, climb on top of his 6 locker and at the prescribed moment launch himself on top of his countryman, who was fast asleep, screaming *Tongs Ya Bas* at the top of his voice.

I never did find out if there was any rivalry between them or not as he didn't last the pace and left the RAF soon afterwards. I don't know what avenue he took on leaving the RAF but I wouldn't be surprised if he turned out to be a *loan shark*. One of his more enterprising ventures involved selling cigarettes.

The majority of my class smoked (me included) and as we weren't paid until after lunch on a Thursday, most people were broke, and didn't have any cigarettes that morning. However, he always had a full 20 packet of either players No 10 or No 6 cigarettes (both makes were small, cheap and crappy). His little scam involved loaning one cigarette on the condition that he was given five back after pay parade. He never failed to make a profit and could be relied upon to be ready for the following Thursday morning's trading.

One of the disadvantages of living *cheek by jowl* is that not everyone observes or indeed is aware of the most basic hygiene requirements. The three years as a boarder at Adcroft had made me mindful of what was required. Unfortunately, there were one or two in my room of 25 personnel that hadn't a clue. As mentioned earlier, we were issued with three collarless shirts and six collars and I think that most people wore a shirt for two days and changed the collar every day.

One particular individual's way of ensuring that he always wore a shirt that was cleaner than the one he took off was, to throw the used article into his locker and take a previously worn article from the bottom of the pile—early recycling, I guess! However, the smell in the room was quite overpowering and rather than run to the flight SNCO and complain, the law was taken into our own hands.

A bath was filled with tepid water, the locker emptied of the offending items and thrown, along with the unsavoury character into the water. He was then covered in Vim (scouring powder) and, despite his protestations, scrubbed with a hard-backed brush. The treatment must have worked because I don't remember him re-offending.

I can't remember how the subject was broached but someone suggested holding a séance using an Ouija board. I didn't really understand what it was all about. It was explained to me that people can receive and relay messages from spirits and many people, including sceptics and non-believers, and to treat it as a form of entertainment. I decided to give it a go.

There were six or seven of us and we went to a small room on one of the unoccupied floors. There were two characters who said that they'd carried out a séance before because between them laid out everything and knew the precise spiel. A table was put in the centre of the room and a circle was made from individual pieces of paper on which the letters of the alphabet and the numbers 0 to 9 had been written.

There were two other pieces of paper positioned inside the circle, one with the word *Yes* and the other with the word *No*. A small upturned glass was placed in the centre of the circle. We all sat down, a candle was lit, the lights turned off and after being told what we had to do, the session began.

We all placed an index finger on the glass and the experienced member started chanting, "Is there anybody there?"

He repeated the chant several times and nothing happened for several minutes. Then, all of a sudden, the glass started to move. I wasn't alone in thinking that someone must have been pushing it but the manner, the positive direction, the exact position it stopped and the speed in which the glass moved, the more obvious it became that it wasn't being controlled by anyone at the table!

People posed various questions to our *spirit;* either asking for a direct yes or no answer which was difficult to corroborate. I became really quite spooked when I asked the *spirit* to spell out my brother Ian's RAF service number. Without a moment's hesitation, the glass moved and very precisely and sequentially stopped at the numbers 6–8–8–4–1–5; a number I can still remember to this day.

I couldn't help thinking at the time, who or what on *the other side* would have known that number? However, I didn't really want to continue and suggested that we leave. But, for whatever reason, one of the guys took his chain and crucifix from around his neck and placed it under the glass.

When we resumed, the response to one particular question caused the glass to move very rapidly between the *Yes* and *No* at which point everyone let go—and that was enough for most of us and we left. The next morning, we were shown the result of the crucifix being placed under the glass—a very neat shape of a crucifix burnt into his chest.

He didn't seem to be in much discomfort and wasn't too concerned, but I don't believe for one minute that he would deliberately scar himself just for a laugh. I never took part in another séance but several others did. I was later told that on one occasion, they'd contacted a devil spirit. When it was asked a question, the glass moved around the table at a great rate of knots before smashing itself against the wall—nobody ever went back.

I think many people associate various times of their lives and experiences with certain music, songs or films. For me, the one record that takes me back to my first few months at Cosford was the soundtrack to the film 'The Good, The Bad and The Ugly'. The only other television event that I remember so vividly was the Apollo Moon landing in July 1969; we were allowed to watch the entire event as it unfolded.

At the end of our first three months, we were given a little more freedom and allowed to venture off the station. As a way of celebrating, a number of us went Roller Skating in Wolverhampton. The only real issue was the fact that we still couldn't wear civilian clothes instead we had to wear our No. 1 uniform with a big hat.

We arrived at the rink and after getting our skating boots, we immediately took off our jackets; we were all really quite concerned about falling over and putting holes in our trousers. Although I'd skated before I took it easy, that was until some gorilla barged his way past me and knocked me for six. I was expecting some bother, but instead, he came back, picked me up, brushed me down and apologised. Fortunately, no damage to my uniform either.

It was at this point that Mick Duffel and I decided to start driving lessons and contacted one of the driving schools based in Albrighton. Lessons cost £1 10 shillings (just under one week's wage). We met the instructor on a Saturday afternoon and went through the introductions.

He asked what driving experience I had and I told him that I'd driven about 100 yards with my brother; Mick was marginally a little more experienced. It was decided that I would drive for the first hour, and then, Mick would drive for the second hour.

I hopped into the driving seat and after being shown the controls was told to pull off and head into Wolverhampton! My steering and gear changes were erratic, to say the least. Every time, I changed gear the car would veer to the left or right, and so as a way of practising, I drove for mile after mile with only one hand on the steering wheel.

Now, I know that Wolverhampton was not as busy in 1969 as it is now but nevertheless, to drive into the city on a Saturday afternoon (football!) was about as frightening as it could get. Anyway, I managed to get through my hour without incident or accident and Mick had his spell in town and drove back to Cosford, again without any problems.

We both paid for the next lesson and arranged to meet the following Saturday for another lesson, unfortunately, I learnt during the week that our instructor had died of a heart attack. I don't know why but I was totally put off driving and didn't resume lessons for several months.

The driving school in Albrighton was ideally situated, however, it was the only school in the area and the next nearest was in Wolverhampton. I resumed lessons later that year and, if memory serves, had a further eight sessions and then felt that I was ready for my test.

It was also early in 1969, I decided to join the Apprentice Band as a side drummer. The band, which comprised entirely of apprentices, was really quite accomplished and was run on a semi-professional basis by a warrant officer bandmaster. Band practice and rehearsals were carried out on a Wednesday evening in preparation for the monthly Apprentice Wing Church parade and more importantly, the relevant entry passing-out parade.

During the summer months, the band spent most weekends playing at various functions, including carnivals and garden parties throughout the West Midlands. The high spot of the year was in July when we performed in the Royal Tournament at Earls Court. I played with the brass band section at Earls Court in July 1969, and with the pipe band section in July 1970, including the full Kilt and associated regalia.

It was also in the spring of 1969, that I began playing hockey, initially for *H* flight, and then, for the apprentice wing team, and eventually, for the RAF Cosford adult team. I was one of only a few left-handed players, or *cack handers* as mentioned earlier. I was in great demand to play on the left wing. There obviously wasn't enough going on in my life because I also joined the Astra Cinema, either selling tickets or refreshments or ushering.

It was whilst I was working at the cinema that I met, a trainee telephonist whom I dated for about two months, what a kisser she was—phew! But things didn't work out and she started dating an adult trainee. I realised later on when my hormones eventually kicked in (late developer!) why she dumped me.

She was after a lot more than just a quick kiss or a snog in the back of the cinema if you get my drift. Good grief, I was only 17 years old, shy and didn't see all of the obvious signs she was giving—what a bugger! Anyway, we remained good friends and she gave me a bottle of aftershave for my 18th birthday. Unfortunately, she was still seeing the other bloke, so, there was nothing else on offer!

All of the extracurricular activities had a disastrous effect on my training because I failed the mid-course electronics exam. I'd also failed a few of the slip tests but had passed most of the other course elements. However, that wasn't enough and in September 1969, I was back coursed to the 214th entry which meant, I had to do an extra four months at Cosford.

Shortly, before being moved, I visited Tom and Edith and shared the train journey to Lime Street Railway Station in Liverpool with my Sergeant Discip who told me that he was disappointed that I'd failed the exam because he had me lined up for promotion, but encouraged me not to give up.

I joined the new entry along with several other failures and decided that I really must try and concentrate on studying. I went home for Christmas and shortly into the New Year took my driving test in Salisbury. The evening before the test, Mum let me drive her Mini to the Cash and Carry outlet also in Salisbury. As I'd had a couple of lessons earlier, I could remember most of the test route.

All was going well until the car started coughing and spluttering and died and no amount of coxing or cursing would start it. Fortunately, Mum was a member of the AA and before too long, the mechanic had the car going again—the problem—we'd run out of fuel.

The petrol gauge, however, had been showing that the tank was half full and the AA man then noticed that a large fly had got into the gauge, died and was jamming the needle! Undeterred, I took the test the next morning and passed.

On 1 April 1970, I was promoted to the position of leading apprentice through my involvement with the band; which some said didn't carry as much weight as a promotion through the flight; but who cared, I got a single room and extra pay for it! One of the advantages of being a leading apprentice was the privilege of being able to go to the front of the meal queue, some people objected but I really wasn't bothered.

There were approximately 15 members of my class, and on those occasions, when we had lessons on the airfield, the walk back to Fulton Block mess for lunch took about 15 minutes. It was always a rush to get back and get in front of the dozens of other classes also heading to the mess.

One little scam that the other leading apprentice in the class and I conjured up was that once we were on the road that ran from the airfield to the camp entrance. We would take turns stopping any junior class in front of ours (one that had no apprentice NCOs) and give the class leader a bollocking for not marching smartly (or whatever excuse we good think of at the time). It continued until such time as our class was in front. It never failed to work.

I mentioned earlier that there were also telegraphy courses going through Cosford. One of the elements of their training involved learning Morse code. Morse code is a method of transmitting text information as a series of on-off tones, lights or clicks. The standardised sequences of *dots* and *dashes* or *dits* and *dahs* were used verbally by the telegrams in the gym changing rooms to pass messages to each other, which, of course, was all very clever. However, after a while, it began to drive us all—Mad!

The majority of equipment fitted to RAF aircraft in the '60s was analogue and used thermionic valves and transistors. Digital techniques and microprocessors were still years away, or at least, they were in training establishments. Consequentially, the equipment boxes were large, slow-to-process information, cumbersome and generated massive amounts of heat.

General fault-findings techniques on the various systems followed the same format. However, for the larger equipment, there were one of two idiosyncrasies that could be guaranteed to catch out the unwary. One such equipment was the rearward facing radar warning system *Red Steer* which was fitted to the Vulcan bomber.

Red Steer had a unique scanning pattern. The mechanism was a maze of cams, motors and balance weights arranged, so that, the dish would repeatedly spiral out from zero datum to about 45 degrees azimuth and elevation. All this happened at about 300 rpm.

Apart from the obvious hazard associated with the mechanical aspects, on one occasion, whilst I was *tweaking* something deep inside the equipment, my knuckles touched one of the test points associated with the transmitter circuits and I received one hell of an electric shock—18k volts. Fortunately, I was uninjured, and luckily, I was stood on an insulating rubber mat.

All servicing bays were equipped with safety mats and when working on live equipment, one hand always had to be in the trouser pocket so as not to offer an earth path in the event of potential electrocution. It was the one and only occasion, when hands in pockets weren't followed up with a bollocking.

For all of 1970, I continued to play hockey, play in the band and work in the cinema as a projectionist. Although, I did fail some of the advanced electronics slip tests, I still passed the radar equipment fault-finding, airfield workshop and aircraft system fault-finding phases. I believed that I was more or less on top of my studies.

Unfortunately, in late January 1971, whilst sitting in the station cinema awaiting an educational film about venereal disease (!) I and several other members of the entry were told to leave and form up outside. We had earlier that week, taken the final, final exam and were told that we had failed and were to resit the exam—no chance to revise or prepare for it!

Three hours later, I was stood to attention in front of the senior training Squadron Leader and told that I'd achieved 58% on the resit (the pass-mark being 60%). He was one of those characters whose face was set with a permanent smile and at first, I couldn't make him out.

However, he went on to tell me that although I hadn't achieved the desired pass mark, based on the results from the various other trade elements, he'd decided to give me the benefit of doubt and allowed to qualify and leave Cosford as a Junior Technician in the trade of L Fitt AR (Electronic Fitter Air Radar)—utter relief!

Of the 20 or so personnel who retook the exam, there was only a handful of us that passed. The remainder had to stay at Cosford and carry out a further 3 months *self-study* revision. I later learnt that three or four people failed that exam and were subsequently discharged from the RAF.

Once the final number of qualified personnel had been determined, the next major event was to sort out who was going where. The process began with lists of all the relevant RAF units where vacancies existed for the air electronics trades being placed on the notice board. Then, names were dropped into a hat for the individual unit.

As I'd visited Lyneham whilst Ian was working in the Hercules Simulator, I put my name on the Lyneham list. There was once a scheme whereby a brother could *claim* a younger sibling to serve on the same unit, unfortunately, that arrangement was no longer available. There were five applicants for three posts at Lyneham, and my name and two other names were drawn out.

Unfortunately, within an hour or so of the selection, there was a complaint from someone whose name, for whatever reason, hadn't gone into the draw and he wanted a re-run. Someone must have been smiling from above because the same three names were selected. So that was it—RAF Lyneham it was to be.

All that was left to do was: to polish the brasses on our ceremonial white webbing, bull our parade boots to a high gloss, go through the details of the final passing-out parade and rehearse the arms drill which was carried out using a Self-Loading Rifle (SLR) with Bayonet fitted.

As a member of the station band, I'd already attended at least a dozen passing-out parades and knew exactly what the procedure was—only this time, I'd be on the receiving end. The one major event that preceded the parade took place on the 15 Feb—Decimalisation Day. The parade of the 17th went without a hitch, and before long, I was on my way to Wiltshire for a spell of leave before moving on to my first operational posting.

214th Entry 17 February 1971
The Final Phew! (I'm 6th from the left, front row)

Chapter Three
Royal Air Force Station Lyneham

(23 February 1971 to 7 July 1972)

RAF Lyneham was situated in the Wiltshire countryside, 10 miles west of Swindon. On the 23 February 1971, following a few days leave, I loaded up Mum's car with what few personal positions I had, and she drove me to the station. There were no guards or entry restrictions at that time and we drove around trying to find Station Headquarters which is where the general office was situated. As we drove up the main drag, it was quite a sight to see upwards of 30 Hercules aircraft parked on the dispersal.

As Lyneham was my first operational unit, I was a little unsure as to the correct arrival procedure, apart from the fact that, I had to wear my No. 1 uniform (with SD Hat) and report to the personnel section in the Station Headquarters. At every new station, everyone is required to carry out the arrivals procedure which entails being given a blue card with dozens of different sections/departments listed.

The first job is to physically visit each section and obtain a signature. It didn't matter whether or not you ever used the section during your tour, a signature was required and the process wasn't considered complete until all the necessary boxes were filled in and the card returned to SHQ.

I was later to find out that the clearance process was even more traumatic. There was no deadline for completing the procedure however it was obviously in our best interest to get it done as soon as possible. I duly found the personnel desk in SHQ and was given the fabled Blue Arrivals Card.

One of the first sections I visited was Engineering Manning, where I learnt that I was to be employed on *B* Line Servicing Squadron based in C2 Hangar. The adjacent C1 hangar was occupied by 216 Squadron which operated the Comet VIP Passenger aircraft. My memory at this point is a little hazy. But I think, Mum took me to the squadron where I met the accommodation NCO; who took me to Beverly block (B Line's designated accommodation), issued me with my mattress and bedding and showed me to my room.

Once I'd unloaded my meagre belongings, Mum left for home and I watched her disappear down the main drag and contemplated what lay ahead. I then went back to *B* line.

B Line had only recently formed following the closure of RAF Fairford and the resident Hercules squadrons moved to Lyneham. The squadron had its own admin section. I was assigned a shift but was told that I would spend a few days learning about the Royal Air Force Transport Command, RAF Lyneham, the role of the station, and more importantly, learn about the Herc radar systems and where I fitted in as a member of the ground crew.

I and a few other new arrivals were then taken by one of the groundcrews in an attempt to finish off some of the more important sections listed on the blue card. One such section was the medical centre where we were each given a questionnaire that covered our basic health details. There was one particular question that I hadn't the faintest idea what the answer was. When I asked for advice, I got a bollocking from the Flight Sergeant for not knowing.

I was told in no uncertain terms that, as a supposedly intelligent individual, I should know what my medical standard was. And when I told him that, I still didn't have a clue what he was talking about, he then proceeded to lecture me in front of everyone—what a twerp! At the end of the sermon, I don't think I was really any the wiser and I never did find out if any of my colleagues knew the answer either.

I later found out that every serviceman and servicewoman is assigned a medical standard which details their fitness to serve in the armed forces. God only knows why the particular alphanumeric were chosen, but in my case, as a fit individual with no medical issues or health problems, my medical standard was:

A4—Fit to travel as a passenger or patient on normal or Aero-Med flights.

G1—Fit for full ground duties applicable to rank and trade, including all general service duties.

Z1—Fit to serve anywhere.

We, eventually, handed in our blue cards and were taken back to B Line.

A traditional flying squadron in the RAF has designated engineers who are responsible for the maintenance of only their aircraft. Lyneham Engineering

Wing however operated a central servicing philosophy whereby two servicing squadrons, colloquially referred to as *A* and *B* Lines, equally shared the responsibility for maintaining the various resident flying squadron's aircraft.

The initial Hercules squadrons were numbers 24 and 36 Squadrons who were joined in February 1971 by 30 Squadron and 47 Squadron when they moved from RAF Fairford in Gloucestershire. Then, in September 1971, 48 Squadron moved from Changi airport in Singapore (70 Squadron was subsequently moved to Lyneham from Akrotiri, Cyprus in February 1975, closely followed by number 242 Operational Conversion Unit (OCU) based at RAF Thorney Island, West Sussex on 31 October 1975).

The Hercules C130K tactical transport aircraft was introduced to the RAF in 1968 and was the workhorse of what was then RAF Transport Command. Despite the colossal number of flying hours achieved, the aircraft maintained a good safety record. Unfortunately, there was one accident on 24 March 1969 where six crew members were killed when XV180 crashed shortly after take-off at RAF Fairford in Gloucestershire.

The aircraft was on a routine training flight when it stalled on take-off and plunged into a ploughed field 300 yards from the end of the runway. There were to be three more crashes during the seven years I was to spend working on the aircraft. The first was on 9 November 1971, when XV216, a 24 Squadron aircraft taking part in exercise *cold stream* with the Italian Air Force, disappeared from the flight formation and crashed into the sea off Pisa.

Apart from the full complement of crew, there were also 46 Italian paratroopers on board but there were no survivors. I was on shift at Lyneham when the news came through and knew that there were several members of our own squadron groundcrew on detachment at Pisa. Fortunately, none were on-board that fated flight. On 12 September 1972, XV194 veered off the runway on landing at Tromso/Langnes airport in Norway and although there were no fatalities, the aircraft's repair status was classed as Category 5 and written off.

The most shocking accident happened whilst I was serving at RAF Colerne and although I didn't see the accident, I heard the crash which was witnessed by several colleagues. It was lunchtime on 10 September 1973, when XV198, a 48 Squadron aircraft on a training flight, lined up with Colerne's runway in preparation for an asymmetric landing and take-off whilst being flown by the co-pilot.

The scenario was such that the aircraft approached the runway and in order to simulate an engine failure the crew would *feather* the propellers of one engine. The landing and overshoot (a *roller*) was then carried out. However, as the aircraft began the climb out of the manoeuvre the *good* engine on the same side as the feathered prop failed.

The asymmetric forces coupled with the height (400 feet) and associated speed of the aircraft proved too much for the crew. The aircraft rolled onto its side and crashed into woodland at the end of the runway. All six crew members perished.

Doncombe Lane, whilst outside of the station bounds, crossed the runway threshold with access being controlled by traffic lights whenever aircraft were taking off or landing. On this occasion, as it was lunchtime there were several cars queuing at both sides of the traffic lights.

It must have been an extremely frightening experience for those people in the cars who witnessed the aircraft zooming close overhead, on its side. The crash site was approximately 20 yards from the road and when the fuel from the burst wing tanks flooded down the road the occupants ran for their lives.

There was also a house just inside the station perimeter adjacent to the runway and I later heard that the lady, who was at home at the time, had a nervous breakdown on realising what had happened.

The work on the Squadron was interesting and varied with a reasonable shift pattern. What a revolution; no more evening bed checks, no more having to get permission to stay out late or having to apply for a 48-hour weekend pass. I had turned 19 years old only a few months before arriving at Lyneham and when not on shift, the time was my own. Fantastic, nobody cared where I was as long as I was back on shift, on time.

I also had more money to spend than I could care to mention (compared to the pittance I had in training anyway). Much of my spare time for the first few months was spent travelling to and from Cosford at weekends with Jamie Millgate (RIP). We were both dating PABX telephonists.

In those days, there were no security implications and hitchhiking in uniform wasn't frowned upon, the advantage of course was that on almost every occasion we could more or less guarantee getting lifts.

In the early 1970s, there was always a requirement to take one or two supernumerary groundcrew members with the aircraft to carry out the after flight, before flight and turn round servicing. This role would later be taken over by SNCO ground engineers who were trained in all the necessary aircraft trades and disciplines. There was no real waiting list as such for the trips.

However, one of the most coveted was a west-about or east-about (around the world via the USA route or the Far East route respectively). I was still relatively new to the squadron and didn't expect to be going anywhere too soon.

However, in July 1971, as I was handing the Land Rover keys into the squadron line control room Flight Sergeant Bert Gough shouted across to me, "Okay, you'll do."

And then, asked for my service number, rank and name which I duly gave him.

I couldn't think what the devil I'd done wrong, instead, I was told to go to the general office and arrange for a NATO travel order as I was off to NASA. In fact, it wasn't the National Aeronautics and Space Administration at Cape Canaveral but Nassau in the Bahamas. I was then coached into what I would be required to do.

The crew in the C130K comprised the captain, co-pilot, flight engineer, navigator and load master. For our trip, the freight bay was absolutely full to the gunnels from floor to ceiling and covered the entire length of the bay. As I remember, there was one other supernumerary crew member; no passengers and we were able to take turns and sit on the bottom bunk bed on the flight deck and smoke.

The Hercules was ostensibly a freight and troop carrier and troop seat comfort must have been the last thing on the designer's mind. I soon learnt that if I sat *in front* of the engines, it was warm but the noise was almost unbearable and ear defenders were needed. However, if I sat at the *rear* of the engines, the noise was bearable but it was freezing. The first stage of the trip was to a United States Air Force base at Lajos in the Azores, where we were scheduled for an overnight stay.

Once we landed, I started to carry out the after flight services by first finding out from the captain what the fuel requirements for the next stage of the trip would be. The fuel bowser duly arrived and we connected the transfer hose to the refuel panel and set the switches to enable the relevant tanks to be filled.

As the refuel was going ahead, I was joined by the air engineer who noticed what appeared to be a crack, about six inches long in the trailing edge of the inboard, starboard flap that was situated directly above us. The refuelling was stopped and further investigation confirmed that the flap skin was indeed split.

The captain was contacted and it was agreed that the damage wasn't that serious and we would continue to Nassau the next day. In the meantime, another Lyneham Hercules had landed and the loadmaster from that aircraft joined us at the refuel point and also noticed the damage to the flap. Our air engineer straight away said that it was deceptive and was nothing more than thawed ice running down the skin.

The flight servicing was completed, the paperwork signed, the aircraft locked and we went off to our accommodation. We'd agreed to meet at the NCOs club later that evening for a meal and a few drinks. Unfortunately, identification cards were needed for access to the club and my I.D. card still showed that my rank was craft apprentice, annotated *CA*.

When I told the rest of the crew that I wouldn't be allowed in they advised that I think of a suitable explanation for the acronym. I arrived at the door and produced my I.D. card.

The doorman exclaimed with a typical American twang, "What in God's name is a *CA*?"

If memory serves, I told him something along the lines that it meant *Corporal aircrew*—it got me in, much to the amusement of the aircrew! The evening, from what I remember of it, was v. enjoyable.

The next morning, after breakfast, I commenced the before flight checks which entailed de-blanking the engines, inspecting the intakes for Foreign Object Debris (FOD) and carrying out a general walk around of the aircraft. A water drain check was also necessary thereby ensuring there was minimal water in the wing fuel tanks.

There had been instances of other aircraft, not necessarily belonging to the RAF, where checks weren't carried out on a regular basis. The volume of water built up to such an extent that the ratio of fuel to water when the tanks indicated full, was minimal, and aircraft jet engines don't operate particularly well on water!

As the specific gravity of Avtur, which is nothing more than glorified Paraffin, was less than that of water; any moisture in the fuel would sink to the bottom of the tank and accumulate close to one of the many drain points situated on the underside of the wings. A sample of fuel (and any water) was drained off by inserting a probe into the relevant drain point.

The probe extended into a long tube, which had a bottle screwed into the end (or if there was no bottle available, a large poly bag). When a sufficient quantity of liquid had been extracted, a clear indication of any water in the system could be seen.

Once the aircraft was prepared for the next leg of the journey, the crew took their positions and commenced the start procedure. The loadmaster and I were positioned outside; he was on a long intercom lead and me manning the CO2 fire extinguishers.

The aircraft integral Gas Turbine Compressor (GTC) was started first of all which generated sufficient b*leed air* to start the first of the four Alison Turboprop jet engines. Number 3 engine was the first to be started (the second from the left when facing the aircraft). When that engine was *burning and turning*, the GTC was closed down as that engine would then generate sufficient bleed air to start the remaining three engines.

The number four engine was next to be started, followed by the number two and finally the number one engine. The specific starting order was chosen due to the inherent safety issues associated with tackling an inboard engine fire, on startup, if the adjacent outboard engine was running.

The onward flight to Nassau was uneventful and the loadmaster periodically checked the damage to the flap with an Aldis lamp shone through the window in the starboard paratrooper door. I'm not sure what would have happened if the split had got worse, because we were in the middle of the Atlantic with no diversion airfield even remotely close.

There were a few occasions when my thoughts wandered, somewhat after we entered the legendary Bermuda Triangle or Devils Triangle as otherwise was known. Between 1942 and 2002, over 90 aircraft disappeared in the area; many vanished within sight of land, whilst being scanned by the ground radar and just about to touch down at runways. Others have vanished over shallow water.

Some had been in radio communication, saying their equipment was acting erratic, or that a *weird object* was harassing them. Sometimes, an unusual object was seen in the aftermath of a disappearance. On a few occasions, a minor piece of debris was found. In one case, containing an unexplained *magnetic particle*.

One thing was the same for them all—they vanished without reason. The most famous of the disappearances took place on 5 December 1945, when Flight 19, comprising five US Navy Avenger aircraft, took off from the US Naval Air Station at Fort Lauderdale. It disappeared from radar and was never seen again.

We duly arrived at Nassau following a fairly uncomfortable flight, most of which was spent in the freight bay. It was impossible to rest on the troop seats, so I climbed on top of the freight midway along the aircraft. There I found a comfy spot quite close to the freight bay roof and managed to get some sleep. Unfortunately, when I awoke, I was a hot, sweaty mess and vowed never to do that again.

Once we'd parked on the dispersal at Nassau International Airport and the engines were shut down. The air engineer had a look at the damage to the flap and informed the captain that the split in the flap was no worse than that seen at Lajos. The captain immediately contacted Lyneham Operations on the HF radio and informed them that the aircraft was grounded due to the discovery of a large crack in the starboard flap!

The decision was taken that a recovery crew would be sent from Lyneham and should arrive within a couple of days. The freight was unloaded, the post-flight servicing was carried out and the aircraft was locked. We were then taken to our hotel.

I don't remember where or what I ate that evening, but I do remember going into a Colonel Saunders Kentucky Fried Chicken restaurant (now known colloquially as KFC) for lunch the next day and was quite blown away by the experience.

It was the first time I'd been inside a fully air-conditioned building, the first time I'd eaten the aptly advertised *Finger Lickin Good* chicken and it was also certainly the very first time, I'd ever drunk Coca-Cola from anything other than a small bottle!

That afternoon, we went to the beach and soaked up the sun for quite a while. Unfortunately, neither of us had any suncream and by the evening, I was glowing like the proverbial and felt quite ill with the sunburn.

Two days later, the repair crew arrived in another Herc and I was to return to Lyneham. The captain of the second Herc was only a Flying Officer which I thought at the time quite strange because both the co-pilot and navigator were Flight Lieutenants. The next morning, we loaded up the aircraft in preparation for the return journey, which this time would be a direct flight to Lyneham and not via the Azores.

The aircraft engines were running, and the pre-flight checks were complete and ready to taxi, when all of a sudden, the captain jumped down from the flight deck and told me to follow him. We ran across the dispersal towards the passenger terminal and once inside told me that two of the members of the crew didn't bother to pick up their full duty-free allowance of booze or cigarettes and that he would use their entitlement.

I don't remember how we got into the duty-free area but we certainly came out with a fair number of goodies.

Once again, the flight was technically uneventful and this time I suffered mild airsickness which wasn't helped by my sunburn. I was probably also dehydrated following the drinks I'd had the night before.

It was whilst we were flying back that I got into a conversation with a rigger who worked on another shift on B Line. I mentioned that I was looking for a cheap car to use as a runaround and he told me that his girlfriend, who lived in Chippenham, had a minivan that she was hoping to sell and would take me to see it when next we were both off shift.

The van was about 10 years old, and considering its age, didn't look too bad from the outside. However, there were no side windows, the seats weren't particularly comfortable, the gear lever was enormous and extended out of the floor, and the starter was a push button also located in the floor. Also, the headlight main beam dip switch was located just to the right of the accelerator pedal, also on the floor.

There was only one dial right in the centre of the dashboard that housed the speedo, fuel gauge and indicators. I had a drive of the van which started okay and wasn't too bad. I noticed a small cutout on the left-hand side of the dashboard and asked what it was for. Apparently, whenever the car was on a steep incline, the radiator would sometimes boil over.

When steam came through the *vent,* it was an indication that you should pull over and refill the radiator. With hindsight, I should have run a mile but I was absolutely desperate for a car and instead accepted that there was a minor problem which I believed would be fairly easy to sort out. I paid £90 for the privilege. What a mug, and I bet there was a lot of celebrating once I'd driven off.

One thing I hadn't considered was that Lyneham is on top of a hill. I hadn't gone too far from Chippenham on the Calne road when steam started pouring out of the vent. Fortunately, there was a large bottle of water in the back of the van and after topping up the radiator, I managed to get back to Lyneham without any more problems.

I learnt an awful lot from that car with regard to maintenance because it was forever breaking down. One of the engines mechs on the squadron suggested that the engine may need a de-coke which may sort out the overheating problem. Rather than strip the engine down, an alternative method of carrying out this task was to use an additive. *Redex* had several engine-related applications.

It could be added to the fuel tank in a measured dose dependent on the tank size and as the fuel travelled through the carburettor, it would clean it internally. But more interestingly, when ignited it helped to remove carbon deposits from the valves.

This could be achieved by pouring the liquid directly into the carb and when left, it would soak away the carbon deposits on the engine valves. It could also be poured into the intake when the engine was running. I couldn't afford Redex so I instead used OM15 hydraulic oil.

So, I set the engine running at quite a high rev rate, slowly poured a small quantity of OM15 aircraft hydraulic oil into the carburettor intake and ran the engine until there was no smoke coming from the exhaust. I decided to carry this out on my next night shift and with the help of a few colleagues parked the car outside of the hangar and proceeded to do as my engine friend had suggested.

To this day, I don't know why the station fire brigade and crash vehicles didn't respond but that little 850cc transverse engine generated so much smoke that half of the hangar was obliterated with thick, grey smoke that billowed over the airfield. After the event, the car was running so rough that I thought I must have unseated every valve in the engine.

I eventually managed to get the car back to the car park. I decided to carry out a proper de-coke later on, and despite help and advice from several *experts,* never did find out why the engine repeatedly overheated when it was on an incline.

I drove home to Durrington late one evening and was just passing Compton Bassett when I was pulled over by a police car. After the normal pleasantries, I was asked why I wasn't displaying any rear lights. I had a look and sure enough, no lights, and when I tried the indicators, they too weren't working. More checks were carried out and I discovered that the windscreen wipers had also packed up.

To make matters worse, I also had a bald tyre and no spare. I lifted the bonnet and the lights came on which obviously pointed to an intermittent electrical fault. Anyway, I received a summons in the post and attended the Magistrates Court in Calne where I gave my view of what happened.

My flight commander gave a character assessment to the magistrate who duly awarded me an £18 fine and my licence was endorsed to that effect (there were no points allocated in those days). I didn't hang onto the car for much longer, however, I did use it on several occasions to drive to Cosford and every trip was a real adventure! Jamie would navigate and try and find a route that didn't involve too many steep hills.

I, eventually, sold it for £25 which cheesed me off because only a week earlier I paid £25 for a new battery and voltage regulator. Shortly after that, I bought my first Mk 1 Ford Cortina. Compared to the Mini, it was an absolute luxury.

An Accidental Flight in a Lightning Jet

Wing Commander *Taffy Holden*, an engineer based at Lyneham in 1966, was conducting engine and taxying tests on a Lightning jet fighter on a runway. It was a relatively simple test which included opening the throttle to simulate a fault that a number of pilots had been experiencing. Unfortunately, he pushed the throttle too far forward and locked the engine into reheat.

The aircraft inadvertently shot forward and quickly built up speed. Before he could disengage the reheat, he was forced to swerve violently to avoid a fuel tanker. Then, after narrowly avoiding a comet passenger aircraft which had just taken off there was only a few yards of runway left, and with a village at the end of the runway, he was forced to take off. Whilst Taffy has flown light aircraft, he'd never flown a jet!

As the jet soared into the air, quickly reaching up to 500 mph, he tried to eject but found the ejector seat had been locked for ground servicing. He also had to do without any contact with ATC as the jet had no radio, nor did it have a canopy. The aircraft was still gathering speed and altitude but he managed to finally disengage the reheat. His thoughts were then centred on landing.

He tried on three occasions to land in the direction of the main runway but all attempts were totally uncoordinated and he probably would have killed himself. He decided to land in the opposite direction where there were no villages ahead. He finally put the aircraft down but with no brake parachute, he had to make do with the ordinary brakes. He finally stopped with only 100 yards of runway left.

That particular Lightning is housed in the Imperial War Museum at Duxford.

Early into 1972, I received notification that I'd been placed on the Preliminary Warning Roster (PWR) informing me that I was soon to be posted to the Persian Gulf. As part of the preparation, I was required to carry out predeployment training on the Bristol Britannia passenger aircraft, one of the mainstays of long-range trooping flights in the '60s and '70s, the other being the Vickers VC10. The course was run at RAF Brize Norton, a sister transport and passenger airhead situated in the Oxfordshire countryside.

The training was from 8 March until 18 April and entailed two weeks of classroom tuition (with a final exam) followed by four weeks of practical servicing and fault-finding of the aircraft radar systems whilst attached to the number 511 squadron.

At the end of the training, if I was successful, I would be awarded a *Q* annotation which indicated that I had carried out formal training for a particular aircraft or system. The alternative qualification was an *X* annotation which was normally awarded following the acquisition of a pre-defined level of **X**perience.

Brize Norton was approximately 30 miles from Lyneham. Rather than commute daily, I opted to live in transit accommodation at Brize during the week, returning to Lyneham at weekends. It was on one such Friday evening whilst walking from the car park to Beverley block, a mere 15 or so yards, that I was approached by a Corporal RAF policeman. He asked why I wasn't wearing my beret and why I had my battledress tunic undone.

When I didn't answer but just stared at him with my hands in my pockets, he ordered me to stand to attention and began to give me a bollocking, and when he noticed that I was wearing civilian shoes he went absolutely ballistic. By now, most of the windows of my block were open and several of my squadron mates were shouting at me and trying to bait the plod, who, unfortunately, didn't rise to the challenge.

He wanted my full details and told me he was going to charge me for being incorrectly dressed and insubordination. I was still somewhat naïve at this point otherwise I may have contested what he said. Anyway, once inside the block, I was asked what it was all about. When I explained, one of the old sweats suggested that I should have asked the plod if he was an acting or a substantive Corporal.

I wasn't aware of the difference at the time, but apparently, even though all RAF policemen under the rank of Sergeant wore Corporal strips, not all were real JNCOs. It was then suggested that I should have established if the plod held an acting rank and if he did, I should have told him to F*** off and act somewhere else—nice one. I contacted Flight Sergeant Bert Gough on B Line and told him what had happened. He told me to forget it and would sort it out on Monday.

I had to return to Brize on Sunday but did hear later on that Bert had contacted the police flight. In no uncertain terms, told them that discipline was his responsibility and that their men should concentrate on security issues and not sneak around the domestic site looking for trouble—charge dropped and end of the problem.

I passed the Britannia conversion course and spent the next three months learning as much as possible about the Hercules systems in preparation for my nine-month tour of duty in the Middle East.

Bomb Threat in the Atlantic

18 May 1972, another day on shift and under normal circumstances it would be no different to any other; after flight or before flight servicing and possibly some radar system rectifications. That was until I was asked by my shift boss to carry out a thorough functional check of the Decca Doppler Radar Navigation system on one of the aircraft.

The analogue equipment was capable of determining the exact latitude and longitude of the aircraft anywhere in the world. I was told that there was little or no margin for error as the crew would be looking for a very small object somewhere within a very large area!

Shortly after 15:00 on that day, Charlie Dickson, finance director of the Cunard Shipping Line, received a call at his office in New York from someone claiming to have planted six bombs aboard the QE2 passenger liner. And it would be detonated by two accomplices on the ship unless a $350,000 ransom was paid. At that moment, the QE2 was sailing across the Atlantic, midway through a cruise from New York to Cherbourg, where she was due to dock with her 1,438 passengers in three days' time.

William Law, its captain, was called and told about the threat, ordering all doors to be sealed and a search for the bombs to start. Meanwhile, the FBI and special branch in London were brought into the ever-widening investigation. Passenger lists were scanned and the MoD dispatched a Nimrod Maritime Patrol Aircraft, to provide immediate assistance and guidance for any rescue attempt. Lyneham operations were ordered to prepare a plan to fly a military team out to the QE2 at a moment's notice.

A four-man team was hastily formed which included the all-important bomb disposal officer, Captain Robert Hacon Williams RAOC. The plan was to parachute two people with the heavy and bulky bomb disposal equipment and a Special Boat Squad (SBS) officer.

The team were told to be ready to parachute to an unnamed ship at sea—something Williams had never done before. Parachuting into water has its complications, especially, in the prevailing conditions with low clouds and over 20KTs of wind.

On the other side of the Atlantic, Dickson was handed a letter from the extortionist, demanding the ransom money be dropped off in a blue bag at a telephone booth several miles north of the city at 21:30.

"Be alone. Any sign of police and you will have a catastrophe on your hands," the note ended chillingly.

Refusing the FBI's offer to have one of their agents handle the drop, Dickson set off with the cash, shadowed by plain-clothed FBI agents.

Meanwhile, on board the Hercules there was growing unease as it reached the drop zone—the weather was atrocious. The team all jumped successfully. Unfortunately, the novice parachutist, Williams, hit the water badly. However, within minutes, the team were picked up by the ship and fully briefed before going to the area where it was believed the bombs needed detonating.

While Williams' team got down to the serious business of combing the ship for suspect packages, Dickson arrived at the phone booth and waited for the extortionist to make contact. At 21:40, he answered a call ordering him to go to a diner a few miles away, where further instructions would be taped under a basin in the lavatory. Dickson left the blue bag containing the ransom cash in a secluded spot as instructed, while the FBI hovered discreetly in the background.

Back on the ship, there was a brief moment of anxiety when a suitcase was found whose owner couldn't be traced. Williams blew open its lock but all it contained was a pile of dirty laundry. Fortunately, by the early hours of the next morning, Williams and his exhausted team concluded that the whole affair had been a hoax.

The FBI's investigation continued and the extortionist was eventually identified. Far from being a criminal mastermind, the man who had sparked the whole crisis was 48-year-old shoe salesman Joseph Lindisi from New York. Charged with attempted extortion and making threatening phone calls, he was found guilty and sentenced to 20 years in prison. I don't know how the bomb disposal team got off the ship—I guess they enjoyed a leisurely cruise back home!

And that was my claim to fame!

Two short months later, I was on my way to the airhead at RAF Brize Norton where I boarded a Bristol Britannia passenger aircraft and departed the UK én route to warmer climes.

Chapter Four
Royal Air Force Station Masirah

(7 July 1972 to 4 April 1973)

My first overseas posting was to Masirah Island in July 1972. The island was approximately 40 miles long by five miles wide, situated south of the entrance to the Persian Gulf and 10 miles off the coast of Oman. I was employed on the Visiting Aircraft Servicing Flight (VASF). There I was primarily responsible for the maintenance of the radar systems fitted to the multitude of aircraft transiting the Gulf én route to the Far East and beyond. The station formed part of the United Kingdom's Near East Air Force (NEAF) whose headquarters was in Cyprus.

Whilst I'd been looking forward to the tour, it was quite an eye-opener as to the way the Arab population lived at the time.

Early in 1904, the Baron Inverdale, a British ship, ran aground at Hallaniyah, an island group north of Salalah. The crew launched the lifeboats and eventually landed on the northeast coast of Masirah. The locals, who hadn't seen a white man before, were very curious. When a member of the crew panicked and fired a warning shot, the locals reacted by massacring the entire crew.

The British sent a gunboat and after meeting with Sultan Faisal the Sultan of Oman, a decree was issued stating that since the locals wished to act like animals, then they would be treated like animals and forbid the use of any permanent buildings for three generations.

To that end, the locals spent the next 90 years living in various types of temporary accommodation, the most common was built from empty 45-gallon oil drums with a flimsy roof covering. The only brick building in the village of Ras Hilf was the school.

My first evening was spent in the NAFFI with a couple of friends I'd worked with at Lyneham. I was somewhat surprised to see people dressed in long-sleeved shirts, jumpers and long trousers especially as I was sweating like a pig. I had taken trousers and a couple of shirts but never really contemplated wearing them. How wrong I was because within a couple of months, once I'd become acclimatised, I began to feel cold in the evening.

The temperature at midday was about 120° F and fell at night to 85° F. A difference of 35° F which in the UK could be compared to a drop in daytime temperature from say 75° F to 40° F—acutely noticeable. Anyway, I don't think I drank too much that evening, but I do remember going back to my temporary accommodation feeling quite pissed. Unfortunately. I hadn't taken into account the effect that dehydration has on the body because when I awoke the next morning I felt like shit.

Masirah was hot, humid and dusty with a permanent on-shore wind and the arrivals procedure was the same as for Lyneham, the only difference was that it was carried out in temperatures of over 100° F. I got dressed into my brand-new cardboard KD and made my way to the general office. I only managed to get a couple of signatures on the blue card and the next stop was the SWO's office (the station warrant officer was one notch above the station commander and two notches below God).

The room was very hot and stuffy, and while I waited an incredible sense of nausea came over me which wasn't helped by an argument that I witnessed going on between an Arab and a member of the SWO's team. Without a moment's hesitation, I opened the door and threw up.

I spent the rest of that day in bed really suffering and it was several days before I could even stomach food. The painful lesson I learnt that day was to always keep hydrated with water and not alcohol. That was a lesson, I was never to forget.

The accommodation at the station was a mix of brick buildings used by the officers and SNCOs. The *other ranks* predominately lived in Twyneham prefab huts, eight people in a room with windows covered by flyscreens and access by doors at either end of the hut. There were no luxuries such as air-conditioning, we had two ceiling fans and that was it!

The windows were left open day and night. There were two Twynehams adjacent to ours with full air con, reserved for transiting aircrew only. The only other buildings on the station that had air-conditioning were the Electronic Supply Group (ESG) and electronics servicing bays. ESG was situated alongside the VASF line hut and it was used extensively by VASF personnel whenever we needed to use the cool toilet facilities.

Drinking water was provided by a desalination plant and shortly before I arrived, the output capacity of the plant was increased resulting in the salt water showers being changed to fresh water. I imagine the desalination technology of today far outstrips that which was available in 1972 because there was always a taste of salt in the drinking water. In an attempt to hide it, we were given free bottles of orange squash. Can you imagine salty orange juice? Tea was equally as disgusting.

Most, if not all, of the Twynehams were infested with bedbugs and the little buggers would hide in the nooks and crannies of the metal-framed beds and come out at night. They were about a quarter the size of a little fingernail and would gorge themselves on blood until they were full, by which time they'd have expanded at least threefold. Most people suffered with the bites, some worse than others and some not at all.

You knew you'd been zapped by the telltale red, itchy spot that appeared a day or two after being bitten and looked similar to a mosquito bite. Throughout my tour, I got bitten several times, but there were one or two people who were repeatedly savaged. Their state of cleanliness was never in doubt in much the same way that mosquitoes don't select people who are dirtier or cleaner than their counterparts.

Insect repellents helped but only killed the live bugs and never eradicated the eggs that were laid in the crevasses of the bed. The most effective method of control was to strip the bed of the linen and mattress, take the metal bedframe onto the bondu, pour on liberal quantities of *Avtur* aviation fuel and set light to it. That killed the bugs and any eggs that hadn't hatched. The trick then was to stop the bugs from climbing from the floor onto the *clean* frame.

This was achieved by taking four empty beer cans, cutting off the tops, half-filling the cans with aircraft hydraulic oil and standing the bed legs inside the cans. This technique worked most times. However, if the bugs fell from the walls or ceiling onto the bed, the infestation would start again and the bed-burning had to be repeated.

The other irritating creatures were the bloody flies. Until my arrival, I'd never come across flies that pestered the life out of someone as much as they did at Masirah. They were generally small, moved like lightning and when shooed away, would immediately land an inch or so away. They were the devil to kill and caused a great deal of frustration; however, whilst they were Arabic flies, it was assumed that they clearly understood English. More often than not, frantic waving of the arms and shouting, "F*** off fly," generally seemed to work!

During the 16 months I spent on the 214th entry, we were constantly harassed by a Corporal who then was a member of the RAF Regiment, a Rock Ape, named after the Barbary Apes that live on the Rock of Gibraltar (he was to subsequently remuster to General Duties). Corporal Herbert's job at Cosford was to maintain discipline on the flight and he was the absolute bane of our lives.

Imagine my surprise and delight when he was posted to Masirah not long before I left. His job title was *Pest Control JNCO* which entailed escorting an Arab who was equipped with a large backpack containing mosquito repellent. He sprayed the buildings on the station. Oh, deep joy, how the mighty had fallen!

VASF operated a three-shift system, each shift having nine tradesmen comprising a mix of ranks and trades, sufficient to service, maintain and repair most types of aircraft that transited through. The cycle began with the day shift starting work at 07:00 and finishing at 12:00, at which point the afternoon shift took over and worked until the last aircraft was serviced, repaired, locked and chocked.

That shift then had a day's stand-down and would start again at 07:00 the following day. So, the cycle carried on for nine months. The work carried out by the electronics trades, or *Fairies* as we were known, was fairly mundane. It got to the stage where Dave Stoddart and I would concentrate on helping the *Riggers* (airframes) and *Sooties* (engines) with replenishing the engine oils, refuelling the aircraft and any other task that would enable us to finish earlier, especially in the afternoon shift.

The flight dispersal or *Pan* as it was more commonly referred to, was an immense expanse of white concrete which, despite the constant on-shore wind, was unbearably hot. By the time the aircraft had been on the ground for about half an hour, it was too hot to work inside and massive diesel, engine-driven air-conditioning trolleys would be needed. The same coolers were also connected first thing in the morning to enable the aircrew to stay relatively cool during their departure preparation.

Another job that was never really fought over was the domestic duties, which gave the lucky man the princely extra sum of 50 p per day. The job entailed emptying the Elsan chemical toilet used on the Hercules or in the case of the

Britannia aircraft, a domestic trolley was used to remove the waste from the two on-board toilets and replenish the tanks with Racasan flushing liquid.

The job wasn't too bad providing a good seal between the aircraft and the Doms trolley was achieved before the vent handle was turned. There was one occasion when our tame Nav Insty, Corporal Ken Butt decided to empty the toilets on a Britannia aircraft that had just arrived from Akrotiri having been serviced by the Tactical Aircraft Servicing Flight (TASF).

Before connecting the trolley, Ken opened the outer skin toilet access panel, removed the inner locking cover from the dump pipe and was immediately hit on the head with a large lump of semi-frozen ice, excrement and water. It wasn't the first time this had happened and we immediately knew the cause. The bastards at TASF hadn't completely emptied the toilet.

Instead, they had closed off the dump valve, refitted the locking cover, and then opened the dump valve again, which filled the pipe with what crap was left in the toilet. Once the aircraft had reached its cruising altitude, the waste in the tube would freeze solid and only start to thaw once the aircraft had landed.

That in itself was unpleasant but what happened next was enough to turn your stomach. Once Ken had pulled the turds out of his hair and finished the servicing, it was time to close up for the night. He decided to go to the shower block that was about 30 yards from Our Twynham. The rest of the shift wrapped up the servicing, closed the section and headed back to the Twynham where we found Ken fast asleep on top of his bed still dressed in his shitty clothes.

We all showered and went back to Twynham. We couldn't wake up Ken, so we left him. He awoke the next morning, got changed into clean clothes, and went to breakfast. We weren't sure when he, eventually, washed but it certainly wasn't when he should have.

One of the early-morning rituals carried out before any ground equipment was moved or disconnected from the aircraft was to check that no scorpions or camel spiders had hidden themselves away overnight. I did find one or two scorpions that could have given a nasty sting. We would also regularly find praying mantis hiding in the chocks.

The clothing we were issued was rather crude and basic comprising of short-sleeved Khaki Dress (KD) shirts, KD shorts which came down to the knees (a quick trip to the Indian tailors would make them look a little more presentable), knee-length socks and Bondu boots. The uniform was expected to last for the full nine-month tour.

However, I, and several other members of VASF had all sorts of problems in trying to get a second, and in my case, a third pair of *Bondu boots*. The clothing stores seemed incapable of understanding that Avtur and OM15 hydraulic oil played havoc with the stitching that held the soles of the shoes in place.

There were no moulded soles then and I was bollocked on more than one occasion for working on the aircraft with a flapping sole. We were also not allowed to work topless on the aircraft; the rationale being that if there was a fuel fire, the shirts would at least offer some protection.

We had a multitude of aircraft overnighting or transiting the island; however, the most eagerly awaited detachment were the Vulcans from Bomber Wing in Cyprus. I'm not sure where the aircraft were flying to, but during my time there, around three detachments each comprising six aircraft arrived. It was always entertaining parking them all on the pan. Another regular visitor was the Shorts Belfast.

The aircraft, operated by 53 Squadron based at RAF Brize Norton, was larger than the Herc. It was roomy enough to carry two single-deck buses. The original RAF requirement had foreseen a fleet of 30 aircraft, but this number was to be significantly reduced as a result of the Sterling Crisis of 1965. The United Kingdom Government needed to gain support for its loan application to the International Monetary Fund (IMF), which the United States would provide.

However, one of the *alleged* clauses for this support was that the RAF should purchase Lockheed C130 Hercules aircraft. The order for the Belfast was subsequently reduced to 10. Unusually, each aircraft was given a name: Sampson, Goliath, Pallas, Hector, Atlas, Heracles, Theseus, Spartacus, Enceladus and Ajax.

The majority of personnel posted in arrived on the Britannia passenger aircraft, there were however occasions when we'd be visited by the VC10. I don't know why, but the aircrew of that aircraft always seemed to regard themselves as something extraordinarily special; more often than not they were impatient. We never had the same rapport as we did with other visiting crews. The VC10 never stayed overnight and only refuelled before continuing to RAF Gan; a beautiful little island that formed part of the Maldives in the Indian Ocean.

There was a great deal to do in our spare time, and on many occasions, once the morning shift was finished, we would get changed, load up with water and cycle to Surf Beach; which was about two miles from the camp. The beach was fantastic and stretched for miles. Swimming was more or less forbidden due to the strong underwater currents and myriad nasties that would do a swimmer some serious harm.

Suncream, if it was available, was expensive. However, a cheap and readily available alternative, which gave a really good long-lasting tan was—Olive Oil. I spent many a relaxing afternoon on the beach and never really got sunburnt which I put down to not trying to hurry the tan. The same unfortunately couldn't be said of *Crinkle* Chris Hardy who I'd known well having worked with him at Lyneham.

Chris was the next new arrival onto VASF after me. By September, I'd achieved a very good deep, all-over tan. Chris, however, being the sensitive sort of bloke, got cheesed off with constantly being referred to as the resident *mooney*. He was very fair-haired and just didn't seem to be changing colour.

So, in a fit of desperation, he liberally smeared olive oil over his shoulders and arms and walked about without a shirt. He was very, very lucky not to have been CasEvacted to the Military Hospital at Akrotiri because his arms and shoulders came up in some of the biggest blisters I have; even to this day, ever seen. I'm sure he must have been scarred for life.

Fishing was exceptional and even the most novice of fisherman really couldn't fail to make a catch. The various messes always had their freezers full of fresh catches varying from queenfish, barracuda, shark and a multitude of other species with visiting aircrew from Cyprus regularly asking for crayfish to take home. I regret never eating any fish throughout my entire tour.

Shortly after I arrived on the island, three firemen drove around the station in a long wheel-based Land Rover showing off their prized catch—a 330 lb shark that they'd caught off the north beach. The head of the shark was against the windscreen and the tail extended over the lowered tailgate.

I can't remember the breaking strain of the line used, but I do remember being shown the tracer line. It comprised three lengths of intertwined aircraft locking wire. The shark was subsequently cut up and shared between the various mess kitchens.

The pay was administered locally. However, I could see no point in having my entire weekly wage paid in riyals. So, shortly after arriving, I made arrangements for a fixed monthly deduction of £110 to be deducted from my wage and deposited in my UK bank account. The savings over nine months would enable me to buy a reasonable car on my return.

Most sections on the station would participate in organised *Bondu bashes*. The trip would take place in a couple of covered three-ton trucks loaded with water, beer and food for barbeques provided by the messes and head off down the island. There were no roads as such, and once through *Tin Town,* the dust tracks quickly degenerated into rock and boulder-strewn trails.

The two most popular places visited were an old WW2 Sea Plane Base on the western side of the island and the Portuguese Fort in the interior of the island.

Golf was played by few people and although the course was effectively one big bunker, the club had carved out a reasonable nine-hole course. The greens weren't green at all and were known as *Blacks* as they were constructed of sand, doused in oil and compressed. Most sports were played on the station and we had a thriving VASF cricket team.

I was selected to play for the station hockey team but was soon dropped because I didn't attend the numerous training sessions. It was all very well and good for those members of the station who only worked daily from 7 to 12 but for me the practices almost always coincided with my being on shift. I was disappointed because the team subsequently played in Gan, Singapore and Cyprus.

Apart from the NAAFI, there were two bars situated about 100 yards from the Twynham; one was the Turtle Club, which doubled as the Masonic Lodge, the other was the Crazy Horse Saloon both of which served a multitude of drinks. There were no draught beers and the only beers on sale, that readily spring to mind, were Carlsbergs (affectionately known as *Charlie Red* and *Charlie Green*) and Tenants which had pictures of scantily clad ladies on the can.

The Charlies cost 6½ pence a can whilst a whisky cost three pence a shot. I don't remember what a pack of 20 cigarettes cost. But I know that on two occasions during my tour each smoker was given a free carton of 200 ciggies. These were the proceeds of confiscations from passengers who either attempted to smuggle the cigarettes into the UK or who had exceeded their duty-free allowance and weren't prepared to pay the necessary duty. Either way, they were gratefully received!

The station was also home to a small dog called Minnie. I'm not sure of her breed but she was about the size of a Jack Russell and would do the rounds, calling in at the various sections for water or to be fed. One particularly clear moonlit evening, Dave Wade left our Twynham and walked towards the Turtle Club. All of a sudden, he came flying through the Twynham door in a real panic.

He told us that as he walked across the bondu, he saw what he thought was Minnie coming towards him. As he got closer and bent down to stroke her, he realised that it wasn't Minnie but a very large camel spider! The spider scuttled off and Dave ran the other way. Now, I know that Dave wasn't the sort to exaggerate and we had no reason not to believe what he'd seen.

One event that caused worldwide condemnation and was to have widespread implications for those of us at Masirah took place on 5 September 1972, in Munich, West Germany. Palestinian commandos armed with automatic rifles broke into the quarters of the Israeli team at the Olympic Village, killed two members of the team and took nine others hostage.

23 hours later, the nine hostages had also been murdered as well as a German policeman. Five of the Palestinian terrorists were killed. The massacre is by far the worst case of violence in Olympic history since the modern games began in 1896. Also, one of the most notorious cases of terrorism on record up until that time.

The Palestinian commandos were part of the then-unknown Black September Organisation (BSO), a band of Palestinian militants founded in 1970, who broke away from Fatah, the Palestinian faction that controlled the Palestine Liberation Organisation (PLO). BSO militants were disaffected with what they perceived to be the PLO's ineffective tactics against Israel.

Their demands in the attack were to secure the release of more than 200 Palestinian guerrillas held in Israeli jails, along with the release of German Red Army members Andreas Baader and Ulrike Meinhof, held in a German prison.

The BSO and the attack were ultimately responsible for the creation of permanent, professional and military-trained forces of major European countries such as: the German Counter Terrorism and Special Operations Unit (GSG 9), the French Gendarmerie Counter Terrorist and Hostage Rescue Unit (GIGN) or the reorganisation of already standing units to such a group, like the UK's Special Air Service (SAS).

Following the Olympics massacre, several suspected BSO activists were rounded up and interrogated. I'm not sure where the interrogations were carried out or by whom, but we were led to believe that confessions were achieved by using Sodium Pentothal, the supposed *Truth Drug*. During one such interrogation, RAF Masirah was mentioned and following further investigations, the Arab school headmaster was arrested when a quantity of explosives was discovered on his Dhow.

The consequence of the discovery of the explosives and subsequent arrest was that the security state of the RAF base was raised considerably and guards were posted during silent hours at the Petrol Supply Depot (PSD) and the saltwater desalination plant.

The PSD was nothing more than half-a-dozen very large cylindrical storage tanks, positioned at the northern end of the island, adjacent to the Water Sports Club, approximately 1½ miles from the station. I was amongst the first to be selected for guard duties.

I and another lad were taken by the RAF police in a Land Rover, shown the area we were to patrol, given a torch and a whistle and also shown where the nearest telephone was situated. Our brief was that in the event of an attack, we were to blow our whistles and phone for help. The fact was that even if we were heard it would take at least 10 minutes for anyone to respond and reach us was an absolute joke!

Weapons were held in the armoury but we were never given access to them. The other area that we had to protect was the desalination plant which I guarded twice and once again I had no weapon to defend myself. At least the PSD had perimeter lights whereas the water plant was built on the side of the Jebel and had no external lighting at all. If a terrorist had decided to attack, the guard wouldn't have known about it until he had been either killed or serious damage caused to the plant.

Number 46 Squadron was permanently detached from the UK and operated the Hawker Siddeley Andover CMK1 aircraft, affectionately known as *Yimkin Airways* (Yimkin is Arabic for maybe) Flights to Seeb International airports in Muscat. Sharjah or Dubai would be carried out on a weekly basis, I believe, on diplomatic missions.

There was always a requirement for the ground crew to accompany the flights and carry out turn around services. Volunteers were taken from either the squadron's own ground crew or from VASF personnel. I went on three flights as it was the only opportunity, not only to see some of the extremely attractive civilian stewardesses that transited through Dubai but also to buy some cheap, well-made clothes from the various souks.

I'm not sure where it came from but Joe Prior managed to acquire a fish tank and in an attempt to brighten up the crew room, he managed to fill the tank with some really beautiful, exotic fish, all caught locally from the sea. Unfortunately, someone also decided to introduce a small baby turtle, which initially, looked quite cute. However, it didn't take long for the fish to start to disappear, the reason; the tank was providing a captive source of food for the turtle, and it was soon removed.

Towards the end of my tour, a request was made via the relevant channels by the Sultan of Oman Qaboos bin Said, for assistance in changing over his desert forces that were on duty in Jebel Akhdar (the Green Mountain) which forms part of the Al Hajar mountain range.

The Jebel Akhdar, at one time, was the scene of conflict between Omani forces loyal to the Sultan of Oman (supported by British soldiers including the Special Air Service), and the Saudi Arabian-backed rebel forces of the Imamate of Oman. The conflict was driven by a struggle for shares in the newly discovered oil wealth and was coordinated from the town of Nizwa.

On 22 February 1973, I flew with a 70 Squadron Hercules and acted as support crew along with two of the squadron's own groundcrew. We landed at Salalah, which is situated on the coast, north of the Yemen border and were briefed as to the precise requirements for the next stage of the operation. We knew that the landing would be at a remote desert location. We, subsequently, prepared the aircraft underbelly for a strip landing.

The preparation entailed taping foam rubber to the leading edges of all lower antennas, undercarriage doors, landing lamps and anything else that may incur damage during landing and take-off. Having prepared and loaded up the aircraft with the necessary equipment and the replacement Omani soldiers, we flew off to the remote desert runway close to the town of Nizwa.

The flight was uneventful and the landing, apart from the unbelievable noise, generated on touchdown, went without a hitch. The Omani forces were to be flown onto their base at the summit of Jebel Akhdar. Unfortunately, the runway wasn't long enough for the Hercules even with its amazing tactical take-off and landing capability.

Instead, the troops and equipment were to be ferried aboard a Skyvan aircraft flown by an RAF Flight Lieutenant who was on secondment to the Royal Omani Air Force. The Skyvan, manufactured by Shorts of Belfast, was a small, unpressurised, square-section fuselage aircraft used primarily for short-haul freight transfer. It was called many things; the most popular being the six-ton budgie, the flying wind tunnel and the whispering nissun hut, but it was never called pretty.

The equipment was loaded and I was asked if I fancied a flight to the summit. There was no room for seats and I was given a headset and told to stand behind the pilot; holding on to whatever was available—no safety harnesses! There were minimal pre-flight checks carried out and the troops were still loading their personnel equipment when we started to taxi. Without further ado, the ramp door closed up and we took off.

The flight and landing on the plateau were hairy, to say the least, and the views on top were breathtaking. After unloading the aircraft, we prepared for take-off. I don't believe the rough landing strip could have been more than about 80 yards long. I was warned that we, probably, wouldn't attain sufficient speed and lift to get airborne.

Instead, we would merely drop off the plateau and pick up sufficient airspeed during the dive and achieve flight; now that really filled me with confidence. However, the guy obviously knew what he was doing because that's exactly what we did; very exhilarating. The flights in the Skyvan continued until all equipment and personnel were transferred. I only flew on the first trip!

By the time I got back to the Hercules, arrangements had been made to take us by Land Rover to the nearby town of Nizwa which, as mentioned earlier, was the centre of the Akhdar conflict in the 1950s. We were taken to the top of a large round tower that formed part of the ancient fort, built around 400 years ago in the centre of the town.

During the conflict, the RAF was called in to assist the Sultan in suppressing the revolt. The tower was bombed and rocketed by Venom jet aircraft. We spent a couple of hours in Nizwa before heading back to the aircraft for the return journey to Salalah.

As we approached Salalah we were *buzzed* by two Omani Air Force BAC 167 Strikemaster light attack jet aircraft. On landing, were informed that shortly after we took off earlier in the day, the airfield had been attacked by rebels who had fired 122 mm Katyusha rockets from the surrounding Jebel. Also, they had successfully blown up a De Havilland DHC-4 Caribou transport aircraft that had been parked next to us.

The attacks were quite a regular occurrence and formed part of the Dhofar Rebellion which began in 1965. The rebellion was fought in and around Salalah by the Sultan of Oman's Armed Forces against guerrilla fighters of the Marxist Popular Front for the Liberation of Oman and the Persian Gulf. The rebellion, which was supported by the newly independent Communist South Yemen and several other socialist states including East Germany, was aimed at overthrowing and deposing the Sultan.

The Sultan was ably assisted by members of the UK and Iranian armed forces as well as support from loan officers from Pakistan and India. The conflict remained active until December 1975; when the guerrillas finally surrendered.

It was during my Masirah tour that I became quite sceptical of some of the officer fraternities and quickly learnt not to trust what they said. Having sailed a little on Lake Shearwater in Wiltshire whilst at Adcroft, I decided to join the Water Sports Club and try my hand at offshore sailing.

There were several boats in the club. However, the majority were in need of repair and renovation which needed to be carried out before being cleared for use in the sea. I joined a small team of enthusiasts, was allocated a boat and between us, we spent several weeks during our spare time restoring and painting our charge.

There were a couple of young officers in the team, who, by all accounts, were experienced sailors and although we never saw them once during the repair phase, once the boat was seaworthy, they were there like rats up a drainpipe. I asked one of the officers if I could crew for him. His response was that he already had a crew.

The boat was only ever used when they and their cronies turned up. Consequently, the rest of the team never got a look in; of course, they were always far too busy (and important) to consider asking those of us who had restored it if we wanted to crew it.

I spent my 21st birthday on the island and as a surprise, Mum baked a cake and gave it to Ian who managed to get it onto a flight from Lyneham to Cyprus and then on to me. It was gratefully received by those on shift. I spent the evening at the Crazy H playing drinking games, the object being to get one, two or more members of the party absolutely legless.

The most popular games played were Cardinal Puff, Rumbo and Fizz Buzz. The rules were easy when sober, but always created a challenge after a few beers.

Cardinal Puff

Each player was given a beer and a whisky (or other spirit).

The game began with the first player chanting, "I'll drink to the health of Cardinal Puff for the first time."

He would tap the top of the table once with his left index finger, tap once with his right index finger and then, tap the underside of the table once with his left index finger and then his right finger. He would then stamp his left foot once, and his right foot once, stand up, sit down and using one finger and thumb take one swig of the beer.

If no mistake was made then the next phase began with same player saying, "I'll drink to the health of Cardinal Puff for the second time."

The same ritual was carried out. Only this time, two fingers were used to tap the table twice, stamp the feet twice, stand up and sit down twice and using two fingers and a thumb take two swigs of beer.

If the player got through the third and final round without making a mistake, the game passed to the next player, whereas, if a mistake was made, then the player downed the short and started again.

Rumbo

Each player decides on a personal *call sign* such as touching his nose, standing up, clapping his hands and so on. The game began with everyone slowly slapping the tabletop with one hand after the other. When the session leader called *Rumbo*, everyone rapidly bangs the table.

The leader gives his call sign and someone else's call sign which he must acknowledge by first giving his own call sign. Then, giving someone else's call sign and so on. The game continues until someone makes a mistake and must take a large swig of beer; he then starts the game again.

Fizz Buzz

Fizz Buzz is a counting game that concentrates on the numbers 5 and 7 and multiples of 5 and 7 with the penalty for making a mistake being exactly the same as for the other games. The players sit in a circle and the first player begins to count from 1, the second player says 2, the third player says 3, and the fourth player says 4. But instead of the fifth player saying 5, he must say *Fizz*.

The sixth player says 6 and the seventh player says *Buzz* instead of the number 7. Number 10, because it's a multiple of 5 is a *Fizz*, and 14 is a multiple of 7 is a *Buzz*, 15 is a *Fizz*, 17 is a *Buzz*, 20 is a *Fizz*, 21 is a *Buzz* and so on.

The number 35, because it is a multiple of 5 and 7, is a *Fizz Buzz*. At this point, if the count has got that far, the direction of the counting reverses. The game goes on until a mistake is made, the culprit takes a drink and the game continues. Hesitating for too long also invokes a penalty.

Having been used to a typical Christmas in the UK where the weather was characteristically cold or damp and generally miserable, the climate in the Arabian Sea made for a surreal experience. Normal operations were suspended for the day, and the airmen's mess presented good, traditional Christmas cuisine after which we just relaxed and sunbathed.

There was no restriction on the amount of beer we could buy. There was, however, a problem in trying to keep sufficient quantities of beer cool for any length of time. Those of us in the Twynham had anticipated the problem and had earlier emptied one of the six-foot lockers and lined it with polythene before filling it with ice and copious cans of amber nectar.

We were regularly visited by natives from the mainland who would sell us various souvenirs and one in particular would call at the Twynham and take orders for specific items; others would regularly sit outside our mess and lay out the wares. Haggling was not only part and parcel of the buying event but was expected to take place.

I and several others from VASF were leaving the airman's mess one evening and witnessed one of the most unique methods of haggling ever seen. A soldier, who I believe was only visiting the island, was in a fierce debate with an Omani; who, instead of trying to knock the price down, kept increasing what he wanted to pay.

So, for example, when the Omani said 10 Riyals, the Pongo would offer 12 Riyals and so on. I really don't think he got the hang of it and the Arab must have thought that all of his birthdays had come at once.

There were two shops on the island: one was the NAAFI where we could buy the very latest in hi-fi technology, cassettes, records, watches and some excellent photographic kit, the other was Kimjis, a small prefab building located just outside the camp boundary and run by Omanis.

Music systems in the early '70s left a lot to be desired and those that were available in the NAAFI were really quite basic. One of my colleagues bought a small Sony AM/FM Radio and a cassette player with the rather innovative capability of being able to copy cassettes and rather than blast out everyone in the Twynham with the twin speakers. He also bought a pair of chunky padded headphones.

There are many *firsts* that I can recollect and one was listening to music in stereo through headphones; the effects were amazing and so completely unlike anything I heard before. I was so taken aback that almost immediately I bought the same system. The song that I'd listened to was 'In the Morning' from the 'Melody Fair' album by the Bee Gees which was the first of my many pirated cassette albums.

In fact, I recently managed to buy a CD copy and when I first listened to it the memories came flooding back. There's one more song that really brings back the emotions associated with that tour of duty, 'Song Sung Blue' by Neil Diamond!

Rain was such a rarity on the island. I only witnessed one storm during my nine-month tour. The downpour started late one evening and was so intense that the noise on the tin roof of the Twynham was deafening. It rained for only a few hours, and in that time, there was standing water everywhere but by the morning most of it had soaked away.

Until then, I'd always thought that the desert island was barren of plant life but within a couple of days, the station began to bloom with grass and a few colourful plants making an appearance. Sadly, the colour didn't last and before long, the plants withered and died back again.

Masirah was also routinely visited by Canberra PR9, a Photo Recce aircraft from 13 Squadron based at Luqa in Malta. On most occasions, the aircraft would arrive with no accompanying ground crew. Therefore, we would carry out the Flight servicing. As I'd worked on the aircraft whilst in training, I was reasonably familiar with the system's layout.

Engine starts were always entertaining; due in part to the two different methods of winding up the engine. The more common method was by using a cartridge that resembled a huge shotgun shell. It was inserted into a specially designed chamber and when fired, the expanding hot gases would turn over the engine enabling it to be started. The explosion from the starter cartridge was impressive with flames leaping from the engine vents with the whole area being wreathed in pungent cordite smoke.

The second more dodgy method was achieved by using Avpin, a nasty explosive fuel that was volatile in the extreme. Avpin or Isopropyl Nitrate, is extremely flammable and burns with a practically invisible flame which presents unique hazards in its handling. The flame is significantly less luminous than hydrogen or methanol flame and is only visible due to the turbulent hot air it generates.

The Avpin was poured into a small reservoir on each engine and when ignited would have the same effect as the cartridge. The only problem was getting the fuel into the little tank without spilling any of the liquid. We would very gingerly pour the fuel from a modest container.

However, on the one occasion, when 13 Squadron groundcrew came from Luqa with the aircraft, one member told us in no uncertain terms, to stop pussy footing about. He took the container, upended it into the tank and split copious amounts of fuel over the surface of the engine and wing. He couldn't understand why he was the only one on the aircraft, whilst the remainder of us were in the middle of the bondu!

The start procedure for the Britannia entailed a somewhat convoluted process requiring at least five personnel to get the four engines running. Once the propeller brakes were released by the aircrew, the props could rotate either clockwise or counterclockwise. To avoid the disastrous consequence of one if not all props rotating in the wrong direction, each prop had to be manually held by the groundcrew until the engine engagement was confirmed.

Tom Gore (Rigger and Shift Boss), Gordon Thornton (Rigger), Bob Combes (Engines), Chris Hardy (Nav Inst), Jack Langridge (Electrician), Me (Radar), Dave Stoddart (Communications) and Alan Johnson (Rigger)

I have some fond memories of my tour at Masirah; not only because it was my first overseas posting and I was only 20 years old when I arrived, but more especially because of the environment we worked and lived in.

I was single and had no commitments in England. Whereas, there were several married personnel who were separated from their wives and families for nine long months. There was the opportunity for personnel to stay with their families at Akrotiri for a two-week holiday and many, even the singles took the break but I didn't bother.

Spring 1973 duly arrived in England in all its glory, and it wasn't until I flew over the countryside on approach to RAF Brize Norton that I realised how absolutely beautiful the English countryside really is; truly a green and pleasant land. Having seen nothing but sand, sand and more sand for nine months, the contrasting colours were stunning.

Chapter Five
Back Home

(April 1973)

One of the first things I did once the hire vehicle was returned; was to get myself another car. Dad had spoken to a family friend, Derek Rowe, who owned a local second-hand car business and asked him to keep an eye out for a reasonably priced motor for when I came home.

Derek showed me a 1968 Metallic Blue 1500cc Mk2 Ford Cortina which was everything I was looking for. It was absolutely immaculate and we did the deal for £400. Showers were the norm in Masirah; there were no baths that I can remember. However, when I took my first bath at Mum's, I must have shed several layers of skin because the tide mark I left on the bath was akin to the devastation left by the Torrey Canyon oil tanker disaster.

The Near Cross-Channel Disaster

It was whilst I was on disembarkation leave in April that Uncle Andy (Dad's sister's husband) asked if I'd fancy sailing to Cherbourg with him and his brother Eddy; who was visiting from America, over the Easter weekend. Andy had recently bought himself a rather smart sailboat and had been attending evening classes learning to sail and navigate. As I'd already carried out some inshore sailing whilst at Adcroft, I accepted.

We arrived at Hamble mid-afternoon and began moving our kit to the boat that was moored in the middle of the river Hamble in an inflatable dinghy fitted with an outboard motor. Andy showed us around the boat, gave us a brief on the various systems and before too long we were on our way. The boat was fitted with a diesel engine as well as traditional sails.

We happily chugged down the river Hamble on a high tide heading towards Southampton Water. We expected to enter the Solent before it got dark. The plan was to sail past Cowes on the Isle of Wight and having passed the Needles, head out into the English Channel towards Cherbourg. Unfortunately, for some obscure reason, Andy got on the wrong side of the concrete marker columns and as we entered Southampton Water we ran aground.

Despite every effort over the next four hours, we were unable to free ourselves. Then, as the tide retreated, the boat began to list. We had a sleepless night and by early light, the boat was high and dry with the water at least 20 yards away. We dug a channel in the shingle for the keel to sit in and hoped that at the next high tide, we might be able to re-float the boat.

The tide duly came in and the boat righted itself but was still firmly stuck. So, we took a long length of rope in the dinghy to the closest marker and using the boat's winch tried to pull ourselves off the bank—no good. By now, the tide was full again and any further delay would have meant another 12 hours stranded. As luck would have it, a very large cruiser stopped and offered to pull us off the sandbank.

Andy was reluctant to accept the tow in the event that the owner might try and claim salvage rights and charge a small fortune to get the boat back. The concern and doubt were needless because once the towline was attached, we were pulled off and, after showing our gratitude to the tow boat, we entered Southampton Water.

We all thought that was a disastrous start to the journey, however, that turned out to be only a minor hiccup compared to what we were to go through over the next four days.

Once we got past the Needles, we shut down the engine, raised the sails and sat in the cockpit contemplating what lay ahead. Rather than all of us staying awake, I was told to get some rest and would be called when it was my turn to crew the helm. I'm not sure how long I was asleep in the Foksal, but when I awoke there was a howling gale and I didn't feel particularly good.

Over the next few hours, we took turns to navigate, crew the boat, eat and drink, and sadly I repeatedly felt sick whenever I was in the galley and threw up over the side several times. Andy, who I thought was a fairly well experienced sailor, also began to feel unwell and during a particularly intense squall, put his head over the side and was violently sick.

When he turned around, he shouted that his top set of false teeth had also gone overboard. Eddie didn't seem to suffer from sickness. The rest of that night and the following day were uneventful. After what seemed an eternity, we eventually, arrived in Cherbourg harbour, moored and went ashore for a well-earned meal and some beers.

The next day was spent tidying up and preparing for the return journey. By mid-afternoon, we were Ship Shape and Bristol Fashion and ready to leave Cherbourg harbour én route for home. Andy was reluctant to use the engine for too long and as a fuel-saving measure chose to hoist the sails.

After four hours or so, the harbour was still well in sight and the wind just didn't want to blow, it was then that I realised what becalmed really meant; which tied in nicely with the other nautical expression *the lull before the storm*. I decided to get some rest and was rudely awoken just before midnight in what could only be described as a massive storm.

Andy and Eddie were both at the helm and I strapped myself in with the safety harness and took over at the helm. For the next eight hours, we took it in turns to crew the boat, with at least, two members always awake. Unfortunately, the battery charging system had broken down and we first became aware when the navigation lights began to dim and eventually extinguished.

So, there we were, three novices sailing across the busiest shipping lane in the world, tired, in the dark and with no exterior lights to warn the tankers that we were there. By early morning, Andy and Eddie were totally knackered and I advised them to get some rest, if that was at all possible in the teeth of a force eight gale. I told them I'd be okay and if I needed help, I'd call.

As dawn broke, I felt quite exhilarated as we raced across the channel and didn't feel in the slightest bit sick or tired. It wasn't particularly difficult navigating because the wind was coming off the starboard quarter which meant I didn't have to tack much, if at all, in order to maintain our course towards the Isle of Wight.

That said, I almost died of fright when the tiller, which is attached to the rudder, parted company and I was left with no steering and the tiller in my hand. I managed to re-engage the two parts and shouted for help. But due to the wind, rain and the waves crashing against the hull, I couldn't be heard.

The storm eventually abated and we found ourselves with land in sight. However, we'd managed to miss the entrance to the Solent and headed towards

Poole Harbour where we pragmatically decided, due to the lack of navigation lights, to spend the night and return to the Hamble in daylight.

We used the motor to sail into the harbour and found ourselves a mooring spot. We hadn't been tied up for very long when we were visited by two customs officials who wanted to know who we were, where we'd come from, where we were going and when we planned on leaving. To make matters worse they thought we may be smugglers or worse still, drug couriers and began a meticulous search of the boat.

We could only stand by and watch and we weren't convinced that they believed the story of what we'd been through. After a couple of hours, they finished their search and found nothing more innocuous than a few of my duty-free cigarettes and my brand-new Yashica camera that I'd bought in Masirah, they let us go.

The weather next day was in total contrast to that experienced the day before and we sailed in full sunshine past the Needles and up the river Solent to Andy's mooring slot. It was then mid-afternoon, and we began to get our belongings together and lowered to the dinghy alongside ready to attach the outboard motor and start to convey our kit ashore.

I only had a rucksack which contained several shirts, spare trousers, underwear and toiletries. I casually leant over the side of the boat and dropped the bag into the dingy. As I let go, the dinghy moved and the bag landed on the central part of the dinghy; very gracefully bounced into the water and floated off down the river.

Andy saw what had happened and told me to jump into the dinghy and paddle after it, which was easier said than done because I jumped in and landed on one of the oars, snapping it in half. The last I ever saw of my bag was it bobbing up and down before sinking a hundred yards or so downstream.

The drama was now turning into a real crisis because Andy and I got aboard the dinghy, attached the outboard motor and headed towards the shore with the majority of our possessions, less mine, of course. As we approached the shore, the intention was for Andy to raise the outboard motor and glide to a stop. However, he was a little late and the propeller got caught up in the shingle and snapped the shear pin.

So, there we were, ashore. Eddy was still on board the boat, with no spare shear pin and no shops open to buy one. Andy, in a leap of desperation, decided to pop into a pub close by and ask if anyone had a spare pin.

I think that was the only thing that went right for us because he returned with a spare and before long the motor was fixed and we were all safely back ashore. That was an Easter I'll never forget and compared to that; the rest of the leave just paled into insignificance.

Chapter Six
Royal Air Force Station Colerne

(4 April 1973 to 21 October 1974)

I arrived at Royal Air Force Colerne in April 1973. Colerne was a relatively small station built on top of Bannerdown Hill which overlooked the city of Bath. The station's role was to carry out Minor and Major Servicings and in-depth modifications to the Hercules C130 transport aircraft. I was employed on the Electrical Engineering Squadron (EES) *C* Flight which comprised a small team of radar, communication, navigation instruments and electrical engineers.

The work was similar to that carried out at Lyneham and Masirah. The team of approximately 15 personnel were a good bunch and amongst other things, I learnt to play golf on a small nine-hole course situated on the airfield. My boss, Chief Tech Ken Bridle, was an absolute star.

By way of supplementing my still meagre wage, I started to work evenings in a pub in the village of Bathampton just to the west of the city of Bath. The *George Inn* was situated across a toll bridge on the main Bath to Chippenham Road. Coincidently, the manager and deputy manager were both named George. The pub was extremely popular and most evenings the pace was frenetic from opening time until the last orders.

Apart from the standard wage the landlord wouldn't allow us to accept drinks from the punters, for obvious reasons, however, he was quite happy for us to accept 10 p, instead, of a drink when offered, which at the end of the evening were added together and shared out. I'd only been working for a couple of months when one of the regular female members of the bar staff commented that of all the barmen who had worked in the pub, I was the only one who hadn't asked her out for a date.

I might have asked her if she hadn't been quite so forthright. From then on, I couldn't help thinking that maybe she was keeping a tally of her pub conquests—either way, she didn't add me to her score!

It was in November 1973, I came very close to killing myself in a road accident. I'd picked up Chris Hardy from Lyneham and went to a reunion at the Lysley Arms pub situated halfway between Chippenham and Calne. I had two pints of beer and a small meal. I took Chris back to Lyneham, picked up some fish and chips from the chippie in Bradenstoke and ate them in a lay-by at the end of the runway.

The next thing I remember was waking up in intensive care at Swindon Hospital! It turned out that I'd crashed the car into a tree on a sharp bend between Dauntsey Banks and Chippenham. The person who discovered me called 999, told the operator of the accident and believed I was dead. I'd been sick, but thankfully, I was wearing my seat belt.

The hospital contacted Mum and Dad who came straight away. I was later told by Mum that up until then, Dad had almost given up believing in God because of everything he'd been through but having seen the state I was in, it seriously reinvigorated his belief that perhaps a God did exist.

The only injuries I sustained were a dislocated toe, bruising to my face, severe concussion and a cut to my mouth caused when I bit through my lower lip. I spent the next 10 days in intensive care, sleeping an awful lot. I also had visits from friends at Lyneham although I never did find out who told them. I was eventually discharged and had to use crutches to get around.

Ian took me to where the accident happened and it looked like I'd driven around a very sharp right-hand bend and instead of straightening up, continued turning and collided with a large tree. There were still parts of the car at the bottom of the tree and I noticed a very large chunk of bark missing from the trunk.

Ian thought that I may have been disoriented by bright lights from a vehicle coming from the opposite direction and couldn't see the road. This was supported by the skid marks on a small lay-by on the left just as the bend started. I later found out the police wanted to breathalyse me but the paramedics wouldn't allow it—I know I wasn't drunk.

The vehicle had been taken to a breakers yard at Christian Mallford where Ian took me to retrieve any personal possessions that may have been left. I asked the yard owners to see the car and the look of amazement on his face was unforgettable. He said he was surprised to see me and commented that not many people would have survived an accident of that nature and took us to the car—what a mess!

As can be seen, the whole front-end had been concertinaed into an area half the original. I was surprised to have only suffered with a dislocation rather than more serious leg and foot injuries. Judging by the position of the steering wheel, I also understood why I'd sustained such serious injuries to my head and face—seat belts definitely do save lives.

It was only 10 days or so after being discharged that I went on holiday to Majorca with Roger King, Dick Dickenson and Dick Grant (known as *Big Dick* and *Little Dick*) I'd worked with them on *B* Line. They turned up at Colerne and picked up my bags. When I started hobbling on the crutches, Dick D said that I wouldn't need them and threw them into my locker. I spent the next week walking a lot and drinking a lot. I was almost always in pain and was told on more than one occasion to stop moaning. I did however have a fantastic time.

I was promoted to Corporal in February 1974 under the time promotion scheme. The system allowed me to achieve promotion after three years, provided I passed the necessary exams and kept my nose clean (the scheme was to be dissolved three years later). Shortly after gaining a promotion, I decided that Colerne wasn't for me and volunteered for another overseas posting.

I fancied RAF Changi in Singapore, Akrotiri in Cyprus or any RAF Station in Germany. I didn't have to wait too long because in April 1974, I was informed that I was to join 70 Squadron at RAF Akrotiri in October of that year. The squadron operated Hercules C130K and Argosy transport aircraft and my tour length, as a *singley*, was two years.

It was a normal practice prior to an overseas posting; to undergo a certain amount of training. However, in my case, due to my relative experience with the Hercs, that wasn't necessary. Although I wasn't familiar with the radar systems on the Argosy, nicknamed the *Whistling Tit*, its systems were very basic and easy to maintain.

It was on 11 April 1974, as I arrived at Salisbury railway station that I was met by Mum and Gillian. I was told that Dad had died that morning. How Mum knew that I was on that train, I'll never know but I was nevertheless devastated. I wasn't truly aware of how unwell he really was, following the removal of one of his lungs due to lung cancer.

He seemed to get over the operation and was recuperating quite well until the decision was taken by some pathetic official that he was fit enough to work and that his benefit was to be stopped. I don't know why he didn't get the proper support from his GP. There wasn't a lot of money left after the sale of the newsagents at Bulford Camp. He, therefore, had to get a job in order to pay the mortgage and provide for Mum and Wendy, who was still at school.

He managed to get a job at Boscombe Down in an office. Unfortunately, there were a lot of smokers in the workplace who wouldn't have the windows open and allow fresh air in. What a terrible environment for someone with only one lung to have worked in. On the few occasions that I saw him, he would come home from work and cough and cough until he was sick.

I don't know how long he lasted on the job, but I firmly believe his forced return to work helped shorten his life. The post-mortem revealed that the cancer had spread to his bronchus which I guess by then was more or less inoperable. He was cremated eight days before Gillian and Pete were married!

I have a vague recollection that sometime, during 1974, I and a couple of other *B Class Drivers* were trained to drive the large vehicles and trucks based at Colerne. It would then enable the release of the trained MT personnel to drive the fabled *Green Goddess Fire Engines* in the event of a planned fireman's strike. As it happens, the strike never materialised.

The preparation for the posting was going well until news came on 20 July 1974, that Turkey had launched an invasion of Cyprus which straight away cast doubts as to whether my posting would still go ahead. The *invasion*, although the Turks referred to it as a *peace operation*, ended in the partition of the northern part of the island along a United Nations Green line which, although, the crossing criteria have been relaxed, is still in existence today.

Cyprus — A Brief History

The island of Cyprus was occupied by a mix of Greek and Turkish citizens all of whom were classed as *Cypriot*. Cyprus for many years had been ruled by the British. However, there was a great desire for independence and in 1955, EOKA, the National Organisation of Cypriot Fighters was formed.

EOKA was an anti-colonial group and not only wanted liberation from the British but also wanted a union with Greece; that union was known as Enosis. Archbishop Makarios was the main protagonist and led the political branch of EOKA. In April 1955, EOKA began launching attacks against the British stationed in Cyprus; sabotaging military installations, ambushing military convoys and patrols and assassinating British servicemen including any Cypriot informers who sided with the British occupiers.

Independence from the UK was eventually achieved on 16 August 1960, with the exception of the two British Sovereign Base Areas (SBAs) located at Akrotiri and Dhekelia which are still there today.

Unfortunately, Makarios reneged on his goal in pushing for Enosis. In 1971, George Grivas, an anti-communist who led EOKA in the 1950s, returned to Cyprus and, angered by Makarios' attitude, took control of EOKA B. The aim was to overthrow him through violent means.

When Grivas died from a heart attack in January 1974, EOKA B came under the control of the Greek Military Junta in Athens. It launched a military coup to overthrow Makarios and installed Nikos Sampson as the dictator of Cyprus. Turkey took extreme exception to the coup which provoked the invasion of the island on 20 July 1974.

Heathrow Plane Spotting

There were one or two geeks on *C* flight who asked me if I would take them to Heathrow Airport so they could do a bit of plane spotting and, as it was a reasonable day, I agreed. We arrived about midday, had some lunch in one of the terminal's restaurants and for the next four or five hours, watched aircraft.

I don't remember where we parked, apart from the fact that it was on open ground, it wasn't busy and was cheap. As we were walking back, one of the lads thought it funny to repeatedly stop and ask people where the nearest toilet was; which you'd think was quite harmless. However, he spoke to them in fluent French.

I and the other spotter wanted nothing to do with him and walked off. He eventually caught us up at the car and we left to go home. As I pulled out onto the dual carriageway, a police car came up behind us with its blue lights flashing and pulled us over. I was shown to the back seat of their car and asked if I'd been drinking. I told them that I'd had two pints and two meals over a five-hour period at which point I was breathalysed.

No new-fangled electronic gadget but a bag with in-line-coloured crystals that would change colour if alcohol was detected. Apparently, the crystals did change colour which meant that alcohol had been detected on my breath and I was taken to the nearest police station.

20 minutes later, I was breathalysed again with the same type of detector and was told that as it was a borderline indication (although I could see no difference in the colours) I'd be given the benefit of the doubt. They then took me back to where my car and the spotters were still waiting. One of the coppers then made a comment to the French-speaking berk, asking why he kept pestering people for the toilet.

I believe because he was acting suspiciously, the coppers wanted to know what was going on and followed us to the car park and it was me who bore the brunt.

Chapter Seven
The Happiest Day of My Life

I'd first visited Uncle Tom and Aunt Edith on my own in the summer of 1973 in my four-year-old Cortina Mk 2 car (it was this car that I subsequently wrote off in November and ended up in intensive care). They had only recently moved to number 6 Coronation Avenue from Freshfield Road in Formby; where they were live-in housekeepers to Mr Bridgewater, an elderly gentleman.

Gran Sowerby had also moved from Milburn and lived with Tom and Edith. The aim of the trip to Formby was to pick up Gran Sowerby and take her back to Durrington for her annual stay with Mum at *Lyndhurst*.

Following the earlier loss of my Cortina Mk 2, I bought an older Mk 1 car which was unreliable and had let me down several times. Rather, that break down whilst Gran Sowerby was with me. Mum let me use her brand-new Chrysler Simca for the journey to Formby and back.

Tom, who had a very dry sense of humour, constantly pulled my leg and told me that he would introduce me to a young lady who lived in Southport. The mother of this *young lady* was Tom's sister, Helen Deal. Anyway, nothing more was said and I took Gran Sowerby back to Wiltshire.

I next visited Tom and Edith in August 1974, this time, I was to take Mrs Bundy, who lived in Cholderton, to Formby and she would be picked up by George Sowerby (Mum's cousin) who, with his wife Fanny, owned the Beechcroft Nurseries in Appleby. I was then to return with Gran Sowerby once again for her annual pilgrimage *down south*.

Once Mrs Bundy had been picked up by George, Tom phoned his sister and mentioned that his nephew, *Flying Officer Kite* (a nickname that he, as an ex-Pongo, invariably gave to anyone in the RAF) was visiting and asked if they and their daughter Patricia were free that evening.

Morley originally had his own salon in Ainsdale and was looking for a suitable young lady that he could train to be a hairdresser. I'm unsure how many people had applied for the job, but one that did was Miss Helen Postlethwaite who not only he employed but later married—and the rest, as they say, is history. Helen and Morley then bought the hairdresser's business in Ainsdale and lived above the salon at 199A Heathfield Road.

Tom, Edith and I were made to feel very welcome and after about 10 minutes Patricia appeared. Now, if anyone ever says that there is no such thing as love at first sight, then I can categorically tell you that, there is. She'd been off work for the day suffering with tonsillitis and had dragged herself out of bed.

It later transpired that I was lucky to catch her in because Friday and Saturday nights were traditionally her nights out. Helen had positioned two chairs next to each other and for the rest of the evening it was like the Spanish Inquisition, they wanted to know all about the both of us.

It was at this point that I discovered that Pat and I were related insofar as we shared the same Aunt and Uncle; Mum's sister Edith married Helen's brother Tom. I also learnt that Helen and Morley had attended the joint marriage of Tom and Edith and Mum and Dad at the church of St Cuthberts in Milburn during the war.

It also transpired that Ian had been visiting Tom and Edith when they were live-in housekeepers to Mr Bridgewater and had visited Helen and Morley and deliberately caught Mumps from John Deal. Helen was the only daughter in the Postlethwaite family and had nine brothers. She and several of the brothers were born in Coronation Avenue, Formby and Trisha was born in Kent Road, Formby (I can't remember the number) on 11 July 1953.

By the end of the evening, I don't think there was much left to tell and Tom reminded me that I had promised to take him to Liverpool the next morning to pick up his new *Datsun Cherry* car and I asked Pat if she'd like to come along. She replied that she couldn't; because she had a driving lesson booked for the morning.

Without a moment's hesitation, Helen said that she'd cancel the lesson and go with Tom and me. As we went to say goodbye, I bent over to kiss Pat on her cheek, she thought I was going to whisper something to her and she also bent down. That encounter was then always referred to as *the missed kiss* (Hot Chocolate. It started with a kiss!)

I picked Pat up at about 11:00 and the three of us went to the Datsun agent in Liverpool. The salesman, as I remember, wasn't particularly quick. After about an hour of waiting, I suggested to Tom that since he was being dealt with, Pat and I would go and I'd see him later on.

He was happy with that arrangement, but he never let me forget and always insisted that we abandoned him in Liverpool with no way home if there was a problem with his new car. Pat and I spent the rest of the afternoon driving around Southport talking, and we went for a walk along Parbold Hill near Ormskirk. She told me that she'd begun her working life as a cadet nurse at Southport Infirmary Hospital.

She loved the nursing aspect having met some really lovely people but she found it difficult to cope with the deaths of many of her very old and infirm patients. She decided as a 16 or 17-year-old that nursing wasn't for her and joined the General Post Office (GPO) as a telephonist, working in Southport main exchange.

I thought this to be more than just a coincidence because one of the girls I'd dated whilst an apprentice at Cosford was a WRAF trainee telephonist. The next, whom I dated for four months whilst I was stationed at Lyneham, was also a WRAF telephonist who worked in the PABX at Cosford—something about telephonists maybe?

We arranged to meet that Saturday evening and she took me to one of her regular haunts, *The Sands* nightclub in Ainsdale. To say she was popular, was an understatement; she introduced me to several of her friends and we spent the majority of the evening there. She drank Cinzzano and lemonade, and she was also wearing *Charlie* perfume, which was one of the most intoxicating scents I can ever remember.

I was due to return to Durrington the next day and asked Pat if I could put off taking Gran Sowerby back until Monday; so, could I see her again. She agreed! When I told Edith that I was stopping for another night and that I was taking Pat out again, her eyes lit up! Was this, the start of a beautiful relationship?

Pat phoned me from the telephone exchange on the Monday morning just before I left for Durrington and if there's one thing that I will remember about her for the rest of my life is her voice. She had the most amazing, soft and sexy voice I'd ever heard. One of her jobs was as a 999 operator and I'm sure that her calm, comforting voice would have reassured even the most panic-stricken of callers.

Anyway, I took Gran Sowerby back to Durrington and carried on with the preparation for my impending posting. I did speak with Pat a couple of times but without today's luxuries of mobiles or the internet, I had to rely on public telephones or by putting pen to paper.

As I wasn't due to leave for Cyprus until the 22 Oct, Mum asked if I'd take Gran Sowerby back to Formby in early October. As I was due two weeks of embarkation leave, I agreed once again to use her car. I phoned Pat and mentioned that I would be going back to Formby and asked if we could meet up again. She said she looked forward to it.

I don't remember where we went for the first few days, I was with her but I do remember that I was totally and absolutely smitten with her and over the next few days we really got to know each other. I'd known Pat for less than two months and had only been out with her no more than half-a-dozen times, but I'd more or less decided that she was so very special and that she was the person that I'd like to spend the rest of my life with.

One evening, whilst we were at the Bold Arms Hotel in Churchtown, Southport I reminded her that I was shortly to leave for Cyprus. Also, because of the trouble on the island, I had no real idea when I would be home again. I then asked her if I was to buy her an engagement ring, would she accept it and wait for me.

The questions surprised her because she didn't say no and asked if I was sure and would let me know the next day (she told me a lot later on, that she wanted to make sure the proposal wasn't something that I'd said in haste and that I might feel different in the morning).

The next day we drove to the *Trough of Bowland*, a beautiful area just east of Lancaster and no mention was made of the previous evening's discussions. That was until, we eventually, arrived at a particularly scenic spot where I pulled into a lay-by, turned the engine off, and asked if she'd decided on my proposal.

She said, "Yes," immediately she added, "Only if you're sure."

I'd never been surer about anything before that day or ever since. The photo was taken just seconds after she accepted.

The rest of the day was just a blur. We drove back to Ainsdale and Pat told Helen and Morley that we were going to be engaged, I think Morley was a bit miffed because I hadn't formally asked him for Pat's hand in marriage! Anyway, they were both pleased and agreed.

I learnt later that Helen would have had her doubts at such a whirlwind courtship if it had been anyone else but me and she would have advised against it. This was based on the fact that she already knew the Lewis family and she knew that I was from good stock!

By the time I'd got back to Formby, my mind was racing. I really couldn't believe that I'd been accepted by someone as stunningly beautiful as Pat and that we were going to be married. I immediately told Edith whose face lit up and was almost as excited as I was.

Tom, on the other hand, was not quite as forthcoming with the congratulations. All he said was, "That was a bit bloody quick, wasn't it?"

Isn't it strange how certain words stick in the mind; those words certainly did! Time was running out before I had to return to Colerne and I asked Pat if she fancied going to Wiltshire and meeting the family. She agreed. I phoned Mum and told her that I'd proposed to Pat and that we'd be spending a couple of days with her.

We arrived at Durrington mid-Friday afternoon. Mum and Wendy immediately took to Pat acting like they'd known each other all of their lives. She really had such a beautiful, gentle nature. Gill, Pete, Pat and I went to the Silver Plough at Pitton on a Friday night. Saturday was spent showing Pat around the area and visiting Stonehenge, and the four of us went to the Mecca Ballroom in Southampton that evening.

The weekend ended far too soon and we left for Southport on Monday morning. Just before I returned to Colerne, Trisha and I met two of her friends, John and Rita Buckley (Rita was to become one of Trisha's bridesmaids). She introduced us to one of the delights of 1970s cuisine, a prawn cocktail, meat fondue and black forest gateau.

The music John played was 'Tubular Bells' by Mike Oldfield, which, whenever I hear it, immediately takes me back to that weekend. Unfortunately, I didn't spend too long with Pat and had to return to Colerne and prepare for the move to Cyprus.

Unfortunately, I foolishly lent the unreliable Mk 1 Cortina to a so-called *friend* who was going through a painful divorce and needed wheels to get about for a while. I also lent him £20 and I'd left my service dress hat on the back seat along with other personal positions. I never saw him again but I later heard that my car had been abandoned in the back streets of Chippenham.

Fortunately, I had a spare set of keys and recovered the car but it was in one heck of a mess. The car had been parked on the street opposite an entrance to someone's driveway and was causing a minor obstruction. Rather than get in touch with the police and try to find out who the vehicle belonged to, the resident simply drove into the side of my car and pushed it out of the way.

In an effort to get it sorted, I drove it to Wolverhampton and left it with an old friend, John Strong; to get it repaired for me. The intention was that I would pick it up at some time in the future when I came home for leave from Cyprus. I eventually cleared Colerne and was taken by some Lyneham-based friends to the airhead at Brize Norton.

Chapter Eight
Royal Air Force Station Akrotiri

(21 October 1974 to 28 January 1975)

I arrived at Akrotiri on board a VC10 passenger aircraft and was met by a couple of lads from the squadron. They took me to my accommodation to drop off my bags and then onto Station Headquarters to begin the tortuous arrivals process. I arrived at the Station Warrant Officer's office with my blue card and immediately recognised Sergeant Gibling, our flight SNCO whilst I was on 214th entry at Cosford.

I don't think he recognised me but started by being very friendly and asked me which unit I'd come from. I told him Colerne and he immediately asked if everyone had such long hair at Colerne and pointed me in the direction of the barber's shop at the end of the corridor—good start to my tour!

I eventually arrived at 70 Squadron and met my new Flight Commander. Partway through the interview, he could see someone at the glass panel of his office door straining to see in; the boss asked him to come in. It was my old shift boss, Chief Tech Jim Chapman. I had worked with him on *B* line, Lyneham in 1971. He was very excited to see me.

I was then introduced to other members of the squadron; some whom I'd known at Lyneham and others that I'd met and worked with when the squadron aircraft had staged through Masirah two years previously.

There was a lot of uncertainty regarding not only the future of the Hercules squadron but also the Bomber and Fighter wings which comprised of Vulcan Bombers and Lightning Air Interceptor aircraft respectively. Before the Turkish coup, the majority of married personnel lived in married quarters and private hirings in the nearby town of Limassol. However, following the invasion, the severe security implications meant that all families were returned to the UK.

The husbands were then accommodated on the Sovereign Based Area (SBA) of Akrotiri in whatever accommodation was available. For the first couple of weeks, I shared a room, which was originally designed to accommodate six people, with at least twice the number of personnel. It was then agreed that as I was one of the few single JNCOs who paid for his accommodation; I should have one of only four single rooms.

There were still major issues and problems associated with the displacement of the Turkish Cypriots who lived in various areas south of the Green Line. Several humanitarian convoys had been set upon by the Greek Cypriots and the aid stolen, there were also demonstrations in and around Limassol demanding that the British leave the island.

One particular demonstration outside of the main entrance to RAF Akrotiri resulted in a demonstrator being run over and killed by a British Army vehicle which further inflamed the population. A night-time curfew for British servicemen was re-imposed until things calmed down.

Several relief flights were organised by the UN in an effort to relocate the Turkish refugees back to the mainland and it was decided that Turkish civilian passenger aircraft would use 70 Squadron's aircraft dispersal. The base at Akrotiri was separated from Limassol by a large Salt Lake, that for certain times of the year, was populated by a massive flock of Flamingos.

Military intelligence believed that when the Turkish civilian aircraft were due to arrive, there was a distinct possibility that the local Greek militia would attempt to blow up the aircraft using surface-to-surface missiles launched from the Limassol side of the Salt Lake.

The station was immediately put on alert and we spent the next few days either at work or on guard. On one occasion, I was put on guard having just completed a day shift. What we were supposed to do if the Greeks did launch a missile attack; I really don't know. Anyway, nothing came of the threat and several hundred refugees were evacuated without incident. It was about this time that I started to think about how and when I might be able to get Pat to Cyprus.

Work on the squadron was no different to what I'd experienced at Lyneham, Masirah or Colerne. Akrotiri, in the '70s, was a very busy air station. Our dispersal was situated at the western end of the runway adjacent to its threshold.

Each weekday morning, two English Electric Lightning air defence fighter aircraft, members of Number 56 Squadron, would taxi to the end of the runway, select reheat and thunder down the runway taking off for their morning dawn patrol (weather sortie really). I learnt from one of the 56 Squadron groundcrew that once the aircraft were positioned on the *Piano Keys* at the runway's threshold and following the pre-take-off checks, many pilots would select the undercarriage up and commence their take-off run.

At this stage, the aircraft's weight on wheels switch was all that was preventing the undercarriage from retracting. However, the moment the aircraft lifted off, the undercarriage instantly retracted. It was an incredibly awe-inspiring sight to see the two aircraft, with reheat engaged, stand on their tails and almost go vertical.

One of the most sensational aircraft based at Akrotiri and one that we saw regularly was the USAF U2 spy plane, nicknamed *Dragon Lady*. The aircraft was introduced in 1970 as Detachment *G* which formed part of the CIA. The Lockheed U-2 was a single-engine, very high-altitude (70,000 feet) reconnaissance aircraft which provided day and night, all-weather intelligence gathering.

Instead of the typical tricycle-style landing gear, the U-2 uses a bicycle configuration with a forward set of main wheels located just behind the cockpit and a rear set of main wheels located behind the engine. This arrangement made it the most difficult plane in the world to land. The rear wheels were coupled to the rudder to provide steering during taxiing. To maintain balance whilst taxiing two auxiliary wheels, called *Pogos,* fitted into sockets underneath each wing at about mid-span, and would fall off during take-off.

Once the aircraft had taken off, it would climb almost vertically before commencing a corkscrew manoeuvre which would continue until it achieved its cruising altitude; at that time, the engine would be switched off, making the aircraft nothing more than a glorified glider. To protect the wings during landing, each wingtip had a titanium skid fitted. After the U-2 came to a halt on the runway, the ground crew would re-install the Pogos; one wing at a time, which enabled the aircraft to taxi back to the hangar.

The role of the U2 in the '70s was to monitor the goings on in the Middle East, ostensibly the Israeli-Egyptian conflict. However, the aircraft had come to prominence in the mid-1950s when a U-2 was shot down whilst flying over the USSR. Following World War 2, the United States and the USSR grew increasingly distrustful of each other.

When, in 1955, the U.S. proposed an *Open Skies,* edict the USSR objected and relations continued to deteriorate. It was then, because of the aura of mistrust, that the U.S. instigated high-altitude reconnaissance flights over the USSR. The aim was to gain vital photo intelligence which, of course, was in an era long before satellite observation was possible. The aircraft of choice, for these covert spying missions, was the U-2.

The Central Intelligence Agency (CIA) took the lead, keeping the military out of the picture to avoid any possibilities of open conflict. By 1960, the U.S. had flown numerous successful missions over and around the U.S.S.R. However, on 1 May 1960, a U-2 spy plane having taken off from the Pakistan Air Force portion of Peshawar Airport and piloted by Francis Gary Powers, was brought down near Svedlovsk in the USSR.

This event had a lasting negative impact on U.S. and USSR relations. Powers was eventually charged, pleaded guilty and was convicted of espionage on 10th August; sentenced to three years imprisonment and seven years of hard labour. He served one year and nine months of the sentence before being exchanged for Rudolf Abel, a jailed, UK-born Soviet intelligence officer on 10th February 1962 on the Glienicke Bridge, Berlin; which connected Potsdam in East Germany with West Germany.

I was single, which meant my tour length was fixed at two years. However, if I was married, there was a remote possibility that Pat might be able to join me at a later date once things got back to normal. Also, hopefully, move into married quarters at the station and finish the tour together.

Several evenings, each week, saw the arrival of a VC10 from Brize and apart from the disembarking passengers, my thoughts would immediately turn to the next mail delivery. I wrote to Trisha three or four times a week, as she did to me. Apart from the handwriting I immediately knew the letter was from her because of the fantastic smell of Charlie—she must have doused the letter in the perfume before sealing the envelope.

There was still a lot of uncertainty regarding the future of the N.E.A.F. and how long I might be expected to stay in Cyprus. So, I decided to fly home and discuss the issue with Pat (I think it was about this point that I started calling her *Trisha*)

I managed to get leave for the first two weeks of December 1974 and arranged a flight with a civilian charter company that took me to Luton airport. Following the earlier fondue we'd had with John and Rita, I decided to take a gallon demijohn of Kokinelli in the hope that Trisha and I could try a cheese fondue. I don't know why, but I was under the impression that I didn't have to pay duty on the wine and casually walked through the *nothing to declare* lane carrying the wine in full view of several customs officials.

I had got about halfway through and looked behind me expecting to see others that I knew were also carrying demijohns, to find myself alone. As there wasn't too much I could do, I continued walking and got away with it! I remember the journey from London to Liverpool Lime Street and on to Formby as being quite tortuous.

Trisha and I spent a while discussing the options and decided to suggest to Helen and Morley that we get married very quickly in a registry office and trust that things would work out with regard to the posting. Helen was not happy and whilst not doubting my sincerity, thought it was much too soon. Also, if we were meant for each other, then a proper marriage could wait. The strange thing was that I had exactly the same conversation with Sgt Brin Jones just before I left Akrotiri. He warned me against making any hasty decisions.

Throughout our entire married life, I never had a cause to complain about Trisha's cooking prowess. However, the cheese fondue was an absolute disaster. The recipe was simple; make a cheese sauce, add a generous amount of wine (in our case Kokinelli) and heat until gently bubbling. Small pieces of bread would then be dipped into the sauce and eaten with salad.

Under normal circumstances such as BBQs or beach parties, Kokinelli tasted okay. But when mixed with molten cheese and presented as a fondue it was absolutely disgusting and despite trying to tart up the sauce the whole pot went down the toilet. It was also during the leave that Trisha and I went to see The Three Degrees in Southport where, amongst others, they sang our favourite song 'When will I see you again' and as usual the time went all too fast and before I knew it, I was back at Akrotiri.

One of the vagaries of the Cypriot weather was made never more evident than when I and several members of the squadron went skiing just after Christmas. We travelled in the back of a three-ton truck to the Rest and Recuperation (R&R) centre in the Troodos mountains. On arrival, we were kitted out with all the necessary skiing equipment and left to our own devices. A couple of days later, I was swimming off Ladies Mile near Limassol.

The New Year came and went without too much ceremony or celebration and the routine work on the squadron continued. It continued until very early in January, when we were told that Akrotiri's Bomber Wing, which comprised of numbers 9 and 35 Squadron, one Fighter Squadron and our transport Squadron were to return to the UK and relocate to their respective bases.

The Vulcans were to be based at RAF Waddington in Lincolnshire, the Lightnings at RAF Binbrook also in Lincolnshire and the Hercules to Lyneham in Wiltshire. The Vulcans had provided a bomber force for the Central Treaty Organisation (CENTO), formally known as the Baghdad Pact, comprising the UK, Iran, Pakistan, Turkey and the USA. The pact's purpose was to provide an anti-communist mutual alliance with the sole aim of containing Russian influence in the region.

Trisha had suffered from repeated sore throats and infections for quite a while. Early in January, I received a letter from Helen telling me that she had been admitted to the hospital where her tonsils had been removed. She was in a children's ward and by all accounts enjoyed the stay eating copious amounts of ice cream.

The next couple of weeks were absolutely manic with the emphasis being on loading our aircraft with all necessary ground equipment, test equipment and aircraft spares as possible ready for the final flights to the UK. When the day for the repatriation of Bomber and Fighter Wings eventually arrived, I witnessed a sight that will live with me forever.

To see two squadrons of Vulcans and two squadrons of Lightning fighters *beat up* the airfield was something that will never be equalled. For some bizarre reason, one or two mindless morons on the squadron decided to trash some of the rooms in our accommodation block and had flown out before anyone really knew what damage had been caused.

I was one of the last to leave and was in my room when the station discip staff arrived to view the damage—they were not happy. My tour of duty lasted a mere three months, and even today, I feel cheated at not being able to complete the tour because of political issues and defence cuts.

As usual, following a tour abroad, all personnel were entitled to a two-week spell of disembarkation leave. Unfortunately, Gran Lewis died a few days before I returned. I waited for the funeral to take place in the small churchyard at Cholderton before heading off for Southport in Mum's car.

I'd only been with Trisha for a couple of days when we decided to once again visit Mum in Wiltshire. I guess that was the beginning of the dozens and dozens of trips we would do between Wiltshire and Lancashire (or Merseyside as the county was later to be renamed) over the next few years.

Chapter Nine
Royal Air Force Station Wattisham

(28 January 1975 to 19 February 1975)

I arrived at RAF Wattisham in Suffolk in January 1975. Having carried out the standard arrivals procedure, I made my way to the Avionics Centre where I was to be employed. After a brief introduction by the bay manager, I was told that as I was familiar with Air Interceptor 23B Nose Radar fitted to the Lightning jet; I could start immediately with the rectification and functional checking of the system!

I told the bay chief that I hadn't the faintest idea what he was talking about and that I'd never worked on the equipment or was experienced on the Lightning aircraft. He immediately got in touch with the general office and told them to speak with my drafting officer at the Personnel Management Centre (PMC) at RAF Innsworth and find out what was going on.

It transpired that some plonker at PMC had missed the fact that I had a *Q* annotation (denoting that I was qualified on the Hercules) and that I should have gone to Lyneham with the rest of the squadron.

In the meantime, I ran into trouble with a Flight Sergeant from the MT section. I'd been to lunch in the airman's mess and was driving back to work. At the end of the road from the mess, was a stop sign which was positioned at the apex of a left-to-right-hand bend. As I approached the junction, I could see that there was no traffic in front of me and nothing to the left either. I drove straight over the junction without stopping.

Within 10 minutes of my getting back to work, there was a message for me to go to the MT yard and report to the SNCO in charge. I was told that I was to be charged with dangerous driving and ignoring the traffic signs. I disagreed with the dangerous driving aspect but I couldn't really argue with the traffic signs issue, anyway, I tried to reason, but was told to get out of the office. When I returned to work, everyone wanted to know what had happened, and when I told them the general reaction was that the man was well known for being an arse.

In fact, it was even suggested that to get my own back on him (once I'd been posted) was to drop a couple of egg whites into his petrol tank. I didn't really understand why; until it was explained that the egg would be sucked into the carburettor (most cars then didn't have an in-line fuel filter) and would solidify when it got warm.

Once the pump stopped sucking, the unsolidified egg white would find its way back into the tank but the fuel line at the carburettor would still be blocked. The only way to clear the blockage was to strip the carb down; and the process would repeat itself until all of the egg white was gone—fantastic.

Unfortunately, I never got to do it. However, that incident caused me to have to stop for an additional two weeks at Wattisham due to the ridiculous time it took to process the charge. I was paraded in front of the Flight Commander who listened to the evidence from the MT plonker. He said that he was walking past the airman's mess and heard the sound of a car accelerating hard with the engine screaming, and that, it then sped across the junction and disappeared at great speed towards to airfield.

I was asked if that was true and told the boss that I didn't stop at the junction because I could see that there were no other vehicles on the road but contested the remainder of the statement—I certainly wasn't speeding. Theoretically, that should have been the end of it, maybe a slap on the wrist, but no!

The Flight Commander, being an indecisive twerp decided that there was a case to answer and passed the charge onto the Squadron Commander. I went through exactly the same procedure with him. He also decided that there was a case to answer and, as he couldn't fine me, he passed it up to the Station Commander.

After 10 days of being messed about, I was paraded in front of the CO who listened to the evidence. He informed me that the stop sign at that particular junction was put there following a major accident where someone had driven into one of the large bollards positioned on either side of the road at the crown of the bend. I later found out that was true but the driver was stoned out of his head and was seriously injured. The Station Commander fined me £3.00 and I was free to go to Lyneham. What a ridiculous and petty farce!

Chapter Ten
Royal Air Force Station Lyneham

(19 February 1975 to 16 July 1978)

Lyneham had changed very little since I left three short years previously. There were a lot more aircraft and personnel following the closing down of various units and the centralisation of the Hercules fleet. I was posted once again onto B Line and caught up with those I'd worked with in Cyprus. There were also one or two familiar faces from my previous tour, and soon, I got back into the swing of things with work.

The shift pattern was reasonable with the time going exceptionally fast, and although, I didn't have a car for the first few months, I still managed to see Trisha a couple of times. It was whilst I was at Southport for one stand-down, Helen mentioned that one of their railway club friends was selling an Mk1 Cortina and thought that I might be interested. It had been looked after, was in a good condition with no rust and I was offered it at a knockdown price, which I took.

From then on, when finances allowed, I visited Trisha most time when off shift. We decided that 26 July would be our wedding day. It would be held at the Sacred Heart Roman Catholic Church in Ainsdale.

But before we could be married, I, as a member of the Church of England, had to undergo a certain amount of religious indoctrination. And so, each week for one month or so, I spent a couple of hours with the RC Priest in Wootton Bassett who taught me about the Catholic faith. However, the tutorial was made all the more tolerable because he was an advocate of homebrew.

At the end of the lecture, I had to sign a document to say that any children we had, would be brought up in the Catholic faith. That document was to be given to the priest in Southport as verification that I had attended the lessons.

Time moved very quickly and before long, my last shift as a singley was over and on Friday, 18 July, I picked up my belongings and drove to Southport.

It was on Sunday that the Lewis' car's jinx surfaced again because my car started to cough and splutter with a complete lack of compression and after some investigation, I decided that the engine head would have to come off. I borrowed some tools from Dougie Price who lived over the road and stripped down the top end of the engine.

Two of the valves had burnt out which I'd need to replace. Unfortunately, one of the valve seats had already been ground down and an oversized valve fitted. I then spent the Monday desperately trying to find an auto shop in Southport that stocked all the bits I needed. Fortunately, one shop came up trumps.

I then spent the next two days in the back room of Helen and Morley's hair salon; grinding the new valves and the other six valves into the valve seats in the head. I had taken the head off of the Mini twice please and the strip down, de-coke and rebuild; including setting the timing was a fairly straightforward process but I even surprised myself when the engine burst into life on the first turn of the ignition. I wouldn't know where to start with a modern engine!

By Thursday evening, everything was more or less sorted. Trisha and Helen had finished with the necessary preparation for the big event on Saturday. Trisha had decided to hold her *Hen* party in one of the local clubs. I, on the other hand, wasn't sure where to go for my stag party and it was suggested that we also go to the same venue which turned out to be a *BIG* mistake.

Trisha and I, more or less ignored each other for most of the evening, and everything was going well until I decided to ask a tall, buxom, blonde girl for a dance. I'd only been dancing with her for a few minutes when Trisha grabbed me, slapped her engagement ring into my hand and stormed off.

I spent the rest of the evening trying to convince her that it was all perfectly innocent, whereas if I'd left the club with the blonde then Trisha may have had something to worry about. By the end of the evening, we were friends again.

Saturday, 26 July 1975, was a truly memorable day. I and Andrew Kirkpatrick, my best man whom I'd known since I was 18 months old, had spent the previous night with Ted and Mabel Fish at their home on Guilford Road, a mile or so from Heathfield Road. I drove the Cortina to Ainsdale Cricket Club where Trisha had arranged the evening function; Andrew picked me up and then drove on to Coronation Avenue where we got changed.

The wedding was scheduled to start at 14:00 and as we had left Tom and Edith's with plenty of time to spare, we decided to call in at the Arion pub in

Birkdale for a little liquid encouragement (not that I really, needed it). By the time we got to the Sacred Heart Church on Liverpool Road, we were running a little late, and as we entered the car park we were met by Edith. Now, if looks could have killed, Trisha would have been a widow even before we were married—although Trisha hadn't arrived. Edith wasn't happy.

The wedding ceremony and the reception at the Railway Club were a bit of a blur. However, the one thing I can still really remember was how absolutely stunning Trisha looked, she was gorgeous. Once the reception was finished, Trisha and I went back to Heathfield Road with Helen; got changed and picked up our honeymoon bags.

Helen asked if we had everything and then said, "Here's something in case you fancy stopping for a nibble."

To which I replied that we wouldn't have time for that sort of thing as we had to get to Heathrow. She just smiled and gave me a pack of sandwiches! We spent a couple of hours at the cricket club before saying goodbye to everyone and leaving in our brightly decorated car.

We got plenty of waves and hoots as we drove towards the motorway, and once on the M6 south of Liverpool, we were overtaken by a bus load of blokes and everyone; without exception, was at the bus windows shouting, cheering and gesticulating some quite suggestive hand and arm movements!

We made it to London in pretty good time and tried to book into a hotel close to Heathrow. I hadn't pre-booked anywhere, instead trusted to luck that something would be available. As we entered the lobby, I remember seeing a cleaner carrying a hoover. As we approached the reception desk, I looked behind to see a long trail of confetti stretching from the main door. The confetti was coming from my trouser bottoms which Gillian had earlier deposited down the front of my trousers.

The receptionist told us and another customer that there were no rooms available and as we turned to leave, the other chap turned to me and said, "Come on, John, we'll go to the Holiday Inn."

I said, "We've never met before. So how on earth did he know my name?"

He told me it was a *London* thing and any stranger was referred to as *John*. We followed him to the hotel where we managed to get a room.

We arose early the next morning, had breakfast and took the complimentary Shuttle Bus to Heathrow. Within no time at all, we were on board the Swiss Air flight to Zurich. I can't remember the aircraft type but I do remember it being relatively small. However, the flight was reasonably comfortable.

When we arrived in Zurich, we boarded a bus and were taken to the railway station for the next stage of the journey, where we boarded the train and set off for Interlaken which was about three hours away. The travel company had arranged everything including the flights, transfers and a delightful three-course meal on-board the train.

We eventually arrived at our destination, the Hotel Jungfrau; a small, friendly and family-run business in the village of Wilderswil which was within reasonable walking distance of Interlaken. Our room was on the second floor and the balcony overlooked the Jungfrau Mountain which forms part of the Bernese Mountain range. The view was absolutely stunning and as the sun began to set, the whole of the Jungfrau turned a brilliant red. This phenomenon only happens at certain times of the year and that night was one of them—beautiful.

As our finances were fairly tight, we spent a lot of the week-long honeymoon walking. We visited Interlaken a couple of times during the day, travelled on a cog train to the top of a mountain plateau close to Grindelwald and cruised on Lake Thun. Breakfast and dinner were included, so, we only had to find lunch.

1 August was Swiss National Day and by way of celebration, the town put on one of the most impressive fireworks displays I have ever seen. There were thousands of people in the park and the display seemed to go on and on forever.

After a couple of hours, a large part of the crowd started to head off in the same direction, and thinking that there must be another event going on, we decided to follow them. I think we must have walked for about an hour, stopped for a coffee on the way and still the crowds kept going.

We thought that whatever the event was, it was going to be big and again joined the throng. All of a sudden, Trisha and I found ourselves in a deserted street, completely on our own, at which point we realised that we had followed the residents of an entire village back to their homes.

As usual, the holiday seemed to be over before it had begun, and we made our way back to the UK. We arrived back at the Holiday Inn at Heathrow and found that the battery on the car was flat. We had to call out the AA to get us going again—I'd left the radio on which had drained the battery.

Mum wanted us to stop with her and Wendy, for a few days before I took Trisha back to Southport, where she would have to wait until a married quarter became available at Lyneham. On the first morning back, which was 4 August,

Mum, bless her, brought us breakfast in bed and also a letter from the family's office informing us that we'd been allocated a two-bedroom quarter at Number 76 Whittle Avenue, Compton Basset.

The small housing estate was situated close to Calne about six miles from Lyneham. Mum was ecstatic and told us that she had done her WRAF square bashing at Compton Bassett during the war. The amazing thing was that I wouldn't have to take Trisha back to Southport as we were scheduled to take over the house on 5 August, the very next day.

Our First Home Together

The whole house takeover or *Marching In* philosophy was alien to me and I really didn't know what to expect. Occupants of service accommodation in those days could opt for either a fully furnished or totally de-furnished house—nothing in between. However, unwanted items of furniture could be returned to the barrack stores at a later date.

We had earlier decided that we needed a fully furnished house which included absolutely everything ranging from cutlery, crockery, bed linen, towels, in fact, everything that newlyweds required to set up home. We used those items that we were given as wedding presents and stored the service items.

The process was quite convoluted and began with the Barrack Warden and the Families Officer carrying out a full inspection with the incoming occupant in attendance and the outgoing incumbent keeping a low profile. The house was checked from top to bottom for dust, dirt, stains and marks on walls and ceilings and the windows were required to be cleaned inside and out.

All barrack items on the inventory were checked for cleanliness and had to be laid out for checking in the appropriate room. Mattresses were inspected for stains and if any were evident the item was scrapped and a bill raised to replace it.

All keys were to be placed in the locks of the relevant doors, cupboards and drawers to which they belonged and all spare keys had to be labelled. Lawns were to have been cut, garden borders dug over and garden tools and lawnmowers should have been cleaned, oiled and placed in the shed.

For some barrack wardens, the cooker was their main focus of attention. In the case of our first March-in the warden had armed himself with a screwdriver, and a torch, wore white gloves and took off every single panel possible on the cooker in the hope of finding hidden grease. He also wiped his gloved hand over door tops, door frames and the top of the toilet cistern.

The process took about an hour, by which time, a very comprehensive handover/takeover had taken place. The warden had found some minor deposits of grease on the cooker ring supports and behind some of the panels. He had also found dust on top of the toilet cistern and decided to fine the outgoing occupant £10. At that point, I was given the choice of taking the money and cleaning myself or allowing professional cleaners to do the cleaning for me.

I chose to take the money. If the house had been dirty, I would accept that a fine was necessary but couldn't believe how petty the warden had been.

The service furniture was reasonable and the two bedrooms comprised of a double bed, a single bed, wardrobes and dressing tables. Downstairs there was a lounge/dinner with a dining room table and four chairs, and for the lounge, just two single armchairs with the most hideous of camouflaged covers imaginable. The kitchen had a small table, a fridge and a cooker.

Trisha was as pleased as punch and soon set about putting everything away (we were to later go to Southport and pick up our wedding gifts). The only aspect that we didn't really care for was the fact that the electricity was on a pay-as-you-go basis with the coin meter located in the outhouse.

It wasn't too long before we got bored with the two single armchairs. I asked the barrack stores if we could have a two-seater settee and was astounded to be told that we weren't entitled unless Trisha was pregnant! I didn't stop to question or argue the point, instead, we went into Calne a few days later and bought our first suite on the *never-never*.

The only electronic entertainment we had was the Sony radio/cassette system bought in Masirah and a small, 12" black and white Hitachi television that I'd bought whilst I was at Colerne.

Over the next few months, we got to know our neighbours and the wives of work colleagues. One such couple was Chris and Jill Hunt. They lived around the corner from us—we were to become very good, lifelong friends and today they are the only people, from our early married life that I'm still in touch with. I first met Chris at Cosford who played the cornet in the brass band.

Trisha had anticipated returning to work but the public transport really left a lot to be desired. She didn't drive and really didn't know what avenue to go down. Neither of us were happy for her to work in a shop behind a counter; her forte was in customer services and I believe she would have liked to carry on as a telephonist.

The gardens were separated by a three-foot chain-link fence and one of our neighbours had two very large Great Dane dogs that really were as soft as they could get and spent a large proportion of the day in the garden. Helen had let it be known that she didn't like dogs at all. When I suggested that Trisha and I had talked about getting an Alsatian, she said that she probably wouldn't visit again.

Now there was a challenge I thought. In the 15 years that Helen was with us, there was only one occasion where I had cause to disagree and argue with her; at breakfast one morning in Southport, where she was giving sweets to Michael and ignored my protests—she later apologised. She was an absolute doll and, hand on heart, a better MIL I couldn't have found. In fact, both Helen and Mum were the perfect mothers-in-law.

Anyway, I digress, Helen was in the garden one morning hanging out some washing and she saw the dogs next door. Normally, the dogs would come to the fence and allow us to stroke them. However, on this particular day, totally out of character they bounded over the fence and ran straight towards Helen.

The first we knew about it was when we heard the screaming. I think the dogs would probably have licked her to death, but poor Helen was quite traumatised and she wouldn't venture into the garden either alone or if the dogs were out.

The prospects of Trisha returning to work soon become immaterial because in February 1976, she found out that she was two months pregnant. It wasn't the fact that she'd missed her menstrual periods that raised suspicions but more to do with the constant morning sickness. She visited the doctors on several occasions and was prescribed various pills but, following the Thalidomide issues, was reluctant to take anything and let nature take its course.

Over the next six months, the poor darling was sick almost every day. We only had an upstairs toilet, so it became a ritual at mealtimes to have the kitchen door open ready for the dash from the dining table to the sink where she would invariably throw up. The only thing she managed to keep down was Lucosade.

If we'd taken into account the amount she was going to drink and bought shares in the company, we'd now be worth a fortune. Apart from the obvious discomfort associated with pregnancy, the summer of 1976 was one of the hottest on record where the temperature regularly reached into the 90s.

There was many a day where she just didn't know what to do with herself. A drought was called and in many parts of the country, hundreds and thousands of people were dependent on standpipes for their water supply. Denis Howell was appointed the Minister for Drought. Within days, he became known as the Minister for Floods as the heavens opened.

Morley was an expert home brewer and turned out some exceptionally strong beers, all of which were made from scratch using hops, barley, yeast and sugar— no beer kits. Trisha did tell me, on more than one occasion, that when she lived at home, Morley would spend a few hours most Sunday mornings, brewing up his latest batch and bottling the previous one.

Whilst she didn't mind the smell too much she absolutely hated him playing his favourite classical music at top volume (the noisiest was Tchaikovsky's 1812 Overture). Trisha and John shared a bedroom which was divided with two wardrobes and was situated directly above the living room. Having heard his music, I can well understand how she must have felt especially after her partying the night before.

The point I'm trying to make is that Morley loved his homebrew (he also had a passion for whisky) and when he, Helen, Ted and Mabel visited Whittle Avenue just before Michael was born. We took them to a pub in the country (can't remember the name), not far from Calne, and introduced Morley to Wadworth's *Old Timer* Real Ale.

During the incredibly hot summer of 1976, the Wadsworth brewery in Devizes couldn't keep up with the demand. In an attempt to keep the pubs stocked with beer, they were delivering kegs of beer that weren't ready for drinking. When the beer was delivered to the pub, the landlord would put a handful of hops into each keg. I believe that helped with the secondary fermentation process and within a few days, the beer had settled and was ready to drink.

The beer was still slightly cloudy but was perfectly drinkable and very palatable. Morley had two pints and when we left, he had a definite stagger and a slight slur. From that day on, whenever the subject of him being drunk was mentioned, he would flatly deny it always; stating that the beer tasted like gnat's pee.

The Cortina was still running fine, however, it really wasn't that comfortable and with Trisha's condition, we looked around for something a little more elegant. I was given the opportunity to buy a Morris 1300 from one of the lads on my shift and after much debate and discussion, we bought it. Trisha reluctantly agreed to buy it but we couldn't really afford anything much better. And once again, it wasn't too long before the Lewis car gremlin struck again—Trisha's intuition proved to be spot on.

It was mid-summer and we'd been to see Mum at Lynton for the afternoon, a journey of about 25 miles. The trip there was fine but, on the way back, just outside of Upavon on the Devizes Road, the car started to cough, splutter and eventually died. It didn't take too long to find out that the fuel pump had packed up.

In desperation, I clouted the pump and to my surprise, I heard it sucking fuel from the tank. I started the engine and drove on. Unfortunately, we only managed to get about a quarter of a mile before the same thing happened. A quick bang of the pump got us going again but the same thing happened every 400 hundred yards or so until we eventually made it back home.

The rest of the summer went quickly and the weather eventually cooled to a more reasonable temperature. Michael was due on or about 24 September but decided he wasn't going to be on time, and after two weeks the decision was taken to induce the birth. I managed to get time off work and took Trisha to Princess Alexandra's Hospital at RAF Wroughton, Swindon.

The hospital was commissioned in 1939, and initially provided 260 beds, by 1943, eight additional wards had been constructed and at the end of 1944, the bed capacity had risen to 1000. Wroughton's busiest period followed the Allied landings in Normandy on 6 June 1945 (D-Day).

The first casualties landed at RAF Lyneham on 13 June 1945, and were ferried by a fleet of ambulances to Wroughton. A team of eight medical officers met the casualties and assessed the treatment required before the men were taken to the wards by Italian PoW porters.

In the next six months following D-Day, 4,811 casualties passed through Wroughton, where it continued as a general hospital treating military patients, until 1958, when it began taking NHS cases as well to relieve the backlog in the Swindon area.

Following a visit to the hospital by Princess Alexandra on 4 July 1967, the Queen conferred the prefix *Princess Alexandra's* on the hospital on 4 October 1967.

Trisha and I arrived at the hospital at 9:00 in the morning and were introduced to a very attractive flight lieutenant doctor who took Trisha to the ward and got her ready. There was a major refurbishment programme underway with workmen everywhere. The building work noise was unbearable so much so that on occasions we could hardly hear ourselves speak.

Trisha was given the drug to get Michael moving and nothing seemed to happen for quite a while; a few breaths of gas and air (for both of us!) and by early afternoon, things were starting to happen. I won't go into the gory details but Trisha was in labour for about six hours and Michael was born at 17:30.

It was such an incredible experience to witness his birth and one that I can vividly recall even today. Mike was bundled up, weighed and placed on his side in a clear Perspex type of crib whilst Trisha was being cleaned up. I sat and just stared at him and I became really quite emotional—he never cried, but he brought tears to my eyes.

I visited every night and Trisha recovered quite quickly but had to spend (I think) about a week before being sent home. It's a fact that everyone, on hearing a certain song, will associate that tune with a specific time or place in their life. For me, I heard the song 'Mississippi' by the American group 'Pussycat' every single night that I travelled from Compton Bassett to Wroughton, and whenever I hear it today, I'm taken back to 6 October 1976.

Quite obviously, Trisha and I were brand spanking new to parenthood and all that every parent wishes for is that their offspring grow up educated. That said, we had a visit from a couple one evening who were promoting Caxton encyclopaedias. They began their sales patter by suggesting that to ensure we were responsible parents; the suite of books would only be sold if we answered a few questions successfully.

Looking back, it was quite obvious that the questions were phrased in such a way that only a total moron would give a negative answer. Questions such as: 'Do you agree that it's important that children go to school, How important is it that children receive a proper education,' and so on.

Needless to say, the answers we gave confirmed that we were considered to be ideal parents! The suite of books was duly delivered but it wasn't too long before we decided that perhaps they were very expensive for what they were. Whilst *cooling-off* periods weren't the norm in 1976, Caxton agreed to take them back.

With Michael, barely a month old, we decided that our little two-bedroom home really wasn't big enough and as there were quite a few vacant quarters at Compton Bassett I applied for a three-bedroom house. We were allocated

Number 3 Atcherly Road almost immediately, and we began the preparation to carry out our first march-out.

We'd only been at Whittle Avenue for 15 months and as the house didn't require additional decorating, coupled with the fact that we still didn't have much in the way of personal belongings, the clean-up and subsequent march-out went without a hitch. After the new tenant had accepted the quarter, I gave him our address. As the house was close to the entrance to the estate, I asked that he drop off any mail on his way to work.

The new house, a two-bedroom semi, was quite unique insofar as our 3rd bedroom, which had two interconnecting doors, was located in the middle of the two properties. Locking either of the doors determined which house had the 3rd bedroom. If memory serves, the house was empty when we took it over, but was clean and presentable.

We'd been in the house for about a fortnight, and there was still no sign of any mail being delivered. So, I called at Whittle Avenue but found nobody at home. I did, however, see a large pile of mail, addressed to us on the window sill adjacent to the front door. I called several times again but never got an answer and I eventually managed to speak to the twerp at work and asked him to drop off the mail.

After a few days, there was still no sign of the mail and I went to the house again. This time, I noticed that it had gone from his window sill and a few days later the *missing* post was delivered by the postman. I was totally confused and couldn't understand why he'd gone to the trouble of redirecting the letters; instead of putting them through our letter box as he was leaving the estate.

There was a post box right outside our door and I often wondered if that's where he posted them from. The man was a complete knob, and fortunately, I never saw him again. I believe he moved out shortly afterwards.

Trisha was a brilliant mother, she was so patient with Michael who was a very placid baby anyway, he was easily contented and cried very little. He started to sleep through the night fairly quickly and was never an early riser, which made things easier for Trisha. She kept the house spick and span and put her cookery prowess to good use. Unfortunately, the main problem she had was, trying to keep Michael quiet during the morning whilst I was sleeping off the night shift.

When RAF Lyneham and RAF Brize Norton were both absorbed into RAF Strike Command on 1 September 1972, it was decided by the authorities that Lyneham would not adopt the same shift pattern that Brize operated. The flying squadrons at Brize operated a three 12-hour day shift, followed by another three 12-hour night shift and the cycle finished with a six-day stand-down period.

Many of the Brize groundcrews were *moonlighting* with some holding permanent jobs during their time off. Lyneham hierarchy, on the other hand, was not prepared to allow their maintenance personnel to be off at the same time as those from Brize Norton. Subsequently, they tried various shift schemes with the sole intent of keeping us a work.

The pattern that was finally implemented was, without a doubt, the most complex and unsociable that I have ever worked on. The day shift cycle began operating from 07:00 until 18:00 on Wednesday, Thursday and Friday. On Saturday and Sunday, the shift was split into two and operated from 07:00 until 19:00 and 19:00 until 07:00.

The day shift on Monday again began at 07:00 but was only half-strength due to the other half sleeping from the previous night shift. However, there were some permanent day workers to supplement the shortage. Tuesday saw the shift at full capacity for the next eleven hours.

The following five days were taken as stand-down. The night shift began on Monday and ran for five days from 18:00 until 07:00 the next morning, and that cycle concluded with four days off before the sequence began all over again.

The entire sequence was a nightmare. I subsequently had acute difficulty in sleeping after a 13-hour night shift which was probably down to being over-tired (if such a thing exists). Following the shift handover, I'd arrive home at 7:30, have some breakfast; usually beans on toast or fried bread, I'd make Trisha a cup of tea and be in bed by 8:15.

Most mornings, I'd be awake by 11:00 and found it impossible to go back to sleep. This process went on for several months, and in a desperate bid to try and get some quality sleep, I made an appointment to see the doctor. His answer was to prescribe Valium. He warned me that they were addictive if taken over a prolonged period, and to be only taken during the night shift phase.

He also told me that the shift system was having a big effect on other workers and that he had prescribed the drug to at least 70% of *A* and *B* line personnel. The Valium didn't really help me to sleep. On many occasions, if I took the pill with my breakfast, then by the time I got to the top of the stairs, I felt like I was drunk and would stagger to bed. I did sleep, but not for that much longer. I woke at about 13:00 and felt zonked out for the rest of the afternoon, and still had more nights to work. I gave up taking the pills after a couple of shift cycles.

We had several visits from relatives at Atcherly Road during 1977 including Tom and Edith whom we took to Bath and saw Queen Elizabeth and Prince Philip who were celebrating their Silver Wedding Anniversary. Michael was only nine months old and we hadn't taken any food with us, instead, we expected to buy something in the city.

Bath was absolutely heaving with tourists and well-wishers. We couldn't find anywhere to sit and give Michael some proper food. Instead, we gave him some quavers and a yoghurt. Edith was not impressed.

Married quarters were fine and I'm sure that if I'd been in any other job apart from the armed forces, I doubt whether we would have been able to get married as soon as we did. We started to look around for a home of our own and called in at a show house on a new development on the outskirts of Calne. The property we viewed was a very spacious three-bedroom bungalow with reasonable gardens both at the front and the rear.

It looked good, we thought, that was until we were told the price, it was £14,000. The average price of a home in 1976 was £12,700, inflation was running at 16.5%, the Bank of England base rate was 14.25% and petrol was 76 p per gallon (16 p per litre). The price of the bungalow straight away dashed our hopes; after all, my entire annual wage was only £3800.

My monthly pay was approximately £317 which after deducting rent of £36.40, income tax of £75.60 and national insurance of £17.75, we were left with about £197 per month to live on. I don't remember what the repayments were at the time, but without a deposit, we just couldn't afford it and resigned ourselves to the fact that we might never be able to get onto the housing ladder.

Despite the unsocial shift hours, Dave Stoddart and I managed to do a bit of moonlighting to supplement our wages. We registered with a local agency and managed to find some reasonable work. Once working in an electronics company in Swindon acting as QA engineers and on another occasion humping and stacking huge lumps of Avon rubber on an industrial estate close to home.

We also registered with Cary Aviation, a London-based agency that specialised in aircraft work at the various airports in and around the capital. Dave and I were offered a week's contract at Luton airport in a Britannia Airline hangar; the only problem was the work involved *Riggering* (Airframe engineers).

We thought about it and tentatively decided to take up the offer. After all, we were telecommunications engineers which had to be infinitely more difficult than bashing bits of metal. If we could follow electronic circuit diagrams, then an aircraft hydraulic system would be no worse and should be a piece of cake.

We were advised that we'd need a complete set of tools, although nothing specific was listed, and also given the address of suitable digs. We arrived at the hangar and met the servicing manager who introduced himself and asked just two questions. The first was to establish if we were servicemen or contractors.

If we were servicemen, he wanted to know how long we were going to be working for and the second was to establish what tools we had. Dave had a fairly comprehensive tool kit whereas mine was pretty basic. I was told that I had an hour to get myself some AF and Whitworth spanners, plus various other specialist tools and directed me to a Halfords store in Luton.

Before I left, he advised us that there was a particular individual on the servicing team who didn't particularly like working with servicemen; he didn't say why but warned us not to let on who we were. I managed to find the Halfords store, bought the necessary tools and was back at the hangar raring to go. Dave and I were allocated a Britannia aircraft belonging to Cyprus Airways.

The first job I was given was to repair one of the two toilets which, fortunately, was a bit of a gift after having worked the system on the RAF Brits whilst at Masirah. Over the next week, we carried out a variety of tasks all of which were well within our capabilities. I was given one particular task that involved working in the aircraft freight bay with the chap whom we were warned about.

It turned out that he was an ex-Royal Navy WAFU, an affectionate nickname given to members of the Fleet Air Arm by the RAF (the acronym WAFU means Wet and F#*#ing Useless, although there are other variations) and as it turned out he was fine. I waffled, lied and blagged it with him for the whole shift.

By the end of the week we had finished and were paid about £100. I'm not sure whether I'd made much money after paying for our digs, meals and my tools but it certainly was an experience.

Under the old *time promotion* scheme, I would have been guaranteed promotion to Sergeant in February 1978, provided I met the relevant criteria (trade exams and assessments). Unfortunately, the format was changed in 1977, to a system where we were examined not on specific trade ability but more oriented towards the organisational structure and function of the F700 aircraft documentation set.

Those of us who wanted to take the new style examination, were given no guidance as to what we were likely to be tested for, or what depth of knowledge was required. We were, however, given the relevant Air Publication (AP) details, which we were assured, would contain all of the information we would need.

I picked up the learning material, totalling some 11 APs, and try as I might. I really couldn't get to grips with learning. There were no classes and all studying was on a self-help basis and suffice it to say I and many other colleagues failed the exam abysmally.

I think the promotional and educational authorities sat up and reconsidered that a certain amount of direction was required due to the high failure rate of the new system. I retook the examination in April 1978 and thankfully passed.

The shift pattern became a little more bearable but no less tiring. Trisha, Michael and I enjoyed the summer of 1977 in our second home. Michael really was a funny little toddler insofar as whenever we went into the garden, he would only play on a blanket as he couldn't stand the feeling of grass on his bare feet.

I'm sure if Trisha and I were to go shopping for a couple of hours and leave Michael, we could more or less guarantee that he'd still be on the blanket when we got back!

I managed to get a couple of trips away during 1977. The first was a night stop at Gander in Newfoundland which was for the benefit of the aircrew and was looked upon as a Nav Ex across the pond. We booked into the Anchorage Hotel in St Johns and later that evening, went to a local bar where I was plied with some quite strong Canadian beer by the aircrew.

Towards the end of the evening, I remember going to the toilets and the next thing I recall was being woken up by the bar staff telling me that they were closing. I'd fallen asleep on the loo and the miserable gits had abandoned me. When I bumped into them at breakfast the next morning, they asked me how I was as they'd thought that I'd had enough and had just gone back to the hotel.

It was whilst I was in the terminal building that morning, that I bought a little teddy bear for Michael which I believe he still has today. We named it *Henry*.

The next trip was to Goose Bay in Labrador, Canada. There we dropped off some equipment for the Vulcan force in preparation for one of their countless exercises in the Canadian outback before carrying on to Offutt Air Force Base in Nebraska. Offutt was situated near Omaha and was the headquarters of the U.S. Strategic Bomber Command. When I arrived at Lyneham in early 1971, each crew member was given a set subsistence allowance and it didn't matter whether you spent it in a 5-star restaurant or in a burger bar; the choice was yours (sufficient funds were held by the imprest officer to pay for hotel accommodation).

However, on this occasion, just before we left Lyneham, a major policy change was implemented with regard to allowances. It was based on the fact that a subsistence allowance was still available but refunds would only be given on actual, receipted costs (up to a maximum limit).

This trip was my first which had a Ground Engineer (GE) as a permanent member of the crew and once the aircraft was serviced, we booked into the hotel. There were major cost cuttings being employed because we had to share a room, anyway, we got changed, went for dinner in a restaurant next door to the hotel after which we went back to the room.

I suggested getting a cab to downtown Omaha and having a few beers but my proposal was met with total disinterest. He told me that he'd been to the city before on a previous trip and couldn't be bothered, at which point he lay down on his bed and fell asleep. Nowadays, I'd have gone on my own but was reluctant to do so. Then, unfortunately, the hotel was just off the freeway and was miles from any built-up area.

So, I sat and watched American TV. It was late evening when my room companion awoke and he suggested we go for another meal; the rationale being that as we were entitled and we'd be reimbursed we might just as well do it—ridiculous!

We left Offutt early the next morning, and headed back to Goose Bay, where we picked up some freight destined for RAF Waddington, the home of the Vulcan Bomber. By the time we got to Waddo, it was quite late in the evening and after shutting down the engines, we refuelled and the movers unloaded the cargo.

We were only on the ground for a short time. However, we were unable to start the number three engine which would motor but not fully engage. So, in a desperate bid to get it started, another Hercules, which was also visiting, was positioned in front of our aircraft in the hope that the jet wash from their engines may be sufficient to windmill our duff engine—all to no avail. The aircraft was parked up and we got a lift back to Lyneham in the other cab.

Over the previous year, I'd learnt how to operate the Watts Datum instrument that was used to ensure the aircraft was set on a precise heading. I was regularly called upon to assist with calibrating the Hercules compass system. The job usually took four or five hours and on a sunny day; it was quite pleasant working on the compass pan situated on the far side of the airfield.

It was on one such day whilst the computations and adjustments were being carried out that I decided to drive to B Line and pick up our pre-ordered hot lunches. The route to the squadron was via the peri-track which was about two miles long and having picked up the meals I set off for the compass pan again.

Halfway around the peri-track, I noticed another Land Rover quite a way behind me, who was keeping pace with me but I took little notice. As I arrived at the aircraft the other vehicle pulled up and told me to report to Air Traffic Control immediately as I'd been seen speeding on the airfield.

I followed him across the active runway and on arriving at the ATC was told by the Flight Sergeant that I was going to be charged for blatantly disobeying airfield driving regulations and asked for my identity card which I didn't have on me. He went absolutely mad and questioned why I wasn't carrying it.

He wasn't the slightest bit placated when I told him that I always emptied my pockets of everything thereby reducing the probability of introducing Foreign Object Debris (FOD) into the aircraft.

Over the next week, exactly the same process was followed as for my last charge whilst at Wattisham. My boss, Flight Lieutenant Al Hayes, was fairly new in post and I think, as I was his first charge, he had to follow the process from a book. He asked why I was speeding and I replied that I wanted to get the meals to the aircraft before getting cold and I repeated the reason why I'd left my I.D card in my locker.

He then started to question the three witnesses and tore to shreds some of their evidence which contained some stark contradictions. However, he decided that there was a case to answer, and referred the case to the Squadron Commander who also thought that there was a case to answer and referred the charge to the Station Commander; I couldn't believe it.

By the time I was in front of the CO, the three stooges from ATC had got their act together; their stories were perfectly coordinated and almost word perfect and I was stitched up like the proverbial kipper. The Station Master fined me £15 and afterwards the Squadron Commander apologised to me stating that it shouldn't have gone that far. What a prick, because he was the only one who could have made that decision.

The next problem we encountered was when the gearbox on the Morris 1300 packed up and left us without transport. Fortunately, one of my work colleagues,

Dick Fiest had a Ford Zephyr which he kindly lent me until I could sort out a replacement. I managed to buy a reconditioned gearbox from an engineering company near the Cowley factory in Oxford. With the help of friends, I managed to remove the engine, replace the gearbox and successfully refit it over a weekend.

One of the worst jobs I had on B Line was when I was employed as the Flight Line Mechanic (FLM) controller. The FLM's prime job was to refuel the aircraft, kick the tyres and do all of the basic, menial tasks associated with the after flight, before flight and turn around servicing. Their role was crap with very little job satisfaction.

Whilst there were a few who were switched on and had the potential to advance further and become specific tradesmen, there were a couple who were as thick as a ton of pig's shit in an aspirin bottle and one such character caused absolute mayhem.

Following the flight servicing, maintenance tasks and relevant repairs, the final serviceability task was for an NCO check to be carried out. The check was designed to ensure that all of the major systems were serviceable and that the aircraft was ready for flight. There were only a few SNCOs on shift and in an effort to spread the workload, authority was given to JNCOs to carry out this final check.

There had been several reports of pools of hydraulic oil, the lifeline of any aircraft mechanical system, being found on the freight bay floor which obviously meant a detailed search in the relevant area to ascertain where the leak was coming from.

Many hours were spent over a period of time trying to find the elusive leaks until someone noticed a disgruntled FLM shooting his OM15 hydraulic oil replenishment gun into the roof of the freight bay and walking off. The little toerag caused so much trouble that he was immediately charged and banned from going anywhere near an aircraft ever again. I believe he was thrown out of the RAF.

The cold-wet protective clothing provided was, more often than not, inadequate and as a means of supplementing what we were issued with, I decided to wear a pair of Trisha's tights under my trousers and Denhams. You would not believe how effective they were at keeping the warmth in, especially, when lying on the concrete dispersal in inclement weather. I'm not sure what the reaction would have been if I'd been involved in an accident and taken to hospital!

By late 1977, I'd had enough of Lyneham, its shift system, Hercules and FLMs and volunteered for employment on the new Sea King HAR 3 Search and Rescue helicopter. Up until then, there were only single trade electronic engineers (apart from the ex-technical apprentices who covered air radar, air communications and navigational instrumentation).

Whereas, in the SAR world, all techies had to be cross-trained, thereby keeping the number of personnel required to maintain the aircraft to an absolute minimum. The requirement was for radar and comms to be cross-trained, electrical and Nav Inst to be combined and Engines and Airframes to be amalgamated.

Within a few short weeks of applying, I learnt that I'd been selected. I was to be eventually posted to RAF Boulmer in December 1978. But first of all, I had to complete 11 months of training commencing at RAF Cosford in January 1978.

My 'Swan Song' after seven and a half years on the transport fleet was to Norman Manley and Sangster, neither of which I'd heard of before and hadn't the foggiest idea where they were. As it turned out, I was off to Kingston and Montego Bay airports respectively, both on the Caribbean Island of Jamaica where we'd be replacing a contingent of British soldiers with fresh blood.

Our first port of call was Gander in Newfoundland where I refuelled the aircraft wearing arctic clothing in subzero temperatures. The aircraft was packed to capacity not only with cargo but also passengers which left very few options as to where to sit, I chose to sit towards the rear of the freight bay.

Toilet facilities on a transport aircraft were very basic and it was always best to *go* before flying. However, when needs must and when you've gotta go, you've just gotta go. Positioned at the rear of and at either side of the freight bay were stand-up urinals, there was also a chemical toilet that was stowed close to the aircraft roof and secured in place with a quick-release pip-pin.

Access was gained by standing on the ramp, reaching up and pulling the pip-pin which would release the toilet, allowing it to slide down on rails into a more manageable position; a vanity curtain could then be pulled around the occupant. I was reading when one of our esteemed Pongo passengers decided he had to use the Elsan. Under normal circumstances, I wouldn't take any notice of people using a toilet but this particular fellow drew attention to himself in quite a unique manner.

He began by unravelling the plastic curtain and stepping behind it which denied everyone seeing what he was actually up to. Over the next few moments, there was a great deal of movement from behind the curtain, which culminated in the soldier's head poking over the top of the curtain which was only a foot or so from the freight bay ceiling. He sat there for a while innocently smiling and eventually reappeared, wrapped up the curtain and took his seat once again.

I couldn't understand what on earth he had done until it dawned on me that instead of releasing the toilet from its stowage position, he had climbed up the freight bay wall and perched himself on top of the toilet. He realised what a plonker he'd been, when a colleague demonstrated, for all to see, how the toilet should have been used.

We eventually arrived at Kingston and unloaded the freight and passengers before flying on to Montego Bay. We had planned on doing a little sightseeing but due to a hydraulic leak in one of the upper wing dry bays and some other minor faults, the GE and I spent most of the afternoon carrying out repairs. By the time we'd finished and got to the hotel, it was early evening and we were asked to go to one of the aircrew rooms for a briefing.

There had been a power cut in the town and as there was no street lighting, we were advised that it would be too dodgy to leave the hotel after dark. I had hoped to pick up a variety of fresh fruit from some of the market stalls in Montego Bay but had to settle instead for some bananas from a small stall at the hotel entrance. The evening was extremely boring.

The next morning, we boarded a minibus and took a drive around the town. The prime purpose was for some of the aircrew to stock up on cheap slabs of beer and after seeing the state of the shanty town area I can well understand why we were advised not to venture out after dark. We loaded the aircraft with soldiers who were returning to the UK and set off for the return trip to Gander and once again the weather at Gander was atrocious.

For the return leg to Lyneham, I sat next to the flight deck and despite the length of time we'd been flying, I felt quite good, that was until we were approaching Lyneham. We'd all been issued with a meal box when we left Gander and the contents had been eaten more or less straight away that was apart from the Pongo sitting next to me who still had a boiled egg.

As we started to descend onto the glide path which would take us safely onto the runway. My friend next to me decided to remove the shell from his egg and bite into it. The egg was obviously rotten because the smell was unbelievable and I immediately reached for a sick bag and threw up. At that point, he just looked at me and enquired if I was all right and carried on eating.

Despite all of the travelling that I'd done, that was the first time I'd been airsick. To make matters worse, I'd put the fresh bananas in a stowage bin in the ramp and when I went to retrieve them, they were black and frozen solid.

Michael celebrated his first birthday in October 1977, we spent Christmas with Helen and Morley in Southport and all too soon January was with us, which signalled the start of my cross-training programme.

Chapter Eleven
Search & Rescue Helicopter Cross-Training

Royal Air Force Station Cosford

(4 January to 31 March 1978)

Chris and Jill Hunt, as mentioned earlier, were our very dear friends at Compton Bassett who were posted to Cosford a few months before the start of my course. As we all got on exceptionally well, it was suggested that Trisha, Michael and I should move into the married quarter with them for the duration of the course which would save me a fortune in weekend commuting costs.

Not only would it help Trisha and me to save money and time, but Jill and Trisha had an awful lot in common. The other bonus was their daughter Emma who was Michael's age and both of them played very well together.

Cosford hadn't changed one iota in the seven years since I'd left and it felt like I'd never been gone. During the three-month cross-training programme, I was to learn about the various aircraft communications and navigation techniques, be trained on specific equipment and carry out system fault-finding and defect rectification.

Day one of the course was spent carrying out the routine arrival procedure, meeting our instructor, an air comms Chief Tech, and more importantly, my future work colleagues. There were six members of the Boulmer course, Sergeant Roger Dingle and the five Corporals were: me, Kel Watson, Brian King, Paddy Malone and Noel Lambert.

I thought I'd seen the last of Sergeant Gibling following my *get your hair cut* greeting at Akrotiri in 1974, but unfortunately, it wasn't to be. I was driving through the main gate with Chris one morning and was pulled over by a Flight Sergeant who asked us why we weren't wearing our berets; no real answer. I then realised who it was—Ex Sergeant Gibling now promoted. I didn't let on that I remembered him.

Trisha and Jill got on really well and it didn't take long for them to get into routine each helping with the normal household chores. We did almost everything together. The one high spot of the week was for the six of us to sit and watch 'Blake's Seven'. Compared to some of the graphics, stage settings, dialogue and storylines available today, that ski-fi programme was pathetic and about as bad as it could get.

But that was 1978, and it was a programme we never missed. As far as home life was concerned, we all enjoyed each other's company, shared the costs of running the house and got through the three months unscathed. To this day, we remain the best of friends.

The training really was a none event. Our instructor was good at what he did, and he managed to get the message across without too much difficulty. I don't remember if there was an end, of course, exam. But suffice it to say, by the end of our three months, we were classed as competent and prepared to move on to the next phase of our training programme.

HMS Daedalus

(7 to 28 April 1978)

Her Majesty's Ship Daedalus, situated near Lee-on-Solent in Hampshire was one of the primary shore-based airfields of the Fleet Air Arm that was first established as a seaplane base in 1917; it later became the main training establishment and administrative centre for the Fleet Air Arm. Our three-week training at Daedalus covered the Sea King MEL Lightweight Radar equipment and was entirely classroom-based.

We were also required to carry out a couple of days of aircraft husbandry training that was designed to enlighten us about the problems associated with operating metal aircraft in a saltwater environment—the two really don't mix well at all.

My course joining instructions stated that I had to be at Daedalus (or *Dead Loss* as it soon came to be nicknamed) on a Sunday evening ready to commence the training first thing on the Monday morning. I arrived at the guard room, booked in and was directed to my accommodation. The rest of the team were already in the room except for Roger who was living in the PO's mess—the boys were not a happy bunch.

The accommodation block we'd been put in was intended for use by transiting personnel and was in a pretty grotty state. Our room, which wasn't occupied, had several lockers and bunk beds which could potentially accommodate up to 40 people. We decided to dismantle some of the bunk beds and, using several of the lockers, segregated the top third of the room for ourselves.

That done, and our beds made, we went for a beer in the NAAFI. When we returned to the block, we were horrified to find our room full of sailors! They turned out to be a part of the ship's company from HMS Blake. I don't think they were too impressed at being packed into the remaining two-thirds of the room—tough!

I'd not come across many naval personnel before and was unfamiliar with the ranks. As we were walking to class on the first morning, we assumed that the three chaps coming towards us must be officers because of the white hats they were wearing. As they got closer, we all saluted them and instead of acknowledging that fact, they just laughed at us. It wasn't until they'd passed that we realised they were only Chief Petty Officers.

I never made that mistake again. By the time we got back to our room after dinner, we were welcomed by the Leading Hand or *Killick* (the insignia worn by leading rates was a single fouled anchor which led to the slang term Killick or Hooky).

He told us that the accommodation was to be part of the Captain's rounds (inspection) the next morning and we were to polish and buff the floors and clean all windows inside and out. Then, thoroughly dust the entire room and *barrack* our beds which entailed stripping our beds and wrapping the sheets and blankets to form a square pack.

Bearing in mind the fact that the room was a real tip, the flooring was made from parquet wood that hadn't seen a lick of polish since Horatio's day. We weren't prepared to take orders from an equal rank. We did, however, agree that we'd clean the windows and nothing else. The Killick was really quite insistent however we told him we weren't interested and went to bed.

The next morning, there was frantic activity from the Matelots; we made our beds and went to our classes. When we returned after lunch, we were met by the Leading Hand who told us we were to report to the Master at Arms immediately.

Unfortunately, once again, nobody was familiar with ranks or positions and hadn't a clue who or what the Master of Arms was responsible for. But we were soon to find out.

We presented ourselves and he began by quoting Queen's Regulations; stating that when two or more people in the Navy collude to overthrow authority a charge of Mutiny will normally be brought against the perpetrators—Whoops! He asked what we thought we were hoping to achieve, and we told him exactly why we thought we shouldn't clean the room to the standards expected—we then got a severe bollocking and were told to leave.

We were expecting to be forced to clean the room but nothing more came of it and by the time we returned in the evening the Matelots had gone. Afterwards, we couldn't help thinking that the ship's company had been put up in the room as a way of getting it cleaned.

During our brief encounter with our Navy brethren, we couldn't help thinking that some of their traditions were carried out not for any practicable purpose but just to be bloody-minded and none more so than the use of the *Liberty Boat*.

Liberty Boats were the small boats that took sailors ashore from the warships for leave or recreation and for some bizarre reason, the ritual was maintained at *dead loss*. Kel Watson tried to get off the base mid-afternoon and was told that trainees couldn't leave until a set time when the Liberty Boat was available, he believed it to be a spoof designed to piss off the *Crabfats*.

He said that he couldn't wait and anyway he was capable of walking on water and left. The nickname Crabfat was and is still used to describe RAF personnel; with the expression going back quite a few years, and lies in the fact that naval personnel would use the grease that the gun shells were caked in to get rid of crabs which they'd picked up after visiting brothels overseas.

The grease they used just happened to be the same colour as the light blue RAF uniform—hence the term.

Lee-on-Solent was only a couple of hours away, and I managed to get home each weekend. It was on the second Sunday afternoon whilst watching television that we heard an almighty noise outside the front of the house. On looking, we found that a taxi had driven into the front of my car. God knows what speed the taxi driver was doing but the collision pushed my car at least six feet backwards (the hand brake was also on) and caved in the front wing, part of the bonnet and the grill.

He reckoned that as he was leaving the estate, he swerved to avoid my neighbour who had pulled out in front of him. Unbelievably, apart from a broken headlight it was still drivable. However, it would be dark by the time, I was due to leave. But then, I was forced to leave early in the morning. The rest of the course went well and we managed to complete it without upsetting our erstwhile Navy types.

Westland Helicopters Ltd

(22 to 26 May 1978)

Whilst it wasn't essential that we attend a manufacturer's course to maintain the Sea King helicopter, we nevertheless spent five days at Westland Helicopters Ltd in Yeovil, Somerset. The course was primarily oriented at familiarising us with the full range of radar and communications equipment. However, we were also given an insight into what made the rest of the aircraft tick and the time spent in Somerset was enjoyable and informative.

Several of the aircraft had already been accepted by the RAF and were in active use by Lossiemouth's aircrew and groundcrew who were the first to commence the training programme at the Royal Naval Air Station (RNAS) Culdrose. Boulmer's aircraft were in Westland's hangar and were scheduled to be delivered to Northumberland by December.

Whilst at Westlands, Trisha received notification that we'd been allocated a married quarter at Boulmer in early July. That gave us a reasonable amount of time to pack up our house on Atcherly road and prepare to move into our 3rd house in less than three years. As it transpired, the move from Compton Bassett turned out to be the most traumatic of all our moves.

The house at Longhoughton was available from around about 3 July. I made arrangements with one of the ground crew on the Whirlwind squadron to act as a proxy and take over the quarter for me. He also agreed to be available to accept the removal van.

I finished work and cleared Lyneham on Friday, 7 July. Unfortunately, the car was still in the garage in Calne and wasn't available to be picked up until mid-afternoon. We, eventually, loaded up the car and set off for Southport where we planned on stopping the night with Helen and Morley. The next morning, we started on the final leg of the journey arriving at Boulmer's Guard Room mid-afternoon where the keys to Number 13 Park Road, Longhoughton had been left.

The house was clean and comprised of a lounge diner, two bedrooms, and a long narrow kitchen with a separate utility room at the end which led to the front of the house. There was a small enclosed garden. Heating and hot water were provided by a Parkray coal burner, that neither of us had used before.

We spent the next few days unpacking and trying to get the house in some semblance of order before the next phase of my training began and as usual, Trisha did her normal wizardry turning the house into a home.

My main concern was not being able to contact Trisha whilst I was away, and for her, to be able to speak with Helen and Morley. However, there was a telephone line to the house that only required connecting in the exchange and Aunt Edith had offered to pay the connection charge. The estate we lived on was a mix of service and civilian accommodation. Unfortunately, we were one of the first families to arrive and consequently, neither of us knew anyone.

Longhoughton village was small but had a pub, The Burnside, a village post office and a small NAAFI which was used by everyone including the civilian residents, the nearest town was Alnwick. Trisha always jokingly maintained that all Southerners (Londoners, I presume), were stuck-up and tended to keep themselves to themselves and wouldn't go out of their way to speak with strangers.

Whilst I wouldn't necessarily agree with that sentiment, when we went into a pub in Alnwick and sat down for lunch, the locals (Northumbrians not Geordies!) immediately made us feel most welcome. The house was close to the busy main Edinburgh to Newcastle railway line, and whilst we couldn't see the HS125 trains until they flashed past, we could certainly hear them coming.

Michael was playing in the garden one afternoon, and all of a sudden, he came running and screaming into the house just as the train went past—the poor lad was half-frightened to death.

By the time the weekend arrived, everything was more or less set up, arrangements had been made for the phone to be connected, Trisha was happy with the coal fire and we'd done sufficient shopping for her and Michael to get by. I left them on Sunday, 16 July, and headed back to Compton Bassett where I spent a lonely night.

The house had been cleaned and prepared for the handover before we left and all that was required the next morning was a quick dust around and as this was our second march-out; I knew what was expected. The normal Family's Officer for some reason wasn't available and as there was no new occupant I handed the house over to a Warrant Officer aircrew.

I was billed for a missing teaspoon and two pillowcases (which we later found in one of the packing boxes). The comment was made about a few cigarette butts that were in the garden. That was it. I then had to drive to Culdrose in Cornwall.

RNAS Culdrose

(17 July to 7 December 1978)

RNAS Culdrose was home, amongst others, to 771 Naval Air Squadron whose principal role was to carry out Search and Rescue duties covering much of the south coast and the western approaches to the UK. The layout of the Air Station was such that the domestic site, where the single accommodation, the Officers and CPO messes were situated, was separated from the operational sites by the main road that ran from Helston to the Lizard peninsula.

The five-month on-the-job training was designed not only to familiarise the aircrew with the aircraft, but also to enable the ground crew to get to grips with the various systems and maintenance procedures. It was also intended to give those of us who weren't familiar with rotary wing operations an idea of the possible events and associated actions that were required.

The Royal Air Force Sea King Training Unit was administered by a few RAF SNCOs. But the main training element was carried out by experienced Fleet Air Arm engineering POs and CPOs. The entire RAF Lossiemouth crew had already been at Culdrose for four months. It was their job to assist in familiarising us during their last month we in turn, towards the end of our programme would help the Coltishall crew who were due to arrive at the beginning of November.

The shift system was straight days and nights, days ran from 8:00 until 17:00 and nights from 17:00 until cease flying. The aircrew were required to carry out a certain amount of night flying but due to lighter evenings in summer, it was invariably late by the time they'd finished. The only change to the scheme was on a Friday when the day shift knocked off at midday and we weren't due back at work until Monday evening which gave us one long weekend every fortnight.

The training began immediately, and I think, I was one of only a handful of people who weren't rotary wing familiar but soon picked up what I needed to know. The yellow Sea King HAR 3, the RAF variant, was based on the proven RN version and was an extremely competent machine.

To enable the RN aircraft to be stored beneath decks on the aircraft carriers, the main rotor blades were capable of being folded such that all five blades were positioned directly over the tail boom. To further save space, the tail rotor pylon would also fold back on itself. These same facets were available on our aircraft.

The rear of the aircraft had a removable polyurethane w*et fit* floor which helped to minimise corrosive seawater ingress during wet winching by the Winchman (affectionately referred to as w*inch weights*). In the middle of the floor was a panel that gave us access to various items of equipment, the most important of these was the radar transmitter/receiver (T/R).

On earlier versions of the Navy aircraft, the T/R was positioned on a rack towards the front of the aircraft. It was quite common for the system to go *off-tune* and the WAFU *Pinkies* would carry out a retune in situ. Unfortunately, the quick retune was invariably never recorded on the aircraft job cards and when the RAF variant was being designed, because it appeared that the radar was extremely reliable; it was moved from its current position into one of the most inaccessible areas on the aircraft.

Now, whether that story is true I don't know, I'm only repeating what I was told—but its validity doesn't surprise me. Whilst the radar was quite reliable, on those occasions where the T/R needed to be retuned once the seal between the cabin floor, the wet fit and the panel had been broken, it was the devil's own job to get a good seal, which unless perfect, would allow seawater to seep into the hold resulting in corrosion.

We'd only been at Culdrose for three weeks or so, when we were told that the station was closing down for a fortnight's *Block Leave* which allowed all of the operational squadrons, including the RAFSKTU but not the RN SAR elements, to have some summer leave.

The journey home was my first and despite the fact it was mid-summer, the drive through Cornwall and Devon was simplicity itself and I know that the same journey today can be a total nightmare. I don't remember specifically what we did during the leave but it was a real treat to see Trisha and Michael, who seemed very grown up all of a sudden.

Trisha also told me that whilst I was away, she'd been visited by the wife of Squadron Leader Derek Nequest, the squadron CO, to make sure that everything was okay—that was a nice touch.

The two weeks off were spent sightseeing and getting to know the area. The Northumbrian coastline, beaches and the surrounding Cheviots Mountains were stunning but even on a sunny day the accompanying wind coming off the North Sea was cool. However, we spent many happy days amongst the sand dunes, close to Seahouses. One delicacy we soon discovered was fresh Craster Kippers and the other was fresh crab—fantastic.

Once again, the time flew by and I soon found myself on the road again. The Morris had been behaving itself since being repaired but all of that was soon to come to an abrupt end. I was travelling on the M6 somewhere, I think, between Knutsford and Sandbach in Cheshire and was overtaking a line of trucks (there were only two lanes on the M6 then) when there was an almighty bang, the oil and ignition lights on the dashboard came on and the engine died.

Luckily, I managed to get in front of the trucks and pulled onto the hard shoulder. The prognosis by the AA man, totally knackered and the Camshaft had smashed through the side housing. So, there I was, stuck 200 miles from home and 350 miles from Helston. The car was towed to a local garage just off the motorway where the owner agreed to store it until I could get back and pick it up.

It was early afternoon, and I was then left with the dilemma of how to get to Culdrose. The only real option was to hitchhike. So, I walked to the motorway junction and stuck out my thumb—it wasn't too long before I was picked up. The truck driver was going to Bristol and it's at this point that my recollection of events is a little hazy.

I know we travelled towards Avonmouth and when he dropped me off, I was told to head back in the direction that we had just come from, so I started walking.

The next thing I knew was that a police car had pulled up alongside me, the policeman in the passenger seat wound down his window and all he said to me was, "Okay! Army or Air Force?"

I told him and he just said, "Get in."

I was apparently hitchhiking on a motorway! I've looked at the map several times but still can't understand precisely where I was. Anyway, I was taken to Gordano Services on the M5 where I managed to get another lift all the way to

Plymouth and the final leg of the journey was by bus to Helston, where I met several of the lads in the Godolphin Arms pub.

The pub became the local to me, Dave Simmons, Merv Roberts, Slim Hammel and Bob Good and we spent many a happy *lock-in* after hours. It was during one such lock-in, not long before we were due to leave, that I mentioned to the landlord that I really wanted to give up smoking but was struggling. I was smoking about 20 a day, had developed a hacking cough and was spending money I couldn't really afford (they cost 50 p for 19 ciggies from a vending machine!).

Trisha had briefly smoked Consulate the menthol cigarette when we first married but never really took to it. Because we all got on so well, the landlord said that he would visit us at Boulmer and he wanted to take us and our wives out for a meal and he offered me a challenge.

If I could give up smoking between that evening and his visit in January 1979 (about 7 weeks), he would give me £20. I accepted immediately and threw away what cigarettes I had in my packet. He did visit Boulmer as promised but unfortunately, we were at Southport. I never saw him again and, of course, never got my £20. There is a plus side though, I haven't, to this day, smoked a cigarette again.

I was billeted along with other members of the groundcrew in a six-man room on the domestic site which was really very comfortable and a far cry from the hovel we lived in at d*ead loss*. The only downside was that if the Captain's rounds (monthly inspection of the block) took place in the morning, we were sleeping off the night shift and we were not allowed to be in bed.

As members of the RAFSKTU, we were entitled to all of the perks afforded to the RN personnel. RNAS Culdrose was classed as a ship even though it was a shore-based establishment; this anomaly meant that everyone was entitled to a monthly duty-free cigarette allowance. The cigarettes or tobacco were issued on the domestic site. However, because of the customs and excise regulations, we were only allowed to carry a maximum of 20 cigarettes a day between the two sites.

The training was comprehensive and whilst the servicing and maintenance concepts are the same for both Rotary Wing and Fixed Wing Aircraft, the operational aspects are totally different. As groundcrew, we were required to be familiar with the many potential emergency situations we were likely to encounter whilst the helicopter was on the ground.

There was one particular airborne emergency response we had to rehearse on a regular basis and that was the *wheels up* landing. Both the air and ground crews knew that what was to follow was an exercise, and the scenario began when the aircraft approached the landing area with the main wheels deliberately retracted. The marshaller was to indicate to the aircrew that the wheels weren't lowered by rolling his arms in a circular motion, and the aircraft would immediately be brought into the hover.

There was an unbelievable amount of static electricity generated by the five blades on the rotor head and before anyone touched the aircraft, it had to be earthed. This was achieved by attaching a large metal hook connected to a pole that, in turn, was connected to a heavy metal weight that sat on the ground via a length of cable.

As many crew as possible had to carry out the procedure, and on this particular day, it was my turn. The line controller began the exercise by tannoying that an aircraft was approaching with its wheels up. At that point, I donned my hard hat, picked up a set of emergency ground locks and ran to the dispersal along with my colleague who was to ensure the aircraft was earthed.

The marshaller signalled to the captain to bring the helicopter into a very, very low hover. I indicated for the earthing strap to be attached, walked forward and positioned myself under the port sponson. The aircraft, by now, was hovering about a foot above my head and I reached up into the undercarriage bay, pulled the release pin and under gravity, the mainwheel oleo dropped. I then fitted a ground lock which secured that particular oleo.

I then walked under the helicopter to the starboard sponson, and unfortunately, when I touched the aircraft, I got an almighty electric shock. I looked around to see that the *earther* had disconnected the earth lead, and instead of staying where he was, he had walked around to my side of the aircraft and in that short space of time, the static had built up and severely bit me.

The weather that day was particularly windy and the aircraft was being buffeted, such that, if I hadn't been wearing a hard hat, I'd have sustained some serious head injuries. I managed to pull the starboard release pin, but the oleo didn't drop. I had to physically haul myself into the sponson bay enabling me to get sufficient leverage to pull the undercarriage down.

I was later told that my feet were at least two feet off the ground whilst I was hanging onto the oleo which eventually dropped. I was able to insert the second ground lock and move away from the aircraft. All credit to the pilot who, despite the blustery conditions, managed to keep the helicopter in a pretty consistent hover.

Shortly after the Morris packed up, John (Trisha's brother) collected the car and took it back to Southport, where he sold it to a local garage. He could only get scrap value for it, which amounted to £25. I thought it was a total scam, especially, as I'd spent £25 on a new voltage regulator and battery only a few weeks previously.

The three months following the block leave went fairly quickly and I managed to get home on three occasions during that time by sharing a car with four other lads, who by then, had moved into Longhoughton. Boulmer was 550 miles from Culdrose, and we normally managed to get a quick beer close to home before eventually arriving just before midnight on the Friday night.

We'd leave for the return journey at 5:00 on Monday morning, getting back to Culdrose in time to start the five-day night shift.

The final month at Culdrose went without a hitch; we helped to train the Coltishall crew and eventually said goodbye to Cornwall.

Chapter Twelve
Royal Air Force Station Boulmer

(16 July 1978 to 9 September 1980)

RAF Boulmer was a small station situated on the coast, east of Alnwick in Northumberland. The station was home to 202 Squadron which operated Westland Whirlwind helicopters in the Search and Rescue capacity. The unit was also home to a large ground radar site, situated about two miles from our site.

Its prime purpose was to act as an early warning facility against infringement of the UK's air space by intruder aircraft, which in the '70s, was predominantly from the USSR. As the UK Air Defence Ground Environment (UKADGE) developed, Boulmer's role gradually increased in importance. By 1974, the station had evolved to become both a Sector Operations Centre (SOC) and the Control and Reporting Centre (CRC).

During this time, fighter controllers from Boulmer routinely detected Soviet aircraft probing the UK Air Defence Region and scrambled Quick Reaction Alert aircraft to intercept them before they reached UK airspace.

Having successfully completed our on-the-job training, we arrived at Boulmer raring to go. We had about a week to get everything set up and ready to take over duties from the incumbent Search and Rescue Westland Whirlwind. There was sufficient manpower to operate a three-shift system and have a few personnel on permanent days. One shift ran for 24 hours on, 24 hours off (but on standby) for two weeks followed by two weeks off. There were individual bunks for shift personnel to sleep.

For the first year at Boulmer, Trisha and I didn't have a car, which somewhat restricted our efforts to take advantage of the time off and we relied heavily on public transport. Our weekly shopping trip on the bus to Alnwick, always culminated in Trisha buying Michael a small matchbox car and me four cans of beer. Unfortunately, I don't remember what her treat was.

We visited a local car showroom and despite the fact that the prices of the vehicles were reasonable, we were shocked at the repayments required for quite an insignificant loan—£50 per month. It was almost a quarter of my monthly take-home wage. We, therefore, decided to save what we could and make do.

One of the joys of working on a Search and Rescue squadron was the amount of assistance and cooperation we got from the other public rescue bodies such as the police, fire, ambulance, mountain rescue and the lifeboat crews.

This was never more evident than when Paddy Malone, a Geordie, who was with us throughout our yearlong Sea King training but had been posted to RAF Lossiemouth in Scotland, learnt that his father had been taken seriously ill and had been admitted to Newcastle General Hospital.

One of Lossie's Sea Kings was scheduled to be delivered to RAF Finningley in Yorkshire for a major servicing. Arrangements were made for the aircraft to divert into Boulmer, drop Paddy off and one of our aircraft would take him to Newcastle. Paddy spent a few hours with his father and when the time came for him to leave, a police car from the Tyne and Wear force was waiting for him.

The car took Paddy to the county border where another car from the Northumberland force was waiting and continued the journey to Boulmer. By the time he arrived, Lossie's replacement Sea King was waiting to fly him back to Scotland—perfectly coordinated.

One of the low spots during our time in Northumberland was when Gran Sowerby sadly passed away in a home in Southport. Unfortunately, we couldn't get to Southport for the cremation. But when I mentioned to one of the pilots that Gran's ashes were to be interred in the St Cuthberts churchyard in Milburn, he suggested that they might be able to drop me off on their way to Ambleside on the west coast where our crews regularly trained with the life boat crews.

I duly contacted the police in Appleby and told them of our proposal. The plan was for me to be winched down onto the village green, attend the interment and the helicopter would return, not land but winch me back into the aircraft. The police were quite happy and would arrange for a local bobby to attend.

The squadron had two Sea Kings at their disposal: one aircraft and its crew were always on immediate readiness and if the second aircraft was required a second crew could be called upon. Two hours before we were due to leave, a call came from the maritime Rescue Coordination Centre (RCC) at Pitreavie Castle, near Edinburgh, putting the crew on standby for the potential rescue of a foreign fisherman who had been seriously injured on a vessel in the North Sea.

RAF Search & Rescue aircraft's primary role was to save downed military aircrew but would always react to calls from mountain rescue teams, lifeboat stations and the police, all of which were managed by the RCC. The costs associated with launching a Sea King on a rescue mission were prohibitive and I believe, in this particular case, there was some dispute as to how serious the man's injuries really were and whether or not he could wait until making landfall.

The duty Captain was obviously very keen to carry out a real-life rescue and was prepared to put the task with the lifeboat on hold. Time ticked away and the RCC decided to launch the Sea King for the rescue, by which time, it was far too late for me to make the church service.

I spoke with the standby captain the next day, who was disappointed to learn that I didn't go. He did say that if he had been on duty, he would have called in the standby crew to carry out the rescue, and would have kept the appointment with the lifeboats and subsequently dropped me off at Milburn.

The British servicemen, despite their dwindling numbers, were and still are held in high regard which is due in no small part to their sheer professionalism and level of training carried out. RAF SAR crews were required to rehearse and practice each and every element of their specialisation on a monthly basis. Whilst most components could be achieved routinely there was one facet that could not—and that was the actual rescue of personnel from a hazardous location.

One way of achieving as realistic a scenario as possible was for volunteers to act as casualties and be *rescued* by the crews. Some members of the ground crew, having been dropped into life rafts out at sea, given various survival items including a UHF Search and Rescue Beacon Equipment (SARBE) were then abandoned by the Sea King whose job then it was to find them.

I volunteered to be rescued, not at sea but on land, and was kitted out with a bright orange immersion suit (a rubberised garment that would give protection against the elements), a *Bone Dome* and a SARBE. I was briefed that I would be dropped on a beach at a remote location, somewhere on the east coast of Northumberland. The helicopter would then fly off out of sight, and I was to hide somewhere at the base of the surrounding cliffs, set the SARBE off and await rescue.

My first attempt was fairly straight forward and I was winched up without too much effort. Once inside the aircraft, I was asked to get myself into a more awkward situation before once again being dropped off and left alone. The next spot was much more complicated for the Winchman; because not only did I find a location where I couldn't immediately be seen but I lay beside some large boulders under a small waterfall. I set the SARBE off and waited.

Whilst I could hear the helicopter, I was a little concerned that, perhaps, the signal from the SARBE was being blocked by the rocks and the crew wasn't picking it up on the aircraft's UHF homing system. However, within a few moments, the helicopter was immediately overhead and the Loady was being manoeuvred into position.

He managed to locate me and despite being in quite an inaccessible position, I was successfully winched aboard—really good fun.

Flights in the aircraft were very easy to come by. We, as ground crew, were often asked if we would accompany the aircraft, sit in either of the two rear seats which had *bubble* windows and act as observers. I went on one such flight believing it to be nothing more than a training exercise with Ambleside Coastguard Rescue services.

I was enjoying the flight until I heard over the intercom that the crew was going to carry out some auto rotations. Being new to the helicopter world, I hadn't the foggiest idea what that meant and if I'd known at the beginning of the trip what was going to happen, then I'd have stayed at Boulmer.

All rotary wing pilots must carry out certain emergency training procedures, and on this particular day, they were going to practice auto rotations. Helicopters do have a certain amount of glide capability, but the pilot has only got one shot at it. For a helicopter, autorotation refers to the descending manoeuvre following the failure of the engines resulting in the disengagement from the main rotor system. The rotor head is then driven solely by the upward flow of air through the rotor blades.

The freewheeling unit is a special clutch mechanism that disengages anytime the engine rpm is less than the rotor rpm; which allows the main rotor head to rotate freely. Now, obviously, as far as training is concerned, nobody in their right mind would deliberately shut down the engines whilst in-flight.

However, the crew could still go through the motions and simulate an engine shutdown. Reducing the engine rpm allows the rotor head to freewheel and as the helicopter falls, the pilot pulls the collective lever which varies the angle of the main rotor blades and hopefully slows down the rate of descent.

This manoeuvre was carried out five times. Each time the helicopter was taken up to about 5000 feet, it was allowed to drop a couple of thousand feet before full control was re-established. I felt dreadful which was compounded by the next stage of very low-level *hedge hopping* flying. Whilst I wasn't physically ill unless I got off the helicopter, I knew I was going to throw up and without any sick bags on board, I'd have to clear up the mess.

I told the Loady that I felt ill and the pilot decided to fly to the top of Helvelin and drop me off for an hour whilst they flew to Ambleside. By the time I'd been *rescued*, I'd started to feel a lot better. The return trip was quite calm, that was until the pilot decided to *beat up* the Officers-married quarter patch.

The Loady was kneeling in the cargo doorway attached by a safety strop, when the aircraft, suddenly, banked and flew around in a very tight circle—that was enough for my stomach. Although I wasn't wearing a safety harness, I undid my seat belt, leant out of the door and threw up. The Loady didn't see me thankfully, and I got back into my seat.

I had to clear up a little vomit when we landed, much to the amusement of the seeing-in crew but I never did find out which officer's house had been painted with my breakfast which neatly leads me on to food!

The airman's mess supplied the raw ingredients for all breakfasts and provided cooked midday and evening meals. However, for the weekends, our shift decided to cook our own main meals. The ingredients, once again were provided by the mess and regardless if it was a Saturday or a Sunday, we always had a *Curry-a-la-Slim*.

One of the more tedious chores associated with the Saturday or Sunday shift was the requirement to hand wash the aircraft; which although dreary was an essential task because of the saltwater environment the aircraft had been flying in during the week.

Slim Hammel had served in the Far East and was a dab hand at cooking curries and we came to an agreement, whereby, if he cooked the curry the rest of the shift would wash the helicopter. Now, whilst curries are not to everyone's taste, as a way of accommodating the different palettes, Slim started off with very mild versions.

I don't remember there being many Indian restaurants whilst I was growing up and the hottest curry that I'd tasted up until then was from a packet. But, by the time I left the squadron, I was up to at least the Madras strength.

When we first moved into the house in July, there was no real need for the central heating, although we did have a *practice* at lighting the Parkray coal fire before I left for Culdrose. Whilst I was away and as the weather conditions cooled, Trisha turned more and more to using the fire. But, despite banking it down each evening, she wasn't able to keep it going and no matter how she tried the fire continually drew in the air.

Because we couldn't regulate the fire, the rooms became too hot, wasted a lot of coal and on many occasions, the water in the tank would boil resulting in the pipes in the attic banging and vast amounts of steam being expelled through the overflow pipe.

I contacted the family's office and they sent around a local plumber to recondition the Parkray door seal. The plumber was a pleasant chap who was really excited at the prospect of becoming a father for the first time very soon. His workmate labourer though was a bit on the dim side and came across as not having full control of all of his faculties.

A few weeks after the repair was complete, we heard on a local news bulletin that Alnwick police were investigating the murder of a local woman and her newborn baby and that a suspect had been arrested—the woman was the plumber's wife and the suspect was the plumber's labourer! We couldn't really grasp the fact that he'd been in our house only a few weeks earlier.

There were some real characters on the squadron whose antics are still fresh in my mind. Al Waters, our Geordie electrician spent many a happy hour in the Fishing Boat Inn (FBI); a quaint little pub right on the beach in Boulmer village. Al was sitting at the bar one particular Sunday afternoon, and was once again late home when his wife Sandra walked in and plonked his Sunday lunch onto the bar, she said nothing and walked out again.

Al, in his typical laidback fashion, shouted to her, "Where's ma knife and fork?"

Not surprisingly, he got no response, the pub though was in absolute hysterics. The landlord lent him some cutlery negating the need for Al to go home and he sat at the bar and casually ate the meal. Another individual who never ceased to raise a laugh was Roger Dingle.

It was Roger who introduced Trisha to the killing and dressing of crabs and never a day would go by without Rog being given recently caught crabs from the local fisherman. His lovely wife Jill was a vegetarian and she hated Rog taking crabs home and boiling them up in front of her. So, Trisha agreed that he could cook them at our home.

One of the main advantages of working within a fairly tight-knit community such as ours was the fact that if any squadron member needed assistance of any kind, there would invariably be plenty of offers of help. *Titch* Harris was within a couple of weeks of being posted and had more or less prepared his married quarter for march-out when one of his children, whilst playing with a box of matches, set fire to some blankets in the bedroom.

Titch managed to extinguish the fire and was incredibly lucky the fire didn't spread beyond the bedroom. Unfortunately, the smoke damage was unbelievable and affected all of the rooms on that floor. I don't believe the house was insured and being so close to moving, he didn't have time to employ a professional painter and decorator and didn't have time to redecorate himself.

He was at his wit's end, knowing full well that the RAF would charge him a small fortune to make good the damage. I don't remember if Titch asked or whether someone offered, but over the next few days, those of us who weren't on shift took turns and completely redecorated the entire upper floor in time for the march-out in record time.

I don't know what it cost him, but even with the materials and the copious amount of beer he bought, it had to be infinitely cheaper than paying for someone else to do the work.

On 12 March 1979, I received notification that I was to be promoted to Sergeant and because Roger was the squadron's established radar and comms SNCO, it meant that I was surplus to requirements. Having spent 11 months of the previous year training only to be told I'd soon be on the move was a bit frustrating. However, promotion was infinitely more important.

Apart from the added engineering and managerial responsibilities associated with promotion, I was soon to be introduced to the finer points of being a Senior Non-Commissioned Officer. Formal dining-in nights, I was informed, were an absolute must to attend, and one such night was scheduled only a week or so after my promotion.

As I was the newest and most junior member of the mess, I was required to carry out the duties of Mr Vice. Seating arrangements were such that the top table was reserved for the head guest, the Chairman of the Mess Committee (CMC) and various other senior members. The various legs that came off the top table were occupied by the remaining mess members with the most senior towards the top end; gradually moving down to the most junior at the bottom end.

My duties as Mr Vice was to call everyone in the bar to the table by yelling, "Ladies and gentlemen, the dinner is served."

I was to be the last one in and once everyone was standing behind their chairs, the Chairman would call, "Mr Vice, Grace."

Protocol dictated that whilst everyone was served at about the same time, nobody could start to eat until the head guest had picked up his knife and fork. At the end of the three courses and before coffee was served, most members were desperate for the toilets and if the CMC was in a benevolent mood he may give permission for an admin break—woe betide anyone who left before.

I've heard of cases of CMCs in some messes refusing to allow the break and members either peeing in empty wine bottles or simply leaving and later suffering the consequences. Once the coffee, liquors and speeches were out of the way, I as Mr Vice, would be called to the top table which allowed the privileged guests and senior members to retire to the bar.

It was then my job to keep the rabble entertained by telling jokes or stories until such time as the guests had been served and the bar was open to everyone else. The whole ordeal was quite nerve-wracking, but the main advantage was that my meal was paid for and I got free drinks all night long.

The Sergeant's Mess was well attended by its members. Trisha, Michael and I would regularly have Sunday lunch there. In fact, there was one time when Helen, Morley and Mabel Fish were visiting and we took them for a meal. Once we'd finished lunch, we retired to the bar, and Mabel, who was always the life and soul, started flirting with the Station Warrant Officer (SWO) and ended up sitting on his knee at the bar.

From then on, whenever I saw him, he would always ask after "Mabel with the blue hair."

According to one of our neighbours, being promoted had several benefits, some less obvious than others. She, very jealously, commented that with the extra money, we could afford to buy *Andrex toilet tissue*—how bitchy! I never really understood the connection, and anyway, how did she know we didn't already use that brand?

As mentioned earlier, being promoted meant taking on more of a managerial role, and in the past, most newly promoted SNCOs were left to their own devices; learning as they went along, which, in most cases (so I was later to be told), created managers who couldn't manage and supervisors who couldn't make a decision to save their lives.

As a means of achieving some sort of continuity, before I got into any bad habits, I was sent on a two-week SNCO Management Training Course at RAF

Newton in Lincolnshire which was to run from 26 July (our 4th wedding anniversary) until 8 August 1979. The course was interesting and taught me an awful lot about myself, but the main thing we were taught was: organisation and prioritisation skills.

There were only two memorable elements of the course: the first was when we were given an A4 sheet of paper that contained a copious list of requirements. The first requirement read:

Do nothing until you've read everything.

The second bullet point read:

Write your name in the top corner of this sheet; which I did.

The remaining bullet points varied from telling the reader to count aloud from 1 to 10, to reciting every second letter of the alphabet, midway through the list the reader was to loudly call out, "I have carefully followed directions."

The list seemed endless until we got to the very last bullet point which read:

Now go back to the beginning and carry out only bullet point two.

You would not believe the number of people who carried out every single bullet point before realising the catch. I, for my part, realised something was wrong and said nothing.

The second was the parachute packing exercise which everyone had to carry out on their own. The scenario was such that I was in charge of the aircraft parachute packing section and had several packers as well as, some drivers for the parachute recovery vehicles. The imaginary RAF station had a squadron of aircraft that used brake parachutes to help slow down the aircraft upon landing.

Each aircraft had one parachute, and once deployed, had to be retrieved, repacked and delivered back to the squadron in time for the next sortie. The exercise ran for about an hour, and as time went by, several spanners were thrown into the works such as personnel going off sick, power cuts, recovery vehicles breaking down, additional parachutes required and so on, until the whole scenario became a total and absolute nightmare.

We were then questioned as to why we took a particular decision; nobody failed as such, but it was excellent learning material. Shortly after starting the course, we noticed that after dinner each evening several SNCOs and Corporals would head off back to their classrooms for what we assumed was additional tuition—it transpired that they were training to become RAF Trade Instructors…more about that later!

Shortly before Christmas 1979, Trisha started to suffer from morning sickness. It wasn't too long before it was confirmed that she was expecting and once again, true to form, she was sick for the majority of the pregnancy. The doctor at her anti-natal clinic suggested that because she'd suffered with sickness when she was carrying Michael there was a very strong possibility that the next baby would be the same sex.

It took us almost a year of saving before we were in a position to contemplate buying a car. Dave Clement, my cousin, who worked for a second-hand car dealership in Southampton, heard from Mum that we were in the market for a reliable motor. He suggested going to Southampton and seeing what he had to offer. So, in early 1980, we travelled to Durrington on the train and whilst Trisha and Michael stayed with Mum, I met with David who showed me a Yellow Renault 12TL.

It was a nice little runner, looked fine and it didn't take me long to decide to buy it. Michael was also very pleased with it because he immediately referred to it as our *Lellow Wenow;* a name that stuck for quite a while. Once we returned to Northumberland and despite Trisha not feeling well, we spent a great deal of time exploring the countryside, the Cheviots, visiting the numerous castles and other tourist attractions as well as the fantastic beaches which stretched from Seahouses to Bamburgh.

A Disaster in the North Sea

On the evening of 27 March 1980, amidst torrential rain, thick mist, and towering waves reaching up to 12 metres, the Norwegian semi-submersible drilling rig, Alexander Kielland, was being towed away from the Edda production platform in the Ekofisk area of the North Sea. The rig was carrying over 200 off-duty personnel at the time.

The rig was initially built as a mobile, floating, drilling rig and delivered to the Stavanger drilling site in July 1976. However, it was never used for drilling purposes; instead, it served as a f*lotel* which provided living quarters for offshore workers. By 1978, additional accommodation blocks had been added to the platform, so that, up to 386 personnel could be accommodated.

A few minutes before 18:30 those on board felt a *sharp crack* followed by some *kind of trembling*. Suddenly, the rig heeled over 30° and then stabilised. Five of the six anchor cables had broken with only the remaining cable preventing the rig from capsizing. Unfortunately, 20 minutes later, that cable also snapped and the rig turned upside down. The rig had seven 50-man lifeboats and twenty 20-man rafts.

Four lifeboats were launched, but only one managed to release from the lowering cables (a safety device didn't allow release until the strain was removed from the cables). A fifth lifeboat came adrift and surfaced upside down; its occupants righting it and gathered 19 men from the water. Two of Kielland's rafts were detached, three men were rescued from them.

Then, two 12-man rafts were thrown from Edda and rescued 13 survivors, another seven men were taken from the sea by supply boats and seven swam to Edda. There were 130 men in the mess hall and cinema and of the 212 personnel on board 123 were killed making it the worst disaster in Norwegian offshore history since WW2.

Crews from RAF Lossiemouth and RAF Boulmer launched their four Sea Kings and flew to the stricken rig returning to their respective bases for fuel before continuing the rescue attempt. I don't remember how many people were rescued by the RAF but it was a true testament to the dedication, determination and professionalism of the crews.

It was shortly after the disaster that I had to opportunity to fly to a gas-pumping platform, a hundred miles or so out into the North Sea and whilst the rig I visited was relatively small compared to some of the main oil platforms, its size was still awe-inspiring. It was hard to contemplate what must have been going through the minds of those poor souls who were trapped inside the Alexander Kielland.

There were many occasions that the Boulmer crew was called upon to successfully rescue sailors or fishermen who were injured at sea, as well as the countless people who found themselves in trouble whilst climbing the mountains. Unfortunately, there were also times when only bodies were recovered. We had two helicopters at our disposal and one always had to be ready to scramble at a moment's notice.

There was one instance when the standby helicopter was in the hangar undergoing primary servicing (a scheduled maintenance procedure) and the principal helicopter had to be taken offline because of a rotor break fault. The aircrew advised the RCC that the aircraft wouldn't be immediately available until the fault was fixed.

Regrettably, not far down the coast near Newcastle, an emergency was unfolding. The RCC contacted our ops informing them that a few people had been fishing off some sort of structure and had been cut off by the incoming tide and wanted to know how long before the aircraft was ready to go (I believe the lifeboat couldn't get in close enough to carry out the rescue because of the severe sea state).

The Riggers had the complete rotor brake system in bits and worked like Trojans to repair, reassemble and test the system before handing over the helicopter to the waiting crew. The fishermen were rescued with little time remaining before they would have possibly been swept away.

One of the annual events on any RAF station is the formal inspection by the Air Officer Commanding (AOC), and Boulmer wasn't exempt from the bullshit and rehearsals that went on prior to the visit. Al Waters and I were detailed to be the seeing-in crew on the day and we were dressed appropriately in white Denhams. Other squadron personnel formed a guard of honour, armed with their Self-Loading Rifles (SLRs) with fixed bayonets.

Al and I marshalled the helicopter in, and once the rotors and engines had stopped, we stood to attention close by as the crew door was lowered.

We waited and waited and waited, and amongst the deathly hush, Al leant towards me and said, "The buggers changed his mind."

Unfortunately, Al had forgotten that he was wearing ear defenders and had shouted the comment, which the entire parade also heard. I don't think the AOC heard or if he did, he never let on. It was mentioned later on that those on the guard of honour could barely contain themselves.

Despite having been promoted almost a year previously, I was eventually notified in April 1980 that we were to be posted to RAF Laarbruch in West Germany but beforehand I'd have to do some pre-employment training. RAF Wittering was not only home to the Harrier Force but also the RAF Arms Support Unit. There, I was to undertake basic training in nuclear physics and learn how to calibrate and repair ionising radiation monitoring instruments using live radioactive sources.

The course began on the 23 July 1980 and would run for two weeks, which meant I'd be away for our 5th wedding anniversary. I arrived at about 21:00 one evening in the midst of total darkness and having never been to the station before, I hadn't the faintest idea of my way around. I booked in at the guard room and was told that a major exercise was underway; I was also given a map and directed to the Sergeant's Mess.

It's one thing driving around in unfamiliar territory but it's something completely different doing so under total blackout conditions. I couldn't pick out any landmarks and even when I found the mess I couldn't orientate myself and find the entrance. I parked up and hadn't walked more than a few yards when I was challenged to stand still, put my baggage down and put my hands up.

One of the guards approached me and once I'd shown him my I.D. and explained what I was doing he directed me to the mess entrance where I *warned-in* and picked up my room key along with directions. My room wasn't in the main mess building but in an annexe some distance away.

For the next two hours, I walked around and around and without any signs or notices, I was unable to find my elusive accommodation. It must have been about midnight and there was still no sign of anybody to ask for directions, I gave up, found an empty room and went to bed. When I awoke the next morning, I was able to see where I should have been and realised that I'd been sleeping in the Officers' Mess annexe.

I quickly packed up my kit and moved into my proper room. There was limited parking for private vehicles on the Arms Support Unit and my joining instructions advised that I catch a bus each morning. I got dressed into my working uniform, unfortunately, I couldn't find my beret which I must have dropped the night before whilst I was wandering about in the darkness.

It's a strict no-no to walk around on the station without headgear, and fortunately, I managed to get onto the bus, having explained my predicament and apologised to a Squadron Leader for being incorrectly dressed, I arrived at the ASU.

The course was educational and as it was too far to travel home for the mid-course weekend, I stayed at Wittering. The fortnight went pretty quickly and once back at Boulmer, the top priority was to apply for a married quarter at Laarbruch.

The allocation of married quarters for personnel posted to units in the British Forces Germany (BFG) was on a points-based scheme with the process beginning on receipt of a posting notice. It was the individual's responsibility to contact his new unit's family's office and establish if accommodation would be available on the relative arrival date. It was an absolute cardinal sin to arrive in Germany with your family unless a *call forward* notice had been issued.

If accommodation was available, then husbands and families could travel together and move in prior to commencing work. However, if no accommodation was available, the individual's name was placed on one of two waiting lists: the Unfrozen and the Frozen lists—only on the *actual day of arrival* at the new station. Points were allocated depending on rank, time served, the number of children, etc.

The number of points would determine where on the unfrozen list a name was added; the rationale being that the name would move up the list as personnel moved from the top of the unfrozen list to the bottom of the frozen list. One of the disadvantages of having very few points was that anyone joining the list with more points simply jumped ahead.

Unfortunately, for a young airman with a family that could be a real problem on stations where there was a large turnover of personnel. However, once a person reached the top of that list and transferred to the bottom of the frozen list, their place was assured and nobody could jump ahead.

I contacted the family's office at Laarbruch only to find that there was no accommodation available immediately. We decided that Trisha, Michael and the new baby would stay with Helen and Morley in Southport until we were allocated a quarter.

Apart from the sickness, Trisha's pregnancy seemed to be going well, that was until one evening mid-term when she began to bleed. The doctor was called, who advised bed rest for a while. I can't remember how long she actually rested but the bleeding eventually stopped and as time progressed it became obvious that once again the baby was going to be late. However, this time, there would be no inducement.

We were watching TV on the evening of 5 August 1980, by which time Trisha was about 10 days late when her waters broke. Trisha had arranged with June Roberts, the wife of Merv who was a rigger on my shift that she'd look after Michael whilst I was at the hospital. I called June, who came immediately and she agreed that she'd stop until things were sorted out.

I got the chance to do the emergency drive to Hillcrest Maternity Unit in Alnwick Hospital and once Trisha was booked in and made comfortable, I was advised to go home because nothing was going to happen for quite a while. Trisha agreed on the condition that the hospital would call me instantly as things started to happen and I went home to bed. I hadn't been in bed very long when June, who'd been sleeping on the settee, woke me telling me to get to the hospital as soon as possible.

My second fast drive that night and I only just got to the labour ward in time to see our second bundle of joy arrive into the world. By the time Trisha and Steven were cleaned up and checked over, it was early morning and I left the two of them to rest. I thanked June for watching over Michael.

As she left, I couldn't help thinking what some of our nosy neighbours would be thinking when they saw a tall, gorgeous, well-endowed, blonde lady leaving early in the day. I'd love to have been a fly on one or two of their walls. I took Michael to the hospital later that morning, to meet his new brother, and later on, we both went to register his birth.

Steven was born one month before our posting to Germany, which obviously, put quite a bit of pressure on Trisha; not only as a mother to a newborn baby but we also had to prepare the house for handover. Trisha had fed Michael with a bottle and he thrived but she fancied breastfeeding Steven. He fed very well whilst in hospital. However, things didn't go quite so well when they arrived home.

Trisha was advised to feed Steven on demand, and if he was still hungry, she could supplement the feed by giving him some cooled boiled water. Unfortunately, the midwife on her regular visits became very concerned when she realised that Steven was losing weight at an alarming rate. After various consultations with the specialists, it was decided that Steven wasn't ill and that breastfeeding wasn't the best way to feed him. Trisha immediately started to bottle feed and the two of them never looked back.

Whilst we didn't have too much in the way of furniture or personal household possessions, we nevertheless had to make arrangements to store those items that we didn't require in Germany. Rather than just selecting a removal company, I was required to get three quotes and choose the cheapest; that way the RAF could at least be assured that they were getting value for money!

I duly phoned around beginning with Pickfords, a company I at least had heard of. I was asked if I'd managed to get any of the other quotes and when I told them that they were the first, they very obligingly offered to get the remaining quotes for me—have a guess which company turned out to be the cheapest. Apparently, that scam was widely used by most if not all of the removal companies. Anyway, we decided on having our bits and pieces containerised and stored in a central depositary, which hopefully would keep them reasonably safe.

The day of the march-out arrived and whilst the house was clean, we were a little behind schedule, so much so, that Trisha was rushing through the side door and loading up the car as the Barrack Warden and the Family's Officer were walking through the front door. She finished just in time and was waiting outside with Michael, at which point the barrack warden came outside and asked her if she'd forgotten anything. She'd only left Steven asleep on the dining room table in his papoose! The handover went without a hitch, and before long, we were on our way to Southport.

My 22 months as a member of a search and rescue squadron was one of the most memorable on record, and was without doubt, the only job I've ever carried out where I achieved a real sense of satisfaction.

Chapter Thirteen
Royal Air Force Station Laarbruch

(9 September 1980 to 4 November 1983)

I spent three or four days at Southport before leaving for Dover to catch the Townsend Thoresen ferry to Zeebrugge—the ill-fated *The Herald of Free Enterprise* that was to later capsize. I'd not travelled on a cross-channel ferry or indeed driven on the continent before and was somewhat apprehensive at what lay ahead.

Prior to leaving Boulmer, I'd agreed to pick up a lad, who worked on the Boulmer Radar site, from Wolverhampton railway station. He was posted to ATC at Laarbruch. By the time we arrived at Dover, a howling gale was blowing and even though the ferry was moored in the harbour it was pitching quite violently. Instead of driving on in a sedate manner as I'd expected, we had to wait to be individually called forward, at the precise moment, that the boarding deck appeared to be level and stable—not a pleasant experience.

The four-and-a-half-hour crossing was reasonable and we arrived at Zeebrugge docks at about 7:00 in the morning. The drive around Antwerp was memorable more so because of the volume of traffic on the six-lane autobahn. Once through that, the remainder of the drive through Belgium, Holland and across the German border went well and we eventually arrived at Laarbruch at midday.

The arrivals procedure was no different to that carried out on any other unit with the exception that the top priority was to get myself on the waiting list for a quarter. Every minute wasted could potentially add weeks before being allocated accommodation. Unfortunately, at that time, both lists were in operation and my details were added to the unfrozen list. At which point, I *warned-in* (a system of signing in) at the Sergeant Mess, was allocated a single room, unpacked and collapsed, absolutely knackered.

Apart from ensuring that my name was on the married quarter's allocation list as soon as I arrived, the next urgent task was to pass the *tick-test*. On arrival in Germany, drivers of British Forces Germany (BFG) registered or military vehicles had to sit and pass the tick-test.

It is designed to help military personnel, civilian staff and family members understand the differences in signage, rules and regulations when driving in Germany and to a lesser degree driving in Belgium, Holland and France. New arrivals were given a grace period, I believe, of one month to pass the test. Failure to do so meant that driving any vehicle in Germany was strictly *Verboten*. Needless to say, I passed!

RAF Laarbruch operated Buccaneer Strike aircraft which possessed a nuclear capability. The station was also home to the number II (AC) Jaguar Photo Reconnaissance Squadron whilst RAF Brüggen, situated some 30 miles to the south, operated Jaguar aircraft in the Strike/Attack role also with a nuclear capability.

The other station in the area, collectively known as the *Clutch* stations, was RAF Wildenrath which operated Phantom FGR2 air defence fighter aircraft as well as the Pembroke VIP passenger aircraft of 60 Squadron. The only other RAF Station in West Germany was RAF Gütersloh, located close to the East German border and operated the AV8 Harrier V/STOL aircraft.

RAF Gatow was the final station in Europe and was located in West Berlin. All five stations were administered by HQ RAF Germany based at RAF Rheindahlen, located close to Mönchengladbach.

I was to be employed on a small specialist team comprising two Sergeants and one Corporal. We were responsible for the repair and periodic calibration of the various radiation monitoring equipment held on all RAF stations and support units located throughout Europe. The equipment would be required in the event of a nuclear war with the USSR.

The section was named the Command Radiation Instrument Servicing Team affectionately known as *CRIST*. The team tended to liaise with the RAF Regiment who carried out the formal Ground Defence Training (GDT) on the main RAF stations and with the Test and Measurement Equipment Coordinators (TMEC) on the various support units. The majority of the work was focused on the main RAF units and Rheindahlen which were visited monthly.

CRIST also visited, on a six-monthly basis any support unit where RAF personnel were employed which included the Supreme Headquarters Allied

Powers Europe (SHAPE) located at Casteau, north of the Belgian city of Mons, the Allied Forces Central Europe (AFCENT) based in Brunssum, Netherlands, the RAFNSU Tongeren near Maastricht, the USAF base at Ramstein near Kaiserslautern in southern Germany and of course RAF Gatow in West Berlin.

The RAF Hospital Wegberg also held various specialist monitoring equipment that would be used in the event of a nuclear accident or an aircraft crash in which nuclear weapons were involved.

Our workshop and offices were located in the corner of a small hangar that was also occupied by members of *L* Troop, 21 Signal Regiment, a band of Pongos who were responsible for Laarbruch's entire telephone network. We shared the *T* bar facility which was run by the regiment administrator *Frau Büsser* a formidable German lady who took no prisoners if messed about by anyone.

We also joined in at their beer calls, barbeques and on one occasion Michael and Steven went to a children's Christmas party. I was eventually made an honouree member of the regiment.

The servicing workshop had metal shutters fitted to all windows and the two access doors were made from thick sheet metal. The rationale was that whilst we were calibrating the instruments, the ionising radiation (alpha particles, beta particles and gamma rays) would have little or no effect on personnel in the surrounding buildings.

For our part, we observed strict handling procedures when using the sources which meant no eating or drinking whilst calibration was taking place, exposure to the sources was to be kept to an absolute minimum and radiation badges and finger stools were worn throughout. We had several live sources at our disposal all designed to cover a specific application.

Our primary radioactive isotope was Strontium-90, used to calibrate the main handheld radiation monitors, the MSR2, of which there were at least 100 items held throughout Europe. The isotope was housed inside a lead ball, about half the size of a football and was capable of being split in half thereby exposing the radioactive material.

We would carry out the calibration of the various MSR2s at the respective units and we would always take the lead ball with us. However, despite the fact that it was housed inside a lead-lined ammunition box it always presented us with security issues. That practice ceased when we adopted a *direct exchange* procedure whereby all monitors were calibrated at Laarbruch and swapped at the relevant units.

Whilst it was hoped that we would never have to use any of the equipment in anger there was one vital piece of test equipment that was used on a regular basis and calibrated by CRIST. Personnel working within the various nuclear weapons storage sites (also referred to as Supplementary Storage Sites (SSA)) at Laarbruch, Brüggen and Güttersloh carried out regular servicings on the various nuclear weapons.

Whenever work was being carried out, s*niffer* test equipment would be used to constantly monitor the ambient air and should a leak be detected klaxons would sound.

The RAF Regiment personnel also used b*eta buttons* to train NBC Shelter Marshalls in the finer art of assessing the level of decontamination required in the event of an individual's exposure to nuclear fallout. The buttons were made of metal (probably tin), which gave off a small amount of radiation but was susceptible to rust.

They were positioned around a volunteer's person often inside clothing and by using the appropriate monitor the potential shelter marshall had to isolate those areas that gave a response. That practice eventually ceased due to issues associated with health and safety protocols.

During my three years on the team, we had to replace some of the sources because their effectiveness had diminished due to the *half-life* phenomenon. Radioactive decay is the process by which the atomic nucleus of an *unstable* atom loses energy by emitting ionising particles (radiation).

The emission is spontaneous in that the atom decays without any physical interaction with another particle from outside the atom and as it decays it gradually changes to a *stable* atom. To change from an unstable atom to a completely stable atom may require several disintegration steps and radiation will be given off at each step.

As more and more unstable atoms become stable atoms, less radiation is produced and eventually the material will become non-radioactive. This decay occurs at a fixed rate and therefore the half-life of a radioisotope is the time required for one-half of the amount of unstable material to degrade into a more stable material.

The half-life of Strontium 90 is 28.8 years, that is to say that every 28.8 years the effectiveness of the source reduces by a half. Cobolt-60, another of our sources, has a half-life of 5 years. There are, however, some radioactive sources with half-lives that are measured in thousands of years.

It was only a week or so after I arrived, I was sitting in the mess ante room reading a newspaper when I came across a photograph of a car being winched out of the river Medway in Kent. I was absolutely horrified to see that the driver had been named as Sergeant Peter (Jamie) Millgate who had died at the scene of the accident.

As I mentioned earlier, Jamie and I trained together while in the RAF Cosford voluntary band, where we both dated WRAF telephonists stationed there. After being posted to Lyneham, we remained close friends for many years. In fact, I had only spoken to him a day or so before departing for Laarbruch.

The newspaper article reported that Jamie was driving his car adjacent to the river with his girlfriend, a divorcee with two children, when a speeding car came towards him forcing him off the road. Jamie's car careered off the road and dragged a young boy who had been fishing on the bank into the river—he tragically drowned. Jamie managed to get his partner and her children out but he became trapped and also drowned. I was absolutely devastated.

I was kept fairly busy for the next few weeks at work, and thankfully, my name moved up the unfrozen list fairly rapidly before my details were transferred to the frozen list. Almost immediately, I was told that I'd been allocated a four-bedroom flat in Weeze early in November.

Due to the close proximity of the clutch air stations to the Warsaw Pact forces in the east, I was to learn almost immediately, that exercises in Germany were taken very, very seriously. The Warsaw Treaty Organisation of Friendship, Cooperation and Mutual Assistance was formed in Warsaw in 1955.

It was the Soviet Union's military response to the integration of West Germany into NATO, the North Atlantic Treaty Organisation. The pact comprised the eight communist states of Eastern Europe namely Albania, Bulgaria, Czechoslovakia, East Germany, Hungary, Poland, Romania and Russia.

I was briefed that at Laarbruch, once every month for 11 months of the year (the only break was in August which gave personnel the opportunity to go on holiday) a generation exercise would be called. Nobody except the station executive officers knew when the exercise would begin and the first that we mere mortals knew was when the station hooter was sounded. At that point, everyone was to report to their place of work, don their Nuclear, Biological and Chemical (NBC) suits, webbing, and tin hat and collect their personnel weapon.

We were also required to carry our respirator and the haversack was to contain only the necessary NBC decontamination equipment and nothing else. The exercise aimed to showcase the flying squadrons and the nuclear bomb dump's ability to prepare and ready a sufficient number of operational aircraft and nuclear weapons within a designated timeframe.

This demonstration was crucial to assure HQ RAF Germany that these assets would be on standby in the event of escalating hostilities with the USSR.

One such generation was called during the daytime in early October which was the first real taste of working under strict exercise conditions, for my part, because I didn't work on a flying squadron, I and several other members of the various Avionics bays would be employed as guards at the *Piccadilly* roundabout which was the main entry point from the domestic site into the technical sites.

The exercise, in this case, lasted for about 18 hours. However, that was generally dependent on the overall serviceability of the aircraft at the commencement and under genuine hostile conditions, the unit would continue to make preparations for the outbreak of war. We were briefed that the next phase would be a three-day Mini Evaluation (Mineval) exercise which would commence towards the end of October.

I was later to learn that the exercise season comprised 11 Generations, nine three-day Minevals, one Maximum Evaluation (Maxeval) and the final exercise of the season would be a full-blown Tactical Evaluation (Taceval).

The Minevals were umpired by our own Directing Staff (Distaff) whilst the Maxevals were assessed by Distaff from other units within RAF Germany. However, the Taceval was assessed by umpires from other NATO countries and the results gained were a good indication of the effectiveness of the unit in fighting a protracted war with the Warsaw Pact countries—woe betide any unit that didn't come up to scratch!

In order to prepare me for and understand the intricacies associated with a station exercise, I was given the low down on what was likely to happen and what I was expected to do. Prior to the commencement of the exercise, the RAF Regiment would plant various dummy Improvised Explosive Devices (IEDs) throughout the unit. Then they assess how long it took for them to be discovered, whether or not the Wing Operations Centre (WOC) had responded appropriately and if the Explosive Ordinance Disposal (EOD) teams could make the devices safe without causing collateral damage or blowing themselves up.

The exercises traditionally began early in the morning of day one, when intruders would attempt to enter the unit and cause as much disruption and chaos as possible, not only to the flying squadrons but to the whole infrastructure of the unit concentrating on the firefighting, medical, bomb disposal and guarding capabilities.

The serious intruders would almost always be members of an elite army unit such as the Special Air Service (SAS) or any one of the Parachute Regiments, who I was later to learn, didn't do things by halves and played for real. Some intruders were made up of volunteers from other units who would try to gain access by various means including hiding in or hijacking vehicles and their occupants or by using false identification cards.

Throughout the Mineval, the station would be repeatedly overflown by *enemy* aircraft, after which a thorough search of the entire station was required and almost always culminated in an Unexploded Bomb (UXB) being reported somewhere or other on the unit. As an aid to personnel operating in the open or travelling between sites, NBC state warning symbols would be displayed throughout the unit so that everyone immediately knew what level of personal protection was required.

A white round symbol signified *All Clear*, a red triangle showed that an air raid was imminent or in progress and a black square denoted that a nuclear, biological or chemical contamination was present. This process would continue for the full three days with meals being provided throughout the day and night in *Hot Lox* tins; breakfast was always an *egg banjo* (a bacon and egg sandwich).

People knew that the exercise was in the final throes by one of two means. Firstly, if a doughnut was served as a dessert for whatever meal, everyone immediately knew that that was the last exercise meal. Secondly, the aircraft would carry out a *Survive to Operate* scramble, whereby they would fly to another unit, which simulated that a nuclear attack on the unit was inevitable.

For those personnel who were left, the NBC alert state would be declared *Black* and movement around the unit was kept to an absolute minimum. Anyone who was required to work outside had to go through a simulated NBC contamination drill before being allowed into the *clean* area. I must admit that the whole scenario sounded intriguing.

Prior to the commencement of my first Mineval, I decided to take leave and I booked the Zeebrugge ferry for the morning after the exercise had ended. I also booked the ferry for the return journey, informed the family's office that I was returning to the UK to pick up Trisha and the boys, and gave them my contact details.

The Mineval began exactly as predicted and followed the precise format. I drew my personal weapon, a Sterling Sub-Machine Gun and joined another guard at the Piccadilly roundabout; one of us would be positioned at the roadblock whilst the other giving covering weapons fire from inside the *sangar* (a small, defensive brick building with a slit hole).

One of the requirements of all passengers in cars, regardless of the air raid or NBC state, was that they were to wear their respirators—the drivers were exempt due to safety issues. However, in a real war situation, they would be required to wear them. I can't remember the number of occasions where I'd have to refuse entry onto the engineering site because vehicle passengers wouldn't dress correctly and there was almost always verbal abuse, especially at shift changeover times.

I know that if they put their respirators on and once through the barrier, they would be taken off—I didn't really care. Each sangar was equipped with a field telephone that was connected directly to the Sector Guard Commander and we were to report each and every event so that the relevant response could be taken. Day one passed without real incident.

However, at midday on the second day, an Air Raid Red was called. We immediately stopped all traffic, lowered the white all-clear sign, raised the air attack red warning sign and took shelter in the sangar. Almost immediately, there was a deafening explosion alongside our shelter and two members of the RAF Regiment stuck their heads inside and told us that we weren't to contact the Guard Commander because we'd been *killed* in the air attack.

The explosion was caused by a thunder flash that had been thrown at the shelter wall (thunder flashes are very large *bangers* used to simulate explosions). The field telephone began to ring and continued ringing which we totally ignored. One of the means of assessing how well the unit can cope with the death of or injury to personnel until reinforcements arrived was to deny the individuals resurrection.

In my case, I was told that I was not to take any further part in the exercise and as proof I was given a *dead chit* which was valid until exercise ENDEX was declared. I still had another two days before I was due to start my leave and once my *body* had been taken away and replaced with fresh guards, I spoke with the Guard Commander, showed him the chit and he just told me to clear off—fantastic.

I returned to the mess, packed my bag and decided to drive to Zeebrugge and get on the next available ferry to Dover. However, before that, I had to get through the station's main gate which was manned by the RAF plods. They were on duty not only to maintain normal peacetime entry checks but were also on the watch for exercise deserters. I showed them my escape chit which fortunately convinced them that I was genuine and they let me go.

I'd only been away for seven weeks or so, and couldn't believe how much Steven had grown. I don't know what Trisha had been feeding him but he was huge! I'd arranged my leave so that we only had a few days in the UK and would pick up Mum. She was going to stay with us, before driving back to Weeze. That was to go horribly wrong and caused me more than a few stressful moments.

Two days before we were due to leave Southport, I received a phone call from the family's clerk telling me that our four-bedroom quarter at Weeze was no longer available, however, we could move into an alternative flat in a few weeks, again in Weeze.

I asked what had happened to our allocated flat, and was told that it had been swapped with someone else who couldn't take over his allocated flat because he was going to be in the UK playing for the RAF Germany Basketball team. I told the clerk that it was totally unacceptable, all arrangements had been made and that we would be arriving at Laarbruch in three days' time. She said she'd call back.

I was in the salon with Helen when the phone rang a couple of hours later, and was told that we'd been allocated a two-bedroom house on the station. For starters, I didn't want a two-bedroom house and I certainly didn't want to live on base. So, with a little bit of quick thinking and a lot of blagging, I told her that a two-bedroom wasn't acceptable because we already had two children and a third was on the way.

Helen, who was standing alongside me, almost died of shock knowing full well that Steven had only been born a couple of months earlier and I'd been away for the majority of that time in between! There was a long pregnant pause from the other end of the phone and once again I was told that I'd be contacted again. I did explain to Helen that I was bluffing—much to her delight.

The phone call the next morning was much more welcoming and gave us some fantastic news. We'd been allocated a three-bedroom house on Feld Strasse in Goch. There was, however, one small problem, the house wasn't available until mid-November—I accepted immediately. I then phoned Ian, who at the time, was a Flight Lieutenant Junior Engineering Officer (JENGO) on 14 Squadron and lived at RAF Brüggen.

When I told him the story and our predicament, he told me that Trisha, the boys and Mum could stop with Ange and him until our march-in date. I wasn't bothered about the baloney associated with not bringing the family to Germany until a *call forward* had been given because as far as I was concerned Trisha, Michael and Steven were on holiday.

The house on Feld Strasse was to be our fourth married quarter and as such we still hadn't built up much in the way of personal possessions in the form of furniture, etc., we were, therefore, still fairly reliant on barrack equipment. The march-in went well with no real problems, and much to our surprise, the barrack warden decided that the living room and dining room carpets had seen better days and were to be changed.

One of the many bizarre anachronisms that were still in force at the time was that airmen's married quarters were not entitled to have fully fitted carpets. Instead, there had to be a gap of approximately eight inches between the edge of the carpet and the skirting board. However, in our case, the new carpets would be fully fitted.

The house was second in a block of four, which had a large attic, and a substantial cellar and the gardens, whilst not particularly big, were separated by a three-foot-high chain-link fence. Once the takeover was complete, Trisha set to work and as usual, turned the house into a home.

Our neighbour on one side was Doug and Brenda McIntosh, who had two young sons, Stuart and Ian, whilst on the other side was Rod and Shelia Craycraft and their older son and daughter.

As members of the British Forces in Germany, we were entitled to several perks and privileges which included the purchase of duty-free cars from specialist retailers, a monthly duty-free petrol or diesel allowance and the purchase of goods from the German shops free from their *Merwesteuer;* which was the equivalent of our VAT.

Whisky and Gin were rationed for the junior ranks who were issued ration cards. However, SNCOs and Officers could buy as much as they liked from our respective messes. For a strange reason, UK-produced tea was also rationed and everyone regardless of rank had to buy it from the NAAFI (coffee, however, wasn't rationed).

We were also given extra untaxed pay in the form of a Local Overseas Allowance (LOA), which, in some cases, added considerably to a monthly wage packet. The autobahns in Germany were exceptional which made travelling a delight, although there were certain times of the year when it was advisable not to travel around cities such as Köln due to the volume of traffic as many holidaymakers headed south.

Use of the fuel coupons was restricted to BP outlets only. As an aid, a map was produced that detailed every single BP filling station throughout West Germany. If we were to travel across the border a 5-gallon Jerry can could be filled up.

There was also a rather unique system of paying for heating and lighting for the quarters, known as the BFG X/Y scheme. Each house or flat whether on base or off, had its own individual electricity meter. Whereas, domestic hot water and heating water were provided from a centralised boiler that covered several if not all houses or flats within a complex. Each householder had a set amount deducted from their pay.

At the end of the year, usually in September, the electricity meters were read, a bill was prepared and added to the communal costs associated with providing hot water and if more was paid in than was used, a refund was shared out. Unfortunately, the use of domestic electricity was the only element that we, as individuals, had any real control over.

The heating system was very efficient and on occasions, the rooms became too hot to comfortably stay in and the only option was to open a window. This was due to the fact that the radiators in all rooms were controlled by an on/off valve only and weren't fitted with thermostats.

There were two main married quarter estates located off base. The biggest one was a couple of miles from the station at Weeze and the other at Goch which was about 12 miles away. Doug informed me that he was a primary callout marshall and that I was one of his designated secondary marshalls. If a genuine alert or generation exercise was called, it was my job, having been woken by him, to go to all the houses that I was responsible for and wake up all the occupants instructing them to report to their place of duty.

Michael, Steven, Stuart and Ian got on well together and I decided to take down the separating chain-link fence and let the four of them share the gardens. All went well for a while although I had to ask Stuart on a couple of occasions not to run around in our garden whilst we were eating.

I might as well have been talking to the moon because one Sunday lunchtime, whilst we were at the dining room table, Stuart and Ian turned up at the window and started pulling faces and banging on the window before running off—the fence went up again that evening! Trisha and I got on well with Doug and Brenda. Unfortunately, their children were wild and totally out of control and, much to Trisha's annoyance, would treat our home and furniture in the same destructive way as they treated their own.

Needless to say, they were not invited in very often. Brenda never really bothered with housework and was more interested in coffee mornings and socialising. Whereas Doug, who was a ground photographer and worked in the Photo Reconnaissance Interpretation Centre (RIC), thought he knew everything about computers and would bore the pants off me with his latest programming exploits (computers in the early '80s really weren't up to much).

The couple were both heavily into Citizens Band radio and treasure hunts and would disappear for hours on end driving around the German countryside with other like-minded people! We were invited to join in on several occasions but fortunately always managed to be somewhere else.

Shortly after Trisha was admitted into Wegberg Hospital for a hysterectomy, Brenda asked if the boys and I would like to go round for Sunday lunch—nothing wrong with that you'd think and so I gladly accepted. We were welcomed at the door. I gave Doug a bottle of wine and Brenda took me into the kitchen to show me what we'd be eating.

She then proceeded to tell me what Stuart and Ian would and wouldn't eat and I wasn't too bothered if they didn't eat too much and that they'd be back later in the afternoon and left me to it! Not only was I stunned and speechless, but I let them get away with it and said nothing.

Michael and Steven, as usual, sat at the table and ate in a civilised manner. Stuart and Ian, however, were like animals in a zoo who wouldn't sit still; constantly got up and down from the table, ran around and were generally a bloody pain. The meal and the whole afternoon were some of the most traumatic I can remember. We visited Trisha the next day, and when I told her of our dining experience she was flabbergasted and told me that Brenda had asked several other neighbours if they would babysit but there were no volunteers.

That was probably the dirtiest and most underhand trick that was ever played on me and our relationship with the Macintoshes was somewhat strained after that.

Drinking and driving was a strict no-no in Germany and anyone caught over the limit could expect to be severely punished not only by the German Polizei but also by the service authorities. It was commonplace to hold an end-of-week beer call in the avionics *T* bar where the boss would pass on the latest news, welcome new arrivals, and say goodbye to the leavers.

The Polizei would almost always have a patrol car somewhere at the side of the road between Laarbruch and Weeze on a Friday evening, and they didn't need an excuse to pull a driver over. The RAF police had a unique method of finding out if anyone had been drinking and driving. Every driver was required to book out and book in at the guardroom after 22:00, and if the driver showed the slightest sign of staggering, slurred speech or whose handwriting was illegible, would be breathalysed.

Brian King, who had trained on the Sea Kings and worked with me at Boulmer, was posted to CRIST towards the end of my tour, and during that time, he was forever in trouble for one thing or another. If it wasn't for getting drunk and fighting with the soldiers of the 21 Signal Regiment, he would try and wind up the RAF police.

One particular night, before his wife had arrived, he'd been out for a few drinks and arrived at the main gate in a taxi, wanting to be taken back to the single accommodation. The taxi drivers were given unrestricted access to the whole of the unit.

When the plod on duty at the barrier asked Brian where he was going, instead of just telling him, he got stroppy and said, "You're a bit nosy for a F****** copper, aren't you?"

His journey ended there and he was up before the boss the next day. I was to learn shortly after I'd returned to the UK that Brian, who was a very complicated character, had committed suicide in the woods behind the camp by gassing himself in his car. I believe he was buried at Rheindahlen Military Cemetery.

Ground Defence Training

All personnel were required to carry out annual Ground Defence Training (GDT), and as mentioned earlier, the training and exercises had to be taken seriously in order to prepare for actual conflict. There were several fundamentals to GDT and covered such subjects as guarding, firefighting, first aid, nuclear, biological and chemical (NBC) protection, and personal weapons care including strip down, cleaning and firing.

One of the more unpleasant elements of GDT was carried out inside the *gas chamber*. The idea was to give confidence to the wearer that the respirator and protective NBC clothing did afford protection against all forms of chemical contamination and nuclear fallout. Once the group were kitted out in their NBC suits and Buddy checked, we would file into the chamber and once settled the RAF Regiment Instructor would light one or two CS tablets.

CS gas (chlorobenzalmalononitrile) was developed and tested secretly at Porton Down in Wiltshire in the 1950s and 1960s. CS was tested firstly on animals, then subsequently, on British servicemen volunteers. The chemical reacts with moisture on the skin and in the eyes, causing a burning sensation and the immediate forceful and uncontrollable shutting of the eyes.

Effects usually include tears streaming from the eyes, profuse coughing, exceptional nasal discharge that is full of mucus, burning in the eyes, eyelids, nose and throat areas, disorientation, dizziness and restricted breathing. It will also burn the skin where it is sweaty and or sunburned. In highly concentrated doses, it can also induce severe coughing and vomiting.

Almost all of the immediate effects wear off within an hour (such as exceptional nasal discharge and profuse coughing), although the feeling of burning and highly irritated skin may persist for hours. Splashing the affected areas with water had no effect, in fact, it invariably made the irritation worse.

Anyway, once the CS gas had completely filled the room, we were required to demonstrate that our respirator was correctly fitted. This was achieved by jumping up and down and if the faintest sniff of the gas was detected—well, there wasn't an airtight seal! Once everyone was contented (!), we were then required to carry out decontamination drills using small pads filled with *Fuller's earth* dust, a clay-like compound with highly absorbent properties.

Everyone had to take a deep breath, close their eyes, remove the respirator and using the pad, dab all around the skin. Once complete, refit the respirator and blow hard to remove any residual gas that may be inside the mask. The

British respirators were really very effective and even had a small drinking tube that could be attached to a special water canister.

Eating and drinking drills also had to be carried out. The main point to remember was that decontamination had to be carried out before and after the removal of the respirator.

There were many occasions in my early career when the RAF Regiment personnel took the sadistic opportunity to *educate* us as to the effect that CS gas actually had on the human body. On completion of the standard procedures, we were required to stand at the end of the room, remove our respirator, open our eyes, and quote our service number, rank and name before dashing outside into the fresh air.

It was always emphasised that the effects were similar to the signs and symptoms associated with mild poisoning by a nerve agent. These symptoms included an unexplained runny nose, sudden headache, sudden drooling, difficulty in seeing, tightness in the chest or difficulty in breathing.

For moderate nerve agent poisoning, the same symptoms would appear but with increased severity, whereas, a casualty suffering with severe poisoning would also suffer with involuntary urination and defecation, convulsions, unconsciousness and ultimately death through respiratory failure. We were also instructed on how to use the auto-injector combo pen.

The medical device is used to deliver a single dose of Atropine in the event of nerve agent poisoning. All personnel would be issued with three such devices only in the event of an escalation in hostilities.

There were many occasions whilst we were behind locked doors that we'd take off our respirators during an NBC Black phase. If the telephone rang, rather than donning the respirator we would merely talk whilst pinching the nose. It seemed to work! However, I think that in the event of real hostilities, the respirator would stay securely fitted and nobody would be able to prize it off even with a crowbar!

World War Three!

There were always tensions between the United States and the Soviet Union. However, they dramatically increased on 1 September 1983. Korean Airlines (KAL) flight 007 was on the last leg of a flight from New York City to Seoul, with a stopover in Anchorage, Alaska. As it approached its final destination, the plane began to veer far off its normal course.

In just a short time, the plane flew into Russian airspace and crossed over the Kamchatka Peninsula, where some top-secret Soviet military installations were known to be located. The Soviets believed that the plane was on a spying mission and sent two fighters to intercept the plane. According to tapes of the conversations between the fighter pilots and Soviet ground control, the fighters quickly located the KAL flight and tried to make contact with the passenger jet.

Failing to receive a response, one of the fighters fired a heat-seeking missile. KAL 007 was hit and plummeted into the Sea of Japan. All 269 people on board were killed.

Two months after that incident, tensions between the two super powers rose to such a height that 8 November 1983, is now recognised as one of the most dangerous moments in the history of the Cold War; when a series of accidents nearly unleashed World War III. On that near-fateful day, senior figures in the Soviet Union had convinced themselves that they were about to come under nuclear attack from the West.

Able Archer 83 was a 10-day NATO command post-exercise that started on 2 November 1983 and spanned the whole of Western Europe. Able Archer exercises simulated a period of conflict escalation, culminating in a coordinated nuclear release. The 1983 exercise incorporated a new, unique format of coded communication, radio silences, participation by heads of government and a simulated DEFCON 1 nuclear alert (DEFCON 1—Nuclear War was imminent).

The realistic nature of the 1983 exercise, coupled with the deteriorating relations between the United States and the Soviet Union and the anticipated arrival of the Pershing II strategic nuclear missiles in Europe; led some members of the Soviet Politburo and the Soviet military to believe that Able Archer 83 was a ruse of war obscuring preparations for a genuine nuclear first strike.

In response, the Soviets readied their nuclear forces and placed air units in East Germany and Poland on alert. This relatively obscure incident is considered by many historians to be the closest the world has come to nuclear war since the Cuban Missile Crisis of 1962. The threat of nuclear war abruptly ended with the conclusion of the Able Archer 83 exercise on 11 November.

Towards the end of my second year on CRIST, I was approached by Laarbruch's RAF regiment boss and asked if I'd like to join the exercise distaff team (umpires), where I'd be primarily responsible for assessing the various NBC decontamination facilities although I'd also assist with many of the other exercise scenarios. One of the most memorable exercises took place in the summer of 1983, when I and another member of the distaff team were carrying out a walkabout on the afternoon before the commencement of the exercise.

We visited a wooded area on the edge of the station that was still within the perimeter and came across members of 2 Para who had been covertly dug in amongst the undergrowth for two days—they were part of an intruder team.

Early the next day, members of the station defence force set up a General-Purpose Machine Gun (GMPG) post at the edge of the wooded area with the aim of defending that particular sector in the event of a ground attack. However, they unknowingly positioned the post about 20 yards from 2 Para and were *exercise killed* immediately after the exercise commenced.

That night, in complete darkness without landing lights, a Hercules aircraft performed a roller on the runway, lowered its ramp, briefly touched down, and released several Land Rovers believed to carry members of the Special Air Service (SAS). The intruders made their way to ATC where they were challenged by an RAF police dog handler.

The plod told the SAS men that unless they stopped, the dog would be released. He really shouldn't have wasted his breath because the intruders didn't stop and when the dog attacked, the poor animal was struck with the butt of a rifle.

The SAS quickly cleared the occupants of ATC apart from a Warrant Officer who had locked himself in the top of the tower and refused to come out; the excuse being that there always had to be someone in attendance for safety and operational reasons.

By all accounts, the SAS man told the WO to come out and if he didn't, he would find a way in—good choice Sir, he came out. As time went by, I would also be asked to umpire exercises at RAF Brüggen and RAF Wildenrath.

We managed to get back to the UK a few times and on one such visit in May 1982, whilst at Heathfield Road, I answered to door to a couple of well-dressed individuals—Jehovah's witnesses—who started their introduction with the normal niceties. They then went on to give their view on the Falklands War and asked for my opinion. I'd been approached before by Jehovah's Witness but never had the reaction that I got from these two.

I told them that as a member of the armed forces, I sincerely hoped that Galtieri and his mob would get a severe stuffing from the task force; stared at them, awaited a response, didn't get one and closed the door.

West Berlin

One of the high spots of my tour was the six-monthly visits to RAF Gatow in West Berlin. The city was a political exclave which existed between 1949 and 1990 and was bordered by East Berlin and parts of East Germany. West Berlin was divided into occupation sectors which consisted of the three conquering powers of WW2, namely America, Britain and France (although I'll never understand why France was ever considered to be a conqueror!).

It was politically closely affiliated with West Germany. However, its administration was formally conducted by the Western Allies. East Berlin encompassed the region occupied and administered by the USSR and was claimed as the capital of East Germany.

The Western Allies didn't recognise this claim, as they asserted that the entire city of Berlin came under the Four-Power administration, nor did they recognise the East German Authorities especially the Volks Polizei (People's Police). The Berlin Wall was built in 1961 to stem the haemorrhage of East Berliners trying to escape to the West, and physically divided East and West Berlin until its eventual fall in 1989.

Because of shortages in foreign currencies, on 1 September 1951, East Germany started to levy road tolls for cars using the transit routes. At first, the toll charged was 10 Eastern Deutsche Mark per car and between 10 and 50 Eastern Deutsche Mark for trucks. However, West German Deutsche Marks could only be exchanged on a 1:1 ratio. On 30 March 1955, East Germany raised the toll for passenger cars to 30 Deutsche Marks, but after West German protests, in June of the same year, it changed it back to the previous rate.

Following an agreement between East and West Germany, starting on 1 January 1980, the Western Federal Government agreed to pay 50 million Deutsche Marks annually, so that, transit passengers no longer would have to pay. The transit routes and surrounding roads were also used by East German domestic traffic. It meant that transit passengers could potentially meet with East Germans and East Berliners at restaurants at the various rest stops.

Since such meetings were deemed illegal by the East German government, border guards would calculate the travel duration from the time of entry and exit of the transit route. Excessive time spent on transit travel could arouse suspicion and prompt questioning or additional checking by the border guards. Western coaches could only stop at dedicated service areas since the East German government was concerned that East Germans might potentially use coaches to escape into the West.

As far as the CRIST was concerned, the process for getting from Laarbruch to West Berlin and back was extremely convoluted. At least a month before travelling, we were required to apply for a movement order from the Commandant, British Sector, Berlin giving all relevant details and the details on the document had to be absolutely precise.

Our vehicle was always a black Ford Escort Estate which had a bright yellow band running the length of both sides of the car and on it was emblazoned, in bold letters, ROYAL AIR FORCE. We always started the trip early on a Saturday morning, and drove to the East German border at Helmstedt. There, we booked in with the army authorities, given our signed movements order and a note made of our departure time.

We were also given a vehicle breakdown pack which contained the relevant military emergency contact details at either end of the corridor as well as two A4 sized cards. If we were involved in an incident, accident or breakdown and the Volks Polizei were in attendance, we were to stay in the vehicle, close all windows and not enter into any dialogue with them.

Instead, we were to show the card with the Deutsche text, which stated that the occupants of the vehicle were members of the British armed forces who required the attendance of a Soviet officer. Once the Soviet official had arrived, we were to show the second card which contained Russian text asking that British military authorities be contacted (there were no mobile phones then).

The fortifications of the inner German border, which were primarily designed to keep the East German population in, comprised a complex system of interlocking fortifications and security zones 858 miles long, several miles wide and ran from the Baltic Sea to Czechoslovakia.

The outer fences and walls were the most familiar and visible aspect of the system for western visitors to the border zone. But they were merely the final obstacle for a would-be escapee from East Germany.

The complexity of the border system increased steadily until it reached its full extent in the early 1980s. An escapee, travelling notionally from east to west, would first reach the edge of the restricted zone (*Sperrzone*), a closely controlled strip of land three miles wide which ran parallel with the border.

Evading the patrols and watchful inhabitants of the *Sperrzone*, the escapee would have reached the first of the border fences. The signal fence (*Signalzaun*), around 1,600 to 3,300 feet from the actual border, was lined with low-voltage electrified barbed wire which activated alarms when touched or cut.

Beyond the signal fence was the *protective strip* (*Schutzstreifen*). It was brightly lit by floodlights in many places to reduce an escapee's chances of using the cover of darkness. Guard towers, bunkers and dog runs were positioned at frequent intervals to keep a round-the-clock watch on the strip. Crossing the *Schutzstreifen*, the escapee would next reach the floodlit control strip, often called the *death strip* in the West.

Tripwire-activated flare launchers were situated at various points to help the border guards to pinpoint the location of an escape attempt. The last and most formidable obstacle was the outer fencing. In some places, there were multiple parallel rows of fences, each up to several feet high, with minefields in between.

The fences were not electrified but were booby-trapped with directional anti-personnel mines at intervals of 33 feet; each one of which was capable of killing at a range of up to 390 feet.

Finally, the escapee had to cross whatever natural obstacles were on the western side of the border fence as well as traversing a strip of cleared ground that was up to 1640 feet wide. While crossing this outer strip, the escapee would appear in clear view and shooting range of the border guards, there were 50,000 guards manning several very tall watch towers.

All of that before, hopefully, reaching the safety of West German territory. The border fortifications were the physical manifestation of Winston Churchill's metaphorical *Iron Curtain* that separated the Soviet Union and Western blocs during the Cold War—all that, not to keep those from the West out but to keep their own people in!

On leaving the British administration buildings, it was only a short drive to the military vehicle lane and checkpoint which was manned by a Russian soldier. We weren't required to travel in uniform and on stopping at the checkpoint, I, as the driver, had to stand in front of the soldier, salute him and present our RAF identity cards and movements order.

He, in turn, would salute me, check the papers and point me in the direction of a small building close by; he would then walk around the car checking the other occupants and noting anything that was left in view. I'm sure he would have been more than a little concerned to learn that hidden in the boot was a lead-lined box containing a lead ball in which a piece of Cobalt was encased.

The radioactive source was used as a calibration source for the radiation monitors. The room was small, unassuming and austere and in the corner was a small hatch where I had to wait until it was opened. At that point, I presented our documents, the hatch slammed down and I waited and waited and waited. It must have been at least a quarter of an hour before the hatch eventually opened and our travel documents thrust through—the hatch was then slammed down again.

Once outside, I had to present the endorsed documents to the Russian soldier. He would check them again before saluting me and I reciprocated—we were then free to continue. The drive through the corridor was uneventful and took approximately two hours and because our journey was being timed, we had to be mindful of our speed.

The speed limit on the corridor was, I believe, 100 kph (60 mph) and if we arrived within one hour, it was obvious that we'd been speeding and a bollocking was guaranteed. On the other hand, if we hadn't arrived in West Berlin within a *reasonable* period, a search party would be dispatched.

I travelled to West Berlin on three occasions during my tour of duty and was really quite shocked at some of the underhand entrapment practices that were carried out by the Volks Polizei on the West Germans travelling through the corridor. On one occasion, we noticed what appeared to be a very large haystack on the autobahn grass verge.

It looked so out of place and on looking a little closer, we could see that a car was hidden underneath and a scanner was sticking out of the front—a crude radar speed trap. A favourite trick and one that I witnessed on my second trip was for temporary speed limit signs to be placed at the side of the autobahn. The limit would reduce from 100 kph to 50 kph, and then, down to 30 kph (18 mph) and for no apparent reason there would be a *no overtaking* sign.

A short distance away, we then saw a car being driven so slowly, it was almost at a standstill and woe betide anyone who overtook it—a fine was inevitable. The practice of fining the West German drivers was commonplace and was a lucrative source of income for the East German economy.

The maximum number of Eastern Deutsche Marks that could be taken into the country from the West was 10; any more and the money would be confiscated and any fine had to be paid in West Deutsche Marks. The commercial exchange rate at the time was 9 East Mark to 1 West Deutsche Mark.

Anyway, we eventually arrived at the Soviet checkpoint which was the entry point into West Berlin without incident. It was here that I had to go through the same procedure that I'd followed earlier; salute, present documents, present documents, wait, present documents and salute before being allowed to continue.

We entered West Berlin on the outskirts of the city and quickly made our way past Spandau Prison to RAF Gatow. The overall visit itinerary followed the same format, there were always two members of the CRIST team and we always took someone from the avionics section for a few days away. Once we'd *warned-in* at the mess and had dinner, we caught the bus to the top of the *Kurfurstendamm* (affectionately known as the Ku'damm). There all the restaurants, bars and nightclubs were located. What a far cry from the Berlin of the late 1940s.

The Berlin Blockade

The blockade of Berlin was the first major international crisis of the Cold War. It began on 24 June 1948 and was eventually lifted on 11 May 1949. During the multinational occupation of Germany following the end of WW2, the Soviet Union blocked the Western Allies' railway, road and canal access to the sectors of Berlin under Allied control.

Their aim was to force the western powers to allow the Soviet zone to start supplying Berlin with food and fuel, thereby, giving the Soviets practical control over the entire city. In response, the Western Allies organised the Berlin airlift to carry supplies to the people of West Berlin.

Aircrews from the USA, the RAF, the Royal Australian, Royal Canadian and South African Air Forces flew over 200,000 flights in one year, providing up to 4700 tons of daily necessities such as fuel and food to the Berliners. By the spring of 1949, the effort was clearly succeeding. By April, the airlift was delivering more cargo than had previously been transported into the city by rail.

The success of the airlift brought embarrassment to the Soviets who had refused to believe it could make a difference. The lifting of the blockade resulted in the creation of two separate German states—the Federal Republic of Germany (West Germany) and the Deutsche Democratic Republic (DDR, East Germany). In remembrance of the airlift, three airports in the former western zones of the city served as the primary gateways to Germany for the next 50 years.

West Berlin was an incredibly vibrant city and no matter what the time of day or night, it never relaxed or slowed down and the buses ran continuously; Saturday night was no different to any other. We walked for a couple of hours, stopping occasionally for a beer and generally soaked up the incredible atmosphere—the West Berliners certainly knew how to party.

President JFK visited West Berlin in the '60s and famously told the locals in perfect Deutsche *Ich Bin Eine Berliner* which he believed meant, *I am a Berliner*. Unfortunately, he wasn't briefed properly because a *Berliner* was the name given to a loaf of bread. There were dozens of clubs on and off the Ku'damm each offering a different degree of entertainment, some fairly innocuous and others quite explicit.

One in particular was the *Puff Puff Club,* where there was a standard rate of admission. However, the more clothes the punter took off at the door, the cheaper the admission became—we paid the full price! I won't go into too much detail but suffice it to say, there were always lots of scantily clad females; most were very pretty, whose sole job was to sit with clients and be bought drinks such as whisky, gin or vodka, and were probably nothing more than coloured water.

Following breakfast on Sunday morning, we once again caught the bus to the Ku'damm and spent the entire day sightseeing. You only have to watch any of the newsreels of the time to realise how much damage and destruction was caused to Berlin during the war not only through the Allies' blanket bombing campaign but also the Russian ground assault from the east.

It was only 31 years since the war ended, and the West Berliners had done an incredible job in rebuilding their part of the city. There were several monuments throughout the city that were designed to be a constant reminder of the destruction and futility of war. One such monument, located on Breitscheidplatz, was one of Berlin's most famous landmarks, the Kaiser Wilhelm Memorial Church, also known as *The Blue Kirche* (The Blue Church).

The church burnt down in 1943 after it was hit by an Allied bomb. Only the broken west tower of the church remained standing which was left as a symbol of Berlin's resolve to rebuild the city after the war. Local opposition saved the structure from demolition in the 1950s and in 1961 a new, octagonal church was built alongside the existing tower. The church is a reinforced concrete structure with blue-coloured glass bricks—hence the name.

At the conclusion of the war, three Soviet war memorials were also built in Berlin, two in the eastern sector and one in the west. They were built not only to commemorate Soviet deaths, especially, the 80,000 who died during the Battle for Berlin but also to serve as cemeteries for those killed.

The one memorial was located in the Tiergarten, which was part of the British Sector of Berlin. It was built from stonework from the Reich Chancellery and was flanked by two Red Army 152 mm gun-howitzer artillery pieces and two T-34 Tanks.

The sign next to the monument explains in English, German and Russian that it is the burial site of some 2,000 fallen Soviet soldiers. However, there are several indicators that this monument was intended not so much to commemorate the dead Soviet soldiers but more for propaganda purposes. It was located in the heart of Berlin along one of the major roads with a clear sight of the Reichstag and the Brandenburg Gate, both potent symbols of the city.

With the building of the Berlin Wall in 1961, the monument was seen as a sign of communist provocation on West German soil, and had to be protected by British soldiers to stop it from being destroyed by the West Berliners.

Throughout the Cold War, Soviet Guards were present at the memorial and were sent out and changed regularly by the Soviet occupying forces in the Soviet sector. The guards would stand for hours, never flinching or moving and it was quite an impressive sight until it was pointed out that, the plinths they were standing on, were very slightly slopping backwards, which meant that they were effectively lying down.

In 1970, Ekkehard Weil a neo-Nazi, shot one of the Soviet honour guards at the monument, severely wounding him.

Monday saw the start of our working day which comprised of a visit to the RAF Regiment Flight where we would spend a few hours servicing and calibrating the MSR2 equipment and Dosimeters. That done, it was a quick dash back to the mess. We had some lunch, got changed into our best blue uniforms and SD Hats, climbed into our service car and headed off to a bank in the city to convert some Western Deutsche marks into eastern currency.

The banks didn't care that we were exchanging and gave us an exchange rate of 9:1. Before going into East Berlin we had to book in with the British military authorities located in the Olympic Stadium complex and advise them of our plans. We were advised that we, as members of the Allied Forces, were entitled to free and unrestricted access to the East.

We were briefed that we were not to enter into dialogue with any East German official and in the event of accidents, incidents or breakdowns, we were to follow the same format as when we drove along the Berlin corridor.

The next stop was at Checkpoint Charlie on Fridrichstrasse, located in the American Sector. The checkpoint had become a potent symbol of the Cold War representing the separation of East and West.

Checkpoint Charlie

By the early 1950s, the Soviet method of restricting emigration was emulated by most of the rest of the Eastern Bloc countries, including East Germany. However, in occupied Germany, until 1952, the lines between East Germany and the Western occupied zones remained easily crossed in most places.

Consequently, the inner German border between the two German states was closed and a barbed-wire fence was erected. Even after the closing of the Inner German border officially in 1952, the city sector border between East and West Berlin remained considerably more accessible than the rest of the border because it was administered by all four occupying powers.

Berlin became the main route by which East Germans left for the West and the Berlin sector border was essentially a *loophole*, through which Eastern Bloc citizens could still escape.

The 3.5 million East Germans, who left by 1961, totalled approximately 20% of the entire East German population with the emigrants tending to be young and well educated. This loss was disproportionately greatest among professionals: engineers, technicians, physicians, teachers, lawyers and skilled workers.

Soon after the construction of the Berlin Wall in 1961, a standoff occurred between U.S. and Soviet tanks on either side of Checkpoint Charlie. The altercation began on 22 October as a dispute over whether East German guards were authorised to examine the travel documents of a U.S. diplomat passing through East Berlin to attend the opera.

By 27 October, 10 Soviet and an equal number of American tanks stood 100 metres apart on either side of the checkpoint. The standoff ended peacefully on 28 October, following a US-Soviet understanding to withdraw tanks. Discussions between US Attorney General Robert F. Kennedy and KGB spy Georgi Bolshakov played a vital role in realising this tacit agreement.

Checkpoint Charlie was designated as the single crossing point (by foot or by car) for members of the Allied forces, who were not allowed to use any of the other sector crossing points.

When we arrived at the checkpoint, we parked up and visited the *Haus am Checkpoint Charlie* (The House at Checkpoint Charlie), which was a private museum dedicated to the determination and creativity of the people desperate to escape. The museum, whilst only small, was crammed with photographs, documents, escape accounts and many of the devices that were used by the escapees.

When the wall was being built, many people tried to climb it or jumped out of the houses that lay right on the border, and during the first days, several people were killed by the eastern border guards. There was a very famous photograph on display; showing a young East German border guard, Conrad Schumann, who escaped on 15 August 1961 carrying his weapon and jumping over a low-lying barbed-wire fence.

In an attempt to stop people from climbing over the wall, the government outlawed the sale of rope and twine. However, in response to that restriction, a large network of tunnels were then built; mostly being dug by college students although many people actually used them.

The first known successful tunnel was dug in a cemetery where people would bring flowers to a grave and pretend to mourn; they would then merely drop out of sight and would never again be seen on that side of the wall. Unfortunately, the tunnel was eventually found and sealed off after a woman accidentally fell into the hole leaving her baby in a carriage.

The most successful tunnel was constructed in the basement of a house at 60 Westerstrasse, where 29 people escaped to freedom. People's ingenuity knew no bounds and some people even flew over the wall. Two families, the Wetzels and Strlzycks, secretly bought small amounts of nylon cloth in quantities that didn't raise any suspicion, and when they had enough, they sewed it together to form a hot air balloon.

They had just enough fuel to get the balloon into the air and floated over the wall, arriving in West Berlin a few hours later—the East German authority's answer was to strictly control the sale of lightweight cloth.

One of the most publicised escape attempts was that of 18-year-old Peter Fetcher. At midday on 17 August 1962, Peter, a bricklayer and his friend Helmut Kulbeik jumped from a ground floor window of a house on Zimmerstrasse into the *death strip;* an area of no man's land leading up to the wall. As they reached the wall, ignoring calls from the GDR guards to halt, they were fired upon with a total of 20 shots.

Helmut made it over the wall but Peter was hit several times and his body lay tangled in a barbed-wire fence, bleeding to death, in full view of the world's media. American soldiers couldn't rescue him because he was a few yards inside the Soviet sector and East German border guards were reluctant to approach him for fear of provoking western soldiers; one of whom had shot an East German border guard just days earlier.

It was believed that Peter died on the spot and more than an hour later his body was removed by the East German guards. A spontaneous demonstration formed on the American side of the checkpoint, protesting at the action of the East and the inaction of the West. A few days later, a crowd stoned Soviet buses driving towards the Soviet war memorial in the Tiergarten.

The Soviets then tried to escort the buses with Armoured Personnel Carriers (APCs). However, they were denied access through Checkpoint Charlie and only allowed entry into West Berlin via the Sandkrug Bridge crossing (which was the nearest to Tiergarten). They were also prohibited from bringing APCs into the West and armed western military units were deployed to enforce the ban.

In all, 5,000 people tried to escape to the west between 13 August 1961 and 9 November 1989. When the wall eventually came down, out of those 5,000, 171 people lost their lives. The first to die was Günter Litwin who was shot on 24 August 1961, and the last to die was 20-year-old Chris Geoffray, who was shot on 6 February 1989. There are several commemorative tablets dedicated to some of the victims of the East German Guards, located next to the Reichstag.

Following our visit to the museum, we booked in with the United States Military Police at the checkpoint and informed them where we intended to go and what time we anticipated returning. We then drove our car, which as you may remember, was emblazoned with the *Royal Air Force* motif, into the Soviet sector having firstly to negotiate several chicanes built from huge lumps of concrete designed to stop even the most determined of potential escapees.

As expected, we weren't hindered or delayed and before long, we were driving in the Deutsche Demokratische Republik (DDR). Initially, we could see no discernible difference between the buildings in the east and the west, all looked fairly modern especially the *Unter Den Linden,* which ran from the Brandenburg Gate towards Alexanderplatz.

However, on leaving the city centre and entering the suburbs, there was a marked contrast with many buildings in a poor state of repair, and some still showing signs of damage caused during the war that had ended some 36 years earlier. The Soviet war memorial in Treptow Park was an amazing sight, somewhat ostentatious but nevertheless impressive.

The park was divided into five large areas where 5000 soldiers were buried and the most spectacular element was the mausoleum on which a 12-metre-high bronze statue was placed; depicting a bareheaded, heroic, Soviet soldier wielding a sword and standing on top of a smashed swastika, into which the sword is deeply cut.

On his left arm, he was carrying a child while staring out over the plaza. In the lead-up to and including the Battle for Berlin itself, 80,000 Russians were killed and a further 275,000 were wounded or declared missing, they also lost two thousand tanks. 150,000 Germans died in the battle.

Once we'd seen the standard Allied forces *touristy* bits, we headed back towards the centre of East Berlin, just driving and taking in the sights. We quickly noticed that there were very few traffic lights, and at almost every major junction, there was a white-coated policeman who stood on a covered pedestal in the centre of the road controlling the traffic.

I didn't notice it at first, until Kev, who'd been to East Berlin before, pointed out that each time we passed a traffic policeman, he would immediately pick up his telephone and presumably take note of the direction we were driving. I imagined that our movements were being closely monitored and tracked at the Stasi Headquarters; which gave us all the incentive to just drive around and around and around.

The Stasi

The Stasi, the Ministry for State Security, was one of the most hated and feared institutions of the East German Communist government and became a highly effective secret police organisation. Within East Germany, it sought to infiltrate every institution of society and every aspect of daily life, including even intimate, personal and family relationships.

It accomplished this goal both through its official apparatus and through a vast network of informants and unofficial collaborators; who spied on and denounced colleagues, friends, neighbours and even family members. By 1989, the Stasi relied on between 500,000 and 2,000,000 collaborators as well as 100,000 regular employees. It maintained files on approximately 6,000,000 East German citizens—more than one-third of the population.

The Stasi also had links to various terrorist groups, the most notable being the Red Army Faction (RAF) who were based in West Germany. During the 1970s and '80s, the Stasi worked closely with the RAF and co-operated with Abu Nidal, the founder of Fatah the Revolutionary Council (a militant Palestinian splinter group), Ilich Ramírez Sánchez (commonly known as Carlos, or *the Jackal*) and the Palestine Liberation Organisation (PLO).

The Stasi also allowed Libyan agents to use East Berlin as a base for operations when carrying out terrorist attacks in West Berlin. Following the bombing of a discotheque in West Berlin in 1986, that killed two U.S. servicemen, the Stasi continued to allow Libyan agents to use East Berlin as both a base for operations and as a safe haven.

One aspect of East Berlin that was acutely noticeable was the number of Trabant cars on the road. The Trabant, which gave Communism a bad name, was powered by a 600 cc two-stroke pollution generator that maxed out at an ear-splitting 18 hp and was a hollow lie of a car. It was constructed of recycled worthlessness (actually, the body was made of a fibreglass-like substance, reinforced with recycled fibres such as cotton and wood).

A virtual antique when it was designed in the 1950s, the Trabant was East Germany's answer to the VW Beetle—a *People's Car*, as if the people didn't have enough to worry about. Trabants smoked like an Iraqi oil fire, when they ran at all and often lacked even the most basic of amenities, such as brake lights or indicators.

Because the car lacked a fuel pump, the fuel tank was placed high up in the engine compartment so that fuel could be fed to the carburettor by gravity; a trade-off for this design was the increased fire risk in front-end accidents. But history has been kind to the Trabi because thousands of East Germans drove their

Trabants over the border when the Wall eventually fell, which made it a kind of automotive liberator.

Once across the border, the none-too-sentimental *Ostdeutschlanders* immediately abandoned their cars. Ich bin Junk!

If you look at the funny side of the famous East German icon, and the sadness associated with life in general in the DDR, you'll appreciate the following jokes:

A customer ordered a Trabant car and the salesman told him to come back and pick it up in nine-years-time. The customer asks if he should come back in the morning or in the evening. The seller said, "You're joking, aren't you?"

The customer replies, "No, not at all. I need to know because the plumber's coming at 3 pm then."

An East German worker's five years were up, and he went to take delivery of his Trabi. He asked the company representative, "Can I have a car with seat belts?"

"Sure," said the representative, "and while we're at it, we can give you a car with two-tone paint, air-conditioning and an AM/FM/Longwave/Shortwave radio!"

Mortified, the customer mumbled, "Now, you're just making fun of me."

"Well," roared the representative, "you started it?"

A West German visitor is driving his Mercedes through East Germany on a rainy night when his windscreen wipers stopped working. He takes it to an East German mechanic, who tells him there are no Mercedes windscreen wiper motors in the DDR, but he will do his best to fix it.

When the businessman returns the next day, to his surprise the windscreen wipers are working perfectly. "How on earth did you find a Mercedes windscreen wiper motor in the East?" he asks the mechanic.

"We didn't," replies the mechanic. "We used the engine of a Trabant."

What would happen if the desert became a socialist country? Nothing for a while, and then, there would be a sand shortage.

How can you use a banana as a compass? Place a banana on the Berlin Wall and East is where a bite has been taken out of it.

Early in the morning, Erich Honecker, the East German leader arrives at his office and opens his window. He sees the sun and says, "Good morning, dear Sun!"

The sun replies, "Good morning, dear Erich!"

Honecker works, and then at noon, he heads to the window and says, "Good day, dear Sun!"

The sun replies, "Good day, dear Erich!"

In the evening, Erich calls it a day, heads once more to the window, and says, "Good evening, dear Sun!"

The sun is silent.

Honecker says again: "Good evening, dear Sun! What's the matter?"

The sun replies, "Kiss my arse. I'm in the West now."

Anyway, once we became bored with driving around aimlessly, and hopefully, having thoroughly pissed off the Polizei, we headed back to Checkpoint Charlie. There, we parked the car before walking back through into the east. Our aim was to walk to Alexanderplatz, which would take about 30 minutes and later that evening, have a meal at the top of the Fernsehturm or Television Tower where there was a rotating restaurant.

As we were dressed in our number one uniform, we stood out like the proverbial sore thumb and people wouldn't look us in the eye and on many occasions acted as if we weren't there. There was polite discourse from the assistants when we went into any of the souvenir shops, and none more so than, when we went into a particular shop that sold glassware.

East German lead crystal was heavy, very good quality and much sought after and as we entered the shop there was one customer being served. We just browsed and once the customer had gone, the proprietor greeted us with the customary Gütten Tag and looked around before beckoning us to follow him behind a curtain where he showed us some amazing pieces of crystal.

I bought a whisky decanter for an absolute steal which was quickly wrapped up, put into a bag and paid for using East German Deutschmarks.

We then headed for the 368 metres Fernsehturm, built between 1965 and 1969, and even today is the tallest building in Germany. We took the lift to the revolving restaurant which was 207 metres above the ground and took one hour to complete one revolution. We were shown to a table and I do remember being quite stunned at the view.

We were given a menu that looked quite comprehensive, although nothing to compare with what we could get in any reasonable western restaurant and ordered a larger to start with. I don't remember what I chose for a starter, but decided on a rump steak for my main and ice cream for the dessert.

The portions were meagre but my steak was quite tasty and was accompanied by potatoes and sauerkraut (pickled cabbage), for those of us who weren't driving, we had another beer; we sat for a couple of hours and watched the sun go down.

Once darkness had fallen, the contrast between east and west was unbelievable. There were very few street lights to be seen in the east, but as we rotated and West Berlin came into view, the contrast was mind-blowing with the whole sector lit up for as far as the eye could see.

There was a very strange phenomenon that was apparent whenever the sun shone on the Fernsehturm's tiled stainless steel dome and that was the reflection which usually appeared in the shape of a crucifix. The effect was neither predicted nor desired and the authorities tried countless ways of correcting it with paint or chemicals but were unable to stop it from happening. The West Berliners immediately named the luminous cross *Rache des Papstes* or *Pope's Revenge*.

The meal, despite its simplicity, was enjoyable and the bill was 40 East, which worked out at approximately 5 DM or the equivalent of just under £2:00 each. The walk back through the checkpoint went without incident, and although, we weren't supposed to converse with the East German border guards, they were polite and wished us *Gütten Nacht*, to which we courteously replied.

The only other area of West Berlin where the Soviet military was allowed was Spandau Prison close to Gatow. After World War 2, the prison was operated by the Four-Power Authorities to house the Nazi war criminals sentenced to imprisonment at the Nuremberg War trials.

Spandau was one of only two Four-Power organisations to continue to operate after the breakdown of the Allied Control Council, the other was the Berlin Air Safety Centre. The four occupying powers of Berlin would alternate control of the prison on a monthly basis, each having the responsibility for a total of three months out of the year. By observing the Four-Power flag that flew at the Allied Control Authority building, you could determine who controlled the prison.

The most famous and longest-serving internee of Spandau Prison was Rudolf Hess who had been the sole occupant after the release of Albert Speer and Baldur Von Scirach in 1966. Rudolf Hess was the eldest of four children, born in Alexandria, Egypt who became a prominent Nazi politician and was Adolf Hitler's deputy in the Nazi party during the 1930s and the early 1940s.

On the eve of the war with the Soviet Union in 1942, Hess flew solo to Scotland in an attempt to negotiate peace with the United Kingdom but was arrested and became a prisoner of war. Hess was trialled at Nuremberg and sentenced to life imprisonment which he served at Spandau Prison, where he was to die in 1987.

The prison was demolished shortly afterwards, largely to prevent it from becoming a neo-Nazi shrine following Hess' death, and to further ensure its erasure, the site was made into a parking facility. A shopping centre comprising shopping, welfare, employment and a broadcasting facility was also built, named The Britannia Centre Spandau.

It was soon nicknamed *Hesscos* after one of our more famous supermarket chains of a similar name. All materials from the demolished prison were either ground to powder and dispersed in the North Sea, or buried at the former RAF Gatow airbase.

Tuesday morning saw us warning out of the mess and heading back to Laarbruch. The same checkpoint procedures were followed for our return trip to the free west.

During the Cold War, Soviet and NATO military observers operated in each other's zone of occupation under the terms agreed at the Four-Power Conference that was held in Berlin in 1945. The British observers went under the acronym BRIXMIS—British Commanders-in-Chief Mission to the Soviet Forces in Germany. The Soviet observers were referred to as SOXMIS—Soviet Military Mission.

SOXMIS and BRIXMIS vehicles were required to display a large yellow sign at the rear of the vehicles with a distinctive black number which was to be clearly visible. There was also a national flag which included the SOXMIS or BRIXMIS symbols. Both groups were relatively small and were designed to instil trust between the occupying powers in Germany.

However, the members of these groups were opportunists and were often suspected of spying on each other's military capability. The SOXMIS group in the British Zone were located in Bad Salzuflen (*Bad Salts* as it was called), located about 10 km from Herford, and they were permitted to use the NAAFI in Harewood Barracks, Herford.

We were issued a card with details of how to recognise a SOXMIS car and were encouraged to report to any military authority when and where such a vehicle was spotted. We were also to report any suspicious activity which included unauthorised observance of military manoeuvres or deviation from the autobahns (they were not permitted to stop at the rest points), unless escorted by British RMP escort.

If suspicious activity such as illegal parking was observed, British military vehicles were to *box in* the offending SOXMIS car and remain with it until a higher authority had resolved the problem. At no time were British service personnel to be discourteous.

Royal Military Police (RMP) personnel from 19 Support Platoon, affectionately known as *White Mice*, usually manned special cars to follow and report suspicious SOXMIS activity. I, for my part, never saw a SOXMIS vehicle and the SOXMIS/BRIXMIS arrangements were terminated when the Berlin Wall came down and the Soviet Union collapsed.

On those occasions, we were required to travel to Belgium; it was blatantly obvious that we'd crossed the border by the general state of the streets. The Belgium streets were probably no different to some of the grotty areas seen in the UK, but the stark contrast was so much more noticeable having just left Germany where the inhabitants were well known for their cleanliness.

The other noticeable indication was the fact that all of the country's autobahns were lit for their entire length which must have incurred a massive electricity bill. Although I'd transited Belgium én route to Laarbruch, I never stopped at a service area and therefore had no real idea how they compared with those in the UK.

It transpired that all rest areas throughout most of mainland Europe were infinitely better than any we'd used in England. However, the one thing I'd not come across in the UK was female toilet cleaners. We'd called in at a service area on the way to Tongeren. Whilst I was standing at the urinal, a woman walked up and casually started to clean the urinal immediately beside me and didn't bat an eyelid—it put me off though!

Life in Goch amongst the Deutsche community was fantastic. Feld Strasse was one of three roads that housed military personnel and the locals were friendly in the extreme. There was a traditional Deutsche Backerie situated at the crossroads very close by, and whenever we shopped there, if we spoke in English the lady owner would only reply in Deutsche. However, if we attempted their language, she would always reply in English!

In the summer of 1981, Helen, Morley, John and Mum came to stay and we kept them entertained like there was no tomorrow. The town officials had agreed that Feld Strasse would be closed off to traffic for the evening of 29 July, so that, the British community could celebrate the Royal wedding of Charles and Diana. I don't remember who organised the street party, but whoever it was, really did make us proud.

The weather for the entire two weeks was exceptionally hot and we visited most of the tourist spots in the area including a holy Shrine at Keveler, Kleve (birthplace of Henry VIII's Ann of Cleaves), Gennep in Holland, Roman ruins at Xanton, a man-made lake at Wisseller See, Arnhem, Venlo and the Philips Museum at Eindhoven.

We also decided to visit Amsterdam and go on a canal cruise. As I'd not been to Amsterdam before, I had no real idea of my way around and headed for what I thought was the city centre. Parking wasn't too difficult and we soon found out why—we'd managed to find our way into the red-light district which didn't look as seedy as I'd expected.

Rather than driving around aimlessly, we decided to leave the cars and walk to the centre. The weather that afternoon was incredibly hot and once we'd spent a couple of hours sweltering on a canal boat, we stopped at an ice cream parlour. Morley and I were the first to be served and were waiting in the street when a rather attractive lady approached Morley and spoke to him in Dutch.

Morley hadn't the foggiest idea what she had said, but knowing we were close to the red-light area, replied, "Sorry, love, I'm too old for that sort of thing."

The woman replied in perfect English (as all Cloggies did), "I only wanted to know where you bought the ice cream."

It was the only time I can ever remember seeing Morley embarrassed.

One annual celebration that was always eagerly anticipated was *Karneval* which in true German style was the time for enforced jollity. The parades were held throughout the country with Düsseldorf and Köln the largest and most well-known. The processions would last for hours with some of the most colourful and creative floats imaginable. And in order to get a good place to watch, we had to be on the street quite early.

It wasn't just about watching the spectacle, it was also about the sweets—the people involved in the parade whether they were walking alongside or actually on board the floats constantly bombarded the spectator with sweets, bags of popcorn and small toys. It became quite a competition between the boys to see who could collect the most.

And it wasn't just the people in the parade who dressed up either, the majority of those who went to watch also dressed up to some extent—they took having fun very seriously.

I arrived home one afternoon to find that dozens of small tree branches had been positioned along the pavements of all four roads leading to the crossroads by the Backerie, and each branch was festooned with ribbons and decorations. Later that evening as we were watching T.V. we heard an Oom-pah band playing on the street and went to see what was going on.

It turned out that the band and the locals were celebrating the 50th wedding anniversary of the owners of the Backerie, and we were invited to join in. We had all sorts of finger food, and every now and then, a large tray of Schnapps would be brought out and passed around.

As the evening progressed more and more residents arrived including one old gent who started talking to me and apologising for what went on in the war. He eventually revealed to me that he had served as a Luftwaffe pilot, flying Messerschmitt 109s from Uedem, an airbase located just a few kilometres north of Goch. He admitted to being responsible for shooting down several British aircraft, leaving me with little to say to respond.

Whilst on the subject of shooting down aircraft, an incredibly bizarre incident happened in 1982, where an RAF Jaguar aircraft was shot down at Wessel, a town north of Laarbruch, not by a hostile force but by one of our own Phantom FGR2 air defence aircraft based at RAF Wildenrath.

It happened during a routine exercise which coincided with a Phantom that was coming off Battle Flight, also known as the Quick Reaction Alert (QRA). It was still equipped with a fully laden Sioux Gun, four live heat-seeking Sidewinder missiles and four live radar-guided Sparrow missiles. The crew took off and decided to join in the exercise and jump a Jaguar that was flying below.

The pilot, for some obscure reason, completely forgot that he was flying a fully loaded live aircraft and let rip with a Sidewinder, which blew the Jag out of the sky. Fortunately, the pilot ejected safely. After the incident, the Phantom pilot attempted to blame it on the missing red tape that usually covers the weapons master arm switch, which warns the crew that live weapons are loaded.

He hadn't considered the fact that he had signed the F700 as accepting the live-armed aircraft and he also failed to notice that the weapons control panel showed eight missiles were fitted. It wasn't too long after the incident that the same two squadrons were at Decimommanu in Sardinia, both taking part in an Air Combat Manoeuvring Instrumentation (ACMI) exercise.

Rumour has it that some wag from 92 squadron placed bowls of milk in front of the Jaguars with a notice saying, *Nice Kitty Kitty*.

Our *Lellow Wenow* was going well until one very cold winter's morning, when I couldn't get it to start due to a flat battery. I was about to give up when Rod Craycraft, our neighbour, came out and managed to tow bump start it. Under normal circumstances, I would have used the main entrance to the station, but on that particular morning, I decided to use one of the side entrances which as it turned out was untreated and very icy.

I drove onto the station and at the top of a reasonably steep hill I gingerly began a very slow descent. I got halfway down the hill and was travelling no faster than walking pace when the front wheels locked up on the sheet ice and I started to slide. At the bottom of the hill was a car, waiting to turn right, and I was getting closer and closer all the while.

I tried steering off the road, pumping the breaks and everything possible, all to no avail and I slid very slowly into the rear of the car that was still waiting at the junction. The driver got out. It was Rod, that really was an exceptional way of thanking him for getting me going earlier. I got the Renault repaired and sold it to someone at the station, and then, bought our first new car—a Volkswagen Jetta.

When we first arrived at Laarbruch, the only television programmes we watched on our little black and white, nine-year-old, 12" portable television were, those broadcast from Holland. Many of the Dutch programmes were made in America or the UK, all with the original English dialogue and Dutch subtitles.

The German broadcasters, however, dubbed all of their programmes. I think it must have been in 1982, when the British Forces Broadcasting Service (BFBS) began to deliver a microwave *Live Link* service from the UK that initially gave us the main news bulletins, some soaps and a few other programmes. The microwave transmitter for Goch and Weeze was positioned at Laarbruch. Unfortunately, there were no TV aerials in any of the married quarters in Goch.

However, the problem was solved by fitting one myself. I also fitted a splitter box and ran the cable from the box to Doug and Brenda's, so that they too could watch UK TV as well. They didn't get to see too many UK programmes because they, and their two tearaways, returned to the UK and we met our new neighbours, Alex and Ann Finlayson and their son Greg who were absolutely brilliant.

The summers in Goch were usually very hot and most evenings, once the boys were in bed, Trisha and I, instead of watching TV, would often relax in the garden with a bottle of wine. Normally, it wouldn't take too long before Ann would stick her head out of the kitchen, wave another bottle of wine and join us.

When I was around about 9 years old, I joined the Cubs and later on the Scouts and enjoyed the camping experience so much, that I suggested to Trisha that we buy a tent and give it a go on the continent. Neither of us were keen on sleeping on the ground and wanted a fair amount of comfort, so we drove to Gennep, a small town in Holland that sold a good variety of tents.

It didn't take too long for us to decide and we bought a Walker Trailer Tent. We'd never seen anything like it before. The trailer was about 5 feet wide by 6 feet long with two folding platforms that tripled the overall width of the tent; under which there were two separate sleeping areas. When the awning was added, the overall length more than doubled which gave the capability of sleeping up to 10 people.

The top end of the trailer housed a large portable kitchen, comprising a sink and a three-ring gas burner. I made arrangements for a tow bar to be fitted to the Jetta and rather than make a fool of ourselves in front of other campers, we decided to make a fool of ourselves in front of the neighbours and practised putting up the tent on the grass area in front of the house.

Holidays

Summer 1981. It was just too good an opportunity to miss, the whole of Europe at our disposal, cheap petrol and no English Channel to have to cross. Our first expedition was to a small campsite in Holland where we planned on stopping two nights. We booked in at the site office and were directed to our pitch where we spent a couple of hours erecting the tent and I must admit it went really well.

We decided on having a barbeque, and I soon discovered that I'd left the metal grill at home, the campsite shop didn't have anything suitable and we ended up buying another complete barbeque. I started to assemble it and found that there were several screws missing that held the individual grills in place. Just when I was beginning to feel hacked off, a Dutch caravan pulled up alongside and told us that we were parked on their slot.

That was it—I was all for packing up and going home, but the Dutch couple insisted that as we were only stopping for a short while, they'd park up in an adjacent area. I don't remember what we ate that night, but the BBQ was not a popular choice. We left two days later, and as a thank you to our new Cloggie friends, Trisha gave them a bottle of wine.

We thought after that nightmare scenario, things couldn't possibly get any worse—how mistaken we were. A few weeks later, we ventured further afield and went to *Camping Sonneneck,* situated alongside the river Rhine near Boppard. It was customary, whenever we visited any campsite for our passports to be retained in reception more for security reasons than anything else. We only stayed for two or three days and thoroughly enjoyed the site and what it had to offer.

We'd also got to know another British couple who were school teachers and lived around the Dortmund area. Came the day of departure; we packed up the trailer tent and went to reception to collect our passports. I was given our two documents and I made a cursory glance inside and noticed that they were the passports belonging to the other Brits. As there were no other British campers at the site, it suddenly dawned on the owner that he'd given them our passports.

Fortunately, they'd left only a few minutes earlier, and he, immediately, jumped into his Merc and disappeared at a great rate of knots; eventually, returning a couple of hours later with our passports.

Summer 1982. Our first major camping trip in 1982 was to Bäd Dürkheim, located on the west side of Germany not too far from the Luxemburg and French border. Only this time, we were accompanied by Helen, Morley, John and Ann. John was following us and we were making good time when for some reason or another he decided to overtake me a couple of klicks from an Autobahn Creuz.

I know he wasn't aware that we had to leave the autobahn or where we were heading to and unless I did something drastic, we would lose them (no mobile phones!). The autobahns in Germany were generally all two-lane affairs and in the particular area where we were driving, there was a restriction on towing vehicles (including trailers) from using the left-hand lane.

As I couldn't get out in that lane, I undertook two or three slow vehicles by using the hard shoulder and managed to flash John to pull in behind us. When we eventually arrived at the campsite, it was a fantastically warm sunny afternoon, and everywhere there were other campers lounging outside their tents and caravans. We got a few strange looks when we pulled up especially when 8 people got out of the cars but with only one trailer.

Over the next two hours or so, we got quite an audience as we put together the tent. That evening, we all went for a meal in the campsite restaurant, and once finished, Helen and Morley decided to walk back ahead of the rest of us and go to bed.

We weren't too long behind them and when we opened the tent flap, we were met with howls of laughter and screaming. Morley was hanging onto Helen's legs and she was dangling over the side of the upper sleeping platform. Unfortunately, Morley couldn't hold her and had to drop her. She landed in a heap and ripped up all the tent pegs trying to find her way up.

When she eventually walked around the tent and through the front, she was absolutely knackered but couldn't stop laughing. Apparently, she'd put her handbag under her pillow, and as she got into bed, it had slipped over the side. Instead of waiting until I got back, she and Morley decided on the rescue attempt. God knows what the other campers thought.

The weather for the whole fortnight was exceptional. Trisha and I waited on Helen, Morley, John and Ann hand and foot. John and Ann fancied going to France for the day but got tetchy when we told them we didn't want to go because it wasn't fair on the boys to have to spend more time sitting in a car sightseeing. All the boys wanted to do was to swim and play in the dinghy on the lake—they went on their own.

We moved on and spent a few days at Camping Sonneneck once again, and made sure our passports were looked after. We visited St Goarhasen and located close by was the famous Lorelei. The Lorelei is a rock situated on the eastern bank of the river Rhine some 120 metres above the water and marks the narrowest part of the river between Switzerland and the North Sea.

The very strong currents and rocks below the waterline have caused countless boating accidents. German folklore tells of the beautiful Lorelei who was betrayed by her sweetheart and was accused of bewitching men and causing their deaths. Rather than sentence her to death, the bishop consigns her to a nunnery, and on the way, accompanied by three knights. She asks permission to climb the rock and view the Rhine once more. She did so and fell to her death.

The one sour point of the holiday was when John and Ann decided they were too tired to help clear up after dinner, and went and lay down following our long day of sightseeing. Trisha was absolutely fuming and told Helen and Morley to leave the washing up to John and Ann and they could do it when they felt up to it!

The six of us then sat by the river. When they eventually got up, Helen had a go at John, telling him that it wasn't fair that Trisha and I should do all of the running around.

Ann's only retort was, "But we're on holiday."

Unfortunately, it didn't end there because when we eventually arrived at Goch, we had to completely clear out the trailer and both cars and put everything away. However, Ann went indoors and sat down complaining that she felt dizzy and was too tired to help, but amazingly, made a miraculous recovery once all the work was done.

Our last holiday in the Trailor Tent was to Bavaria. We visited a small campsite very close to Berchtesgarten and despite the fact that the site was busy, we found the perfect place to set up camp—or did we? Our spot gave us the most perfect view down a fairly steep valley and it was later that evening, just before dark, that the heavens opened.

It absolutely poured down and a sight that still lives with me today was watching bolts of lightning striking the sides of the valley. It was early the next morning, that we realised why our spot had been left vacant—following the earlier storm, water from all directions had cascaded down and culminated exactly where we were. Fortunately, we slept off the ground, but nevertheless, several possessions were soaked.

There was one redeeming fact, the weather was glorious and it didn't take long to dry everything. We then noticed that the campsite was situated directly beneath the Kehlsteinhaus (known in English as the Eagle's Nest) a Nazi-constructed building erected atop the summit of the Kehlstein, a rocky outcrop that rises above Obersalzberg.

It was used exclusively by Adolf Hitler and senior members of the Nazi Party for government and social meetings.

Later that day, we met up with another English couple, John and Carol Owen and their two sons Jason and Stevie. They were a fantastic family, and we spent the next few days together visiting the Eagles Nest before moving on to Lake Bodensee (Lake Constance) and Neuschwanstein Castle near Füssen where the film 'Chitty Chitty Bang Bang' was filmed.

Travel was so easy on the autobahns and we made the most of the duty-free petrol allowance by travelling far and wide. On one occasion, we left early in the morning and drove to the USAF base at Ramstein, a mere 200 miles away just to do a bit of shopping in the American Base Exchange. There was almost always a host of the latest American-electrical devices on sale, unfortunately, most operated off 115vts however there were some which ran off 240vts.

I could get into the BX on my service I.D. card and Trisha and the boys had their passports endorsed as families of Allied Forces Personnel. Once upon a time, the commissary at Ramstein was *the* place to go for food (steaks, etc.). Unfortunately, that privilege was withdrawn shortly before we arrived in Germany; when a busload of families from RAF Wildenrath descended on the facility and quite literally cleaned the place out leaving nothing much for the American families to buy.

On the way home, we diverted to Rüdesheim am Rhine. Trisha had holidayed in the town with some of her friends and wanted to reminisce and specifically revisit the Drosselgasse. The Drosselgasse is one of the most famous streets in the world and is situated in Rüdesheim's old quarter. From early afternoon until after midnight, live bands play popular music including brass and dance as well as serving regional dishes and local wine.

It was whilst we were on our way home having visited the UK that we had our one and only brush with the Polizei. We were driving past Weeze; keeping to what I believed was the speed limit of 60 kph, when I was overtaken by a police vehicle. He must have been hiding because the first I was aware of was when an illuminated *lollipop* was stuck out of the driver's window as he overtook me.

The wand was waved in such a manner that I knew I had to pull over. The policeman, who spoke very good English, told me that I'd been speeding and I had to pay an on-the-spot fine of 50 DM. I'd previously been warned not to argue and just pay up, and managed to just scrape together enough to pay. I was absolutely convinced that I'd not been speeding.

However, it wasn't until a few days later that I was told that before we left for England the speed limit on that particular stretch of road, which I'd used countless times before, was 60 kph but had been reduced to 50 kph whilst we were away—typical!

The service medical facilities were generally top-rate; unfortunately, the same couldn't be said of *some* of Laarbruch's military doctors. We had to take Steven to the medical centre late one evening because he was repeatedly sick and struggled to keep anything down. There was always a medic on duty, who, if the need arose, would contact the duty doctor at his home for advice. And on that particular night, it was the Sergeant medic who really should have stayed at home.

We went through the normal question and answer process and I got the impression that he thought he was God's gift to the medical profession; especially, when he authoritatively suggested that because Steven had drunk some milk and later orange juice he was suffering from a classic case of curdled milk!

Trisha wasn't happy and asked that the duty doctor be contacted. We didn't hear the telephone conversation but within a few minutes, the idiot returned and told us that his diagnosis was correct. Steven had an uncomfortable night and come the morning, he was still retching and we were forced to take him back to the medical centre, the revised diagnosis—Gastroenteritis.

Not content with worrying us about *normal* childhood illnesses, Steven decided to go one better and cause us some serious concerns for his health. When he began to hallucinate, became confused and disoriented, couldn't tolerate light and developed a stiff neck. Trisha took him to a clinic that was held every weekday morning at Goch's Deutsche Kaserne (German Army Barracks).

The RAF duty doctor thought he was suffering from a viral infection that would clear itself in due course. However, he contacted Wegberg Hospital for a second opinion and then told us to get Steven to the hospital without delay. By the time we got to Wegberg, the doctors were waiting and immediately took him from us and carried out a lumbar puncture.

They needed to establish if Steven had contracted meningitis and unless that was confirmed very quickly it could become life-threatening because of the proximity of any inflammation to the brain and spinal cord. As far as I can remember, the spinal fluid was clear although there was some inflammation of the lining of the brain. He was admitted to the children's ward until things had calmed down. I believe he spent almost a week in the hospital.

Our last out-of-hours visit to Laarbruch's medical centre was on Christmas Eve 1982, and by the time we got home again, it was the early hours of Christmas day. Both Michael and Steven didn't seem to be tired and, in an effort to get them to bed quickly, I told Trisha that I think I may have heard Santa's sleigh bells in the distance deathly silence.

I went into another room and very gently jangled the bells from the Angel Chimes and the boys were up the stairs like a flash.

Goch was located in the Nordrhein-Westfalen region of Germany which bordered Holland and the area witnessed some of the fiercest fighting following the Allied invasion of Europe on the 6 June 1945. Many of the dead were buried in cemeteries that today are maintained by the Commonwealth War Graves Commission. The closest to Goch was the Reichwald Forest War Cemetery which we visited several times.

It was a very sobering experience to walk amongst the headstones and to learn that the majority of those whose bodies were interred there were very young, and most in their late teens and early to mid-20s. There were also several war museums in the area, whose sole purpose was to act as a reminder of the horrors of war, and keep alive the memories of those who gave their lives.

The Reichwald Forest War Cemetery

The Reichwald Forest War Cemetery is situated five kilometres southwest of Kleve (Henry VIII's fourth wife *Anne of Cleves* came from the town). It was created after the Second World War, when bodies were brought in from all over western Germany, and is the largest Commonwealth cemetery in the country. Some of those members of the land forces buried there died in the advance through Reichwald Forest in February 1945.

Others died crossing the Rhine; among them members of the airborne forces whose bodies were brought from Hamminkeln, where landings were made by the 6th Airborne Division from bases in England. Some of the airmen buried in the cemetery lost their lives supporting the advance into Germany, but most died earlier in the war in the intensive air attacks over Germany.

Their graves were brought in from cemeteries and isolated sites in the surrounding area. There are now 7,594 Commonwealth servicemen of the Second World War buried or commemorated in the cemetery, including 79 war graves of other nationalities, most of them Polish, and 176 of the burials are unidentified.

Overloon National War and Resistance Museum

The museum is situated in Holland some 40 km south of Nijmegen, and consists of a 35-acre park, which is the very location of one of the fiercest tank battles of World War II. Here, the American 7th Armoured Division and the British Infantry met with stubborn resistance from the Germans and fought for

20 days in 1944. The Allies had not come up against such hostile opposition since June, on the beaches of Normandy.

Their losses included three aircraft, some forty tanks and 1,878 men. The Germans lost about 600 men and a number of tanks. Harry van Daal, a citizen of Overloon, was so shocked by the events that had taken place, that he proposed preserving part of the battlefield and erecting a museum on it as a monument.

On 25 May 1946, General Whistler, the commanding officer of the British troops who recaptured Overloon, officially opened the museum; where visitors can wander through the park and encounter tanks, planes, guns, antitank devices and many other remnants of World War II.

The Airborne Museum and the War Cemetery at Oosterbeek

Following the Normandy landings of June 1944, the Allied advance through northern Europe was extraordinarily rapid and on 11 September 1944, the Second Army entered the Netherlands just south of Eindhoven, the first Allied troops to set foot in the country since its fall in May 1940. Their next aim was to cross the Rhine before the Germans had time to reorganise after their recent setbacks, securing crossings over the rivers and canals that stood in their path at Grave, Nijmegen and Arnhem.

In September 1944, the Allies launched *Operation Market Garden,* a major offensive from the Dutch-Belgian border across the south of the Netherlands through Eindhoven and Nijmegen toward the Rhine Bridge at Arnhem; with the goal of crossing the river and bypassing the Siegfried Line in preparation for the final drive towards Berlin.

The operation would involve the United States 82nd and 101st Airborne Divisions, the Commonwealth 1st Airborne Division and the Polish Parachute Brigade. On 17 September 1944, the 1st Airborne Division began landing west of Arnhem, but German resistance, bad weather and problems with supplies and reinforcements led to heavy losses and their objectives were not taken. They were forced to form a perimeter at Oosterbeek which they stubbornly held until 25 September; when it was decided to withdraw the remnants of the division across the lower Rhine.

The museum *Hartenstein* in Oosterbeek is a museum dedicated to the Battle of Arnhem, fought in September 1944. During the battle, the building was the headquarters of the British forces fighting in and around Oosterbeek and Arnhem. The museum shows a diverse and extensive collection of original weapons, tanks, uniforms and equipment, alongside interviews, pictures and videos about the battle.

Arnhem Oosterbeek War Cemetery contains the graves of most of those killed during the September landings and many of those killed in later fighting in the area. There are now 1,680 Commonwealth servicemen buried or commemorated in the cemetery, 245 of the burials are unidentified, two casualties are commemorated by special memorials, and there are 73 Polish burials and eight Dutch graves.

One of the many advantages of living in married quarters, especially when serving abroad, is the fact that most of the accommodation would be subject to fairly regular redecorating programmes. One such spruce-up in Feld Strasse involved the painting of the walls and skirting boards. The German civilian painters duly arrived and once they'd finished in the main rooms, rolled up the stair carpet and left the roll on the landing.

They then painted the walls and the end of each step from bottom to top. We were advised to walk only in the centre of the stairs, and they would return the following day and refit the stair carpet.

The contractors eventually turned up and secured the carpet. It was later that evening that Trisha noticed a large portion of the wall at the top of the stairs hadn't been painted. The strange thing was that the unpainted portion matched exactly where the rolled-up carpet had been lying—the lazy gits had merely painted around it!

One of the other duties we carried out in the CRIST was safety and radiation leakage checks on microwave ovens held in various messes throughout RAF Germany. We also used to unofficially carry out the same checks, when requested, on domestic microwave ovens.

I received a call from the boss telling me that there was a new piece of RF test equipment, the NARDA, on the market which we'd require for checking high-power RF sources and that I was to go to RAF Locking near Weston-Super-Mare and attend a one-day training course. Rather than go through the nausea of arranging flights, I decided to drive and take Trisha and the boys along and intended to drop them off with Mum at Durrington whilst I went on to Locking.

I was the sole attendee on the course, which was run by a Group Captain medical officer and whilst the training was intense in the time available, I learnt sufficient to be competent in the equipment use. Just before I left, I was asked to take a complete test system back to Laarbruch and was advised that I could make a claim for the carriage of service equipment in a private vehicle. The kit took up about half of the boot space!

When I arrived at Laarbruch and I first registered the equipment with the test equipment coordinator, I submitted the transport claim. Imagine my surprise when the claims section refused to pay and argued that I hadn't received prior authorisation from them. Whilst it wasn't a great deal of money, I challenged the decision and stated that when the Group Captain gave me the equipment, the last thing I was interested in was asking him if he had the authority. I never did get paid.

Prior to leaving for RAF Gatow on my last visit, I was asked to take along the NARDA and carry out a leakage check on the industrial microwave oven held in the airmen's mess. Apart from the fact that the oven was in a pretty grotty state; with a lot of food debris inside and around the door, there was a massive leak from around the door seal and no amount of cleaning would reduce the level of leakage.

I warned one of the cooks that it was too dangerous to use and by way of making sure that they didn't use it again, I removed the complete power cable. They weren't happy but when I told them it would be infinitely cheaper to buy a new one than try to repair it, they reluctantly agreed.

My tour length at Laarbruch was for three years. Although, I did manage to get a two-month extension to allow for a proper handover to my replacement. Under normal circumstances, protocol dictated that reasonable notification would be given prior to a posting. However, the first indication that I had was when I was called to Cosford for an interview; which meant only one thing—instructor duties!

I was told by colleagues who had been instructors that there was very little I could do to get out of it. I subsequently flew to the UK and caught a train to Cosford arriving late afternoon. My interview was scheduled for mid-morning the next day, and for what it was worth the MoD could have saved a lot of money and me a lot of time. I was introduced to a Squadron Leader who had my full-service history in front of him and he asked me what I thought about becoming an instructor.

I had earlier thought about pulling the race trick insofar as telling them that I couldn't possibly teach ethnics (although I don't believe that word was in the vocabulary then). I even considered carrying out the interview with an acute stutterer but decided against both options. One concern I had centred on my ability to stand in front of a class of students and spout.

However, because I'd struggled as a student with some of the more detailed, technical aspects of electrical and electronic theory, I felt distinctly uneasy at the prospect of teaching those same principles to people who had infinitely more qualifications than I had. I was reassured by the fact that most people have the same misgivings and following formal training, who knows, I might even get to enjoy the experience.

Without further ado, I was told that I was an ideal candidate and bid goodbye. The interview lasted for approximately 20 minutes, and I think the same effect could have been achieved by carrying it out over the phone, instead of dragging me all the way from Germany. If anyone had told me when I left Cosford in January 1971 that one day I'd return as an instructor, I would have had them certified.

Our first march-out from an overseas posting went without a hitch. The house was cleaned from top to bottom, handed over to the Barrack Warden who complimented us.

Chapter Fourteen
Royal Air Force Station Cosford

(4 November 1983 to 3 December 1986)

I'm not sure if airmen's married quarters were in short supply or not, but a few officer's houses on Lancaster Road had been set aside for SNCOs. The house was enormous and we still had to rely on some items of barrack furniture just to try and fill it. I don't believe the place had been lived in for a while because it was cold and to a certain degree it felt damp.

The heating comprised of an open coal fire in the lounge (the back boiler had been taken out), hot water and downstairs central heating was provided by an oil burner. There was no heating in the bedrooms apart from wall-mounted electric bar fires and a similar device in the bathroom, each bedroom also had a sink. I don't know who selected the carpets in the lounge, but whoever it was, clearly hadn't considered the effect that an open coal fire would have on a white carpet!

Later that day, Pickfords arrived and we were both surprised to see our belongings had been taken out of the sealed containers and were loose in the removal van. I questioned why and was told that as there were no vans available that could accommodate the containers; our items were removed and placed in a normal van. I couldn't prove otherwise and reluctantly had to accept what I was told.

We'd barely finished unpacking when I was awoken early one morning by the sound of sirens from a fire engine followed by a knock at the door. When I opened it, I was greeted by a callout marshall telling me that an exercise had been called and I was to report to my place of duty; as I hadn't the faintest idea where I'd be working, I went back to bed! Trisha eventually got the house into some semblance of order; Michael was registered at the junior school in Albrighton and my disembarkation leave was over.

Helen and Morley spent Christmas with us and whilst we enjoyed their company, they later said that they wouldn't visit us again because it was absolutely freezing. The windows throughout were metal framed and in most cases, there was a gap between the actual frame and the window which allowed cold air to billow through.

The only way to stop the draughts was to fill the gaps with copious amounts of cotton wool. On one occasion we awoke to find ice on the *inside* of the windows and the dripping tap in our bedroom sink was frozen solid.

Gnat Line

I was to be employed on Gnat Line, a small section comprising one Chief Technician and four Sergeants; jointly responsible for instructing trainees in the various techniques associated with the ground-handling of aircraft. The section was located in an old-fashioned single-story wooden hut on the airfield very similar to those seen in the *Battle of Britain* film.

The building had two offices, a classroom, a student's tea bar and a room that was used as a first-line office where the necessary aircraft documentation was kept and maintained. Heating for the building was provided by wall-mounted electric heaters. But in the line office, there was a very old-fashioned wood/coal burner situated in the centre of the room with the chimney sticking out of the roof.

The section had at its disposal six of the ex-Red Arrow display team Folland Gnat aircraft, all of which were fully serviceable and whilst not cleared for flying, the engines could be started and the aircraft taxied. I sat in on several classes making copious notes on what was to be covered, observing the various teaching techniques and participating in the practical lessons.

But before I could be let loose on a class of my own, I had to pass the infamous TIT (Trade Instructional Techniques) course. The RAF, in its infinite wisdom, had decided that two weeks was sufficient to train us in the art of teaching, and hopefully, make us proficient in the task.

But before I attended the course there was the small matter of the married quarter and the ridiculous amount of money, we were throwing away just trying to stay warm. It was time to move out and buy our own home. However, as usual, finance was a problem. Apart from a branch of Lloyds bank, Cosford also had its own Building Society Centre which was managed by an ex-RAF man, Chalky White.

Trisha and I met with Chalky who recommended we start a 25-year low-cost endowment scheme. The plan was for us to pay a standard monthly insurance premium and once a mortgage had been arranged, we would only pay the interest of the loan with the capital being paid off when the insurance policy matured. In addition, there would also be a substantial lump sum.

The beauty (then) of the scheme was that if we were to move back into married quarters, we could continue to pay the insurance premiums, build up a cash lump sum as well as having life insurance. And so, for the princely sum of £32 per month, we signed up with *Standard Life* which gave us cover for a mortgage of up to £25,000 and we started house hunting.

We decided on a small 3-bedroom link-detached house (each house being separated by a garage) in the nearby market town of Newport. The repayments for a £22,500 mortgage were reasonable and in March 1984 we moved into 40 Oak Avenue.

Partway through the house purchase process, I left for the TIT course. I was to attend course number 462 which was held at RAF Newton and was structured such that following the introduction by the training staff we were split into syndicates. Over the following two weeks, we were required to prepare and deliver several lessons to our fellow classmates. The lesson content was our choice and didn't have to be trade-related.

The first lesson was to last for approximately five minutes; with each subsequent lesson lasting a little longer and the course culminated (as far as I can remember) in a 20-minute lesson being given to the entire course. We were advised that for every 10 minutes of lesson time, at least 1 hour of preparation time was required.

As there were no computers or PowerPoint Presentations available, course material (handouts) had to be handwritten and all text and graphics had to be put onto transparent slides and presented on an overhead projector.

One of the first things we were taught was the difference between a lecturer and a teacher. It was impressed on us that both sources may well deliver the necessary information, but a lecturer merely spouts information and doesn't receive any direct feedback from the class, and therefore, cannot fully assess if the students have grasped what's being taught. The onus is on the student to get the information he needs.

Whereas a teacher will engage with the student. I've sat through courses where the teacher has thrown an open question in the hope that someone will reply, and if nobody responded, the answer would be given. The main problem with that technique is that lazy students will always rely on someone else to respond.

However, we were taught a tried and tested method which entails asking a question and nominating someone to answer (putting hands up was not allowed). That way, everyone has to pay attention never knowing whether or not they'll be next *picked on* to answer a question.

Adequate preparation for a lesson was essential, and I soon began to realise what those people I'd seen returning to the classroom each evening whilst on my management course, were actually doing. They were still putting together the material for the next day's lesson. I too had to return most evenings but always gave myself a cut-off time of about 21:00 and not work past that time (it also always gave me time to get a beer or two in the mess).

We were also advised that once the lesson was more or less ready, not to fall into the trap of starting to make changes. There had been cases where students had made changes which altered the whole theme or context of the lesson, and subsequently, ended up going round and round in circles, and basically, not having a subject to teach.

Whilst everyone was anxious when giving their lessons, nothing compared to the state that one of my syndicate colleagues got into. He found acute difficulty in presenting his specialist subject (I think, he worked in Air Traffic Control). He stumbled, hesitated, sweated profusely and really was a nervous wreck. No amount of coaxing or support from the rest of our syndicate seemed to help.

As a way of getting through the final lesson, he made an appointment with the doctor who prescribed him Valium, in the hope that he could relax—how ridiculous! On the final day, he popped a pill and gave a reasonable lesson. Unfortunately, the hierarchy decided that he shouldn't be reliant on the drug just to be able to give a lesson, and he, subsequently, failed the overall course.

I think that of all the courses I've attended whilst in the RAF, the TIT course was probably one of the most demanding. Anyway, I passed it and was deemed suitable to be let loose on the unsuspecting trainees.

I assumed the techniques being taught were the universal methods of engaging with the class and getting the message across to the students. However, once the TIT course was over, whenever I attended any subsequent courses or presentations, I couldn't help but mentally criticise the instructor for faults in their technique, and I'm sure they would have been equally critical of mine.

On my return to Gnat Line, I was given the opportunity to sit in on a couple more courses before taking a class of my own. We taught from a master set of OHP slides and notes, there was no need for me to prepare my own.

The two-day course started with a couple of hours of classroom work discussing the finer points of aircraft towing, ground-handling and the use of Ground Support Equipment (GSE). This was followed by a session where the students would hand manoeuvre (push) an aircraft around the hangar trying not to damage their aircraft and others that were parked. One of the main points taught was the phenomenon known as *Swept Wing Growth*.

During aircraft ground movements, whether being taxied or towed, the wing tip clearance is not always constant and this fact is more noticeable with aircraft whose wings are not perpendicular to the airframe but *sweep* backwards. Wing tip growth has to do with the *at-rest* wing tip clearance.

For example, a hangar wall or other obstruction, and the fact that when pivoted on its main wheels, the wing tip appears to grow in span when turning which ultimately decreases the overall clearance as the wing tip arc moves outward. The VC10 aircraft has always been a good example.

The afternoon session began with classroom instruction on the Gnat engine startup and shutdown procedures, hand signals, the use of the relevant GSE, emergency procedures and the use of the portable CO_2 aircraft fire extinguisher. In the meantime, the aircraft and ground equipment would be towed out to the ground running pan and positioned ready for the practical lesson by two other instructors.

The main method of starting the Gnat engine was by a Palouste, a small, extremely noisy, portable jet engine whose primary purpose was to deliver a high flow rate of compressed air which would initially turn over the aircraft engine. Once the basic classroom work was complete, the instructor would make his way to the Gnat and carry out a pre-ground run safety check, climb into the cockpit and prepare for the engine ground runs.

The students, in the meantime, were being reminded of how to operate the Palouste and were given a résumé of the procedures they were to carry out. There were typically 8-10 students per class. Each in turn had to act as the aircraft ground handler, Palouste operator and fire extinguisher safety man—there were always two instructors to cover the three positions.

The purpose of this element of the course was to familiarise the students with starting an aircraft engine safely and, despite the surrounding noise and other potential distractions, be able to confidently and firmly signal to the pilot what was happening in the immediate environment.

Hand marshalling signals are the chief means of providing critical communication to the pilots and the safe operation of the aircraft. Once all the relevant internal safety checks had been carried out, and the canopy closed and secured, the Palouste was started and the instructor in the cockpit would signal to the handler, who was stood immediately in front of the aircraft; that the engine was ready to be started.

The student, having ascertained that the area was safe, would give a confirmation signal, the instructor would raise his right thumb in the direction of the Palouste operator and (with his left hand on the throttle lever) depress his right thumb which was the signal for the air to be delivered.

The engine igniter button would be depressed and at the same time, the throttle lever would be advanced. Once the engine had eventually stabilised at *Ground Idle,* the handler would be signalled to disconnect the Palouste hose. It was vitally important that the Palouste operator remember to switch off the compressed air before disconnecting the hose, otherwise, it would snake and flay everywhere.

Once everyone was clear of the aircraft, the signal was given to check the function of the flaps by lowering and raising them and provided there were no obstructions the handler would confirm as appropriate. By way of ensuring that he was aware of what was happening, there would be occasions when the flaps would not be fully retracted. It was the handler's responsibility to alert the instructor in the cockpit to that effect by signalling non-compliance.

The next signal from the cockpit was to advance the engine to max rpm. The handler was to look around and ensure there was adequate clearance behind the aircraft and, when content, he gave the clearance. The engine throttle would then be advanced and held at max rpm for a minute or so before decelerating back to ground idle and once stabilised, the signal to shut down was given.

The procedure was repeated until all of the students had carried out all three positions. By way of getting the message across that safety is paramount, there were occasions when one of the instructors would deliberately walk towards the rear of the aircraft once clearance for the engine start had been given—the idea was that the handler was to recognise a potential hazard to personnel and stop the startup procedure.

There were times that inadvertent hazards were caused and one of the most spectacular was if the throttle was advanced before the bleed air was delivered and, as a consequence, fuel would build up in the exhaust which would then catch fire once the engine ignited resulting in long sheets of flame coming from the jet pipe. By the end of the first day, the entire class were reasonably proficient and confident in the general ground-handling techniques required.

The second day concentrated on marshalling the aircraft in a confined space. Once again, the day began with a classroom presentation and a precise briefing of what was required. The purpose of this element of the course was to give the trainees a feel of standing in front of a moving aircraft and direct the pilot using hand signals.

Marshallers on an active flying squadron invariably become proficient in the various hand signals associated with a specific aircraft and will eventually become blasé. As far as our students were concerned, our intention was to show them how to use the prescribed marshalling signals, and what they did once on their operational squadrons was of no real concern to us.

The session began with the instructor once again carrying out a complete safety check of the aircraft before climbing into the cockpit and awaiting the arrival of the starter crew. The same start procedure was carried out and once the engine was *burning and turning* the starter crew jumped into the Land Rover and were taken to the marshalling area.

Clearance was then requested from the ATC tower for the Gnat to be taxied. There was no steering wheel in the cockpit, instead the aircraft was turned using the differential braking method. In other words, if the aircraft needed to be turned to the port, the tip of the left rudder pedal was depressed which applied the brakes to that side of the nose wheel which caused the nose to move in that direction.

The marshalling area comprised a long taxiway and a fairly compact area between the hangars—a basic figure of eight. It was always very easy to direct an aircraft that was coming straight towards you; if the aircraft was required to go to the right the marshaller merely pointed with his right hand and waved his left hand, in other words, go in that direction. However, if the marshaller was on the inside of the turn confusion nearly always ensued.

I cannot recall the number of times that the marshaller pointed with his left hand meaning that the aircraft was to go around him, assuming the man in the cockpit would understand what was required. Prior to the exercise, the marshallers were briefed that the man in the cockpit would go in *precisely* the direction we were told to go—even if that meant taxing towards the hangar doors, which on many occasions we did.

As an aide memoir, the students were initially told always to point at the wheel that the aircraft was to *pivot* on and providing they remembered that, there was not normally a problem. Some of the students realised the error of their wayward instruction, whilst others merely waved their arms in a more frantic manner; hoping that the aircraft would eventually turn in the correct direction.

The other instructors would not intervene unless absolutely necessary. However, the man in the cockpit would never compromise the safety of himself, the marshallers or the aircraft. The whole exercise lasted for about an hour and I don't remember any class ever saying they thought that it was a waste of time—all seemed to have enjoyed the experience.

To ensure that we, as instructors, didn't get into any bad habits and were fully conversant with the various emergency procedures associated with operating the aircraft, an annual assessment was carried out by a Squadron Leader pilot from RAF Halton.

During the annual GDT training, great emphasis was always placed on an individual's ability to effectively carry out all elements of first aid. Fortunately, I'd not had to put any of that training into any real practical use; however, during the early part of the summer of 1985, things were to change. Many of the smaller hangers on the airfield had seen better days and were in desperate need of a serious makeover.

The main problem was the rusting of the external steel sheets and the basic internal hangar roof steel support structure. Contractors were brought in who treated the roof structure with anti-corrosion paint and once finished, scaffolding was set up in readiness for the removal of the old single-skinned corrugated panels and replacing them with insulated aluminium panels.

The external work had been going on for a couple of weeks without incident; however, one afternoon whilst I was in the classroom with some students there was a knock at the door. A student from another class burst in and told me that one of the contractors was lying injured on the grass outside the hut. The other Gnat Line instructors were all away. So, I ran outside to find the man on the ground and all his workmates were just standing around not knowing what to do.

He had a massive gash to the side of his head, and burns to his face and hands; he was shaking profusely and obviously in shock. He then began shouting for somebody to do something. I told some of the students to get water and keep dousing the burns whilst I called for an ambulance.

I ran to our office only to find that the telephone wasn't working and the first aid kit didn't have the necessary bandages to treat such a serious head wound. I jumped onto my bike and cycled to the nearest office where I called for assistance.

By the time I got back, the poor fellow was in a real state, fortunately, for him, there was no blood coming from the gouge to his head, but by then, he was in a state of deep shock and extremely pale. The medics duly arrived and bundled him into the ambulance and took him to the medical centre.

Just as the ambulance was leaving, the OC Station Services Squadron (SSS) arrived wanting to know what had happened. I'd spoken with his work colleagues and repeated what I'd been told. The guy had been on the top level of the scaffolding, which was at least 30" off the ground, cutting away some of the old wall support beams with a petrol-driven disc cutter.

Everything was fine until he raised the cutter above his head and inverted it, whereby the petrol gushed out of the tank, spilt over his head and was ignited by the sparks. With his head alight, he dropped the cutter which caught the side of his head causing a deep cut which went right through to his skull although I don't believe it penetrated—he was incredibly lucky.

He then jumped from the scaffolding and on landing, crawled across the grass. It later transpired that he'd shattered both of his heels when he hit the ground.

Two weeks later, I was visited by my boss, Squadron Leader Peck who showed me a letter he'd received from the MD of the company concerned. The letter thanked OC SSS for his prompt action in giving the appropriate first aid and alerting the medics without which the injured man may well have sustained more serious, long-lasting damage and potentially life-threatening injuries—what a bloody cheek! Anyway, S/L Peck duly pointed out that the thanks should have gone to me.

Apart from being drafted into areas of conflict, all vacancies in specialist posts were normally filled by volunteers with the requirements being promulgated via Station Routine Orders (SROs). Early in 1985, an advert appeared asking for a volunteer to join the Kuwait Liaison Team. The vacancy called for a Sergeant air radar engineer with a comprehensive knowledge of the

Hercules aircraft. I don't remember seeing many adverts where I fitted the requirements criteria so exactly and immediately applied.

The accompanied tour of duty was for three years with accommodation and schooling for any children being provided free of charge by the Kuwaiti government. There were only two applicants for the job and both of us were stationed at Cosford.

Following a little bit of *digging around,* I found out that my opposite number was relatively inexperienced and hadn't spent that much time on the Hercules. Whereas, I had spent seven years on the airframe in a multitude of posts and I sincerely believed that the job was mine.

Imagine how pissed off I was when I received notification that I was unsuccessful. It later transpired that my desk officer at PMC had spoken with my Flight Commander, asking for a character reference and my suitability to do the job. Instead of getting in touch with me or checking my record, he merely told PMC that he didn't really know me and therefore couldn't comment. However, the other applicant's boss gave him a glowing report—experience obviously counted for nothing.

It was also in May of 1985 that I received a call from Ian telling me that there was some very good news on the way and went on to mention that he'd recently sat on the Sergeant to Chief Tech promotion board where my name had come to the fore. He immediately pointed out to the other promotion board members that I was his brother and there was the potential for a conflict of interest and asked to be allowed to leave the room.

When he returned, he was told that I was initially placed 33rd in a field of 240 candidates but after reviewing my service record and annual assessments the board decided to raise my position to number 11; there were to be only 40 promotions that year. Ian advised me not to mention anything and to act surprised when the notification eventually came through.

Sure enough, a couple of weeks later, I was summoned to S/L Peck's office and told that I'd been selected for promotion and duly signed the acceptance form—surprised or what? There was no mention on the form as to the precise promotion date but I was advised that I'd be notified by PMC in due course. The weeks went by and there was still no sign of when I was to be promoted.

I happened to be in the general office on 17 July on a completely unrelated enquiry and asked my desk manager if PMC had been in touch, imagine my surprise when I was told that the promotion was effective from *that day.* I immediately went to stores, picked up a couple of sets of Chief Tech shoulder tabs and went back to work.

When I mentioned the news to the rest of the section, there were congratulations all around and then Jeff bollocked me for being incorrectly dressed. I wasn't wearing the correct rank badges! As I didn't have a needle and cotton to hand, I stapled the rank tabs together which did the job until I got home.

So, there I was, a newly promoted C/T and loving every minute of it. A call came later that same morning from Ted Bottomley, who worked on the maintenance section, asking for someone to drop off the Palouste outside one of the hangars in preparation for some ground runs later that morning. I cordially obliged and returned to the Gnat Line.

Shortly before lunch Jeff was called to our admin office and informed that several cars had been severely damaged that were parked outside the workshop's classrooms. It turned out that the maintenance boys hadn't moved the Gnat and the ground equipment to the authorised concrete pan, but had, instead, carried out the ground run outside of the hangar on the tarmac!

The jet pipe on the Gnat was oriented such that it pointed downwards at an angle of about 30°; something that was obviously not considered because once the aircraft engine was started and run for several minutes, the tarmac began to melt and was blasted towards the cars that were parked about 50 yards away.

As is the norm with any major incident a formal investigation into the circumstances is carried out. Colloquially referred to as a Board of Enquiry, the questions asked were far-reaching and as such I was called to give evidence. When questioned I was asked why I'd positioned the Palouste where I did. My response to the board was that I was asked to deliver the equipment to the requested location and nothing more.

I was then asked if I'd considered that the ground runs may well be carried out alongside the hangar. Once again, I reiterated that my responsibility ended at the drop-off point. I naturally *assumed* that the maintenance boys would tow the aircraft and ground equipment to the ground running pan, and that they would have enough intelligence not to run the aircraft where they subsequently did.

The moral to that story, from my perspective was, *Never assume, check*. I don't remember the overall outcome of the enquiry, but I was absolved of any blame.

It was shortly after that incident that I was told of my impending move to RAF Stanley in the Falkland Islands.

Chapter Fifteen
Royal Air Force Station Stanley

(22 July 1985 to 9 October 1985)

The Falkland Islands are approximately 8000 miles from the UK and the only major island group in the South Atlantic, about 300 miles east of Argentina and the continent of South America in the Strait of Magellan. There are two main islands, West and East Falkland and more than 100 smaller ones. The Buenos Aires government, which had declared its independence from Spain in 1816, claimed sovereignty over the Falklands.

Britain began settling the islands and declared a colonial administration in 1842. Argentina never recognised the claim and historically has demanded that the islands be part of that nation. They say that *Ownership is 90% of the law*, and the islands have been continuously occupied by residents who have always demanded the right to remain British subjects.

The islands were occupied by the forces of Argentina's Military Junta on 2 April 1982 following the country's fading public support for military rule, and so the leadership decided to engage in popular theatrics. Argentina had never been happy with our long-standing occupation of the Falklands, or Malvinas as the islands are known in Argentina, and it seemed like a simple enough exercise.

The islands were small, the main industry was sheep-herding and it was assumed that it would be extremely difficult, expensive and too risky to try and conduct a military campaign over such an enormous distance. It was further assumed that Britain would do no more than bluster.

However, General Galtieri severely underestimated the will of our Prime Minister, Margaret Thatcher, in a way that even her most contemptuous enemies back home wouldn't have considered. After various ultimatums were ignored, Britain's military machine went into top gear, throwing together a counter-invasion fleet in a round-the-clock effort.

The Vulcan bomber was also seen as a useful asset for the conflict. Five B2s were selected to fly under Number 101 Squadron in the *Black Buck* campaign, as it was codenamed, with a mad scramble to get the aircraft ready for operations. The idea was to operate the Vulcans out of Wideawake Airfield on Ascension Island in the mid-Atlantic for strikes on the Falklands. Even from Ascension, it was a long journey and numerous Victor tankers would be needed in stages to provide in-flight refuelling support.

During the Falklands War, there had been several complaints from the troops that their DMS boots had let in water causing severe cases of trench foot. The troops had just cause to complain following the incredible distances, walked prior to re-taking Port Stanley and the two expressions that epitomise that incredible feat are *Yomping* and *Tabing*.

A Yomp is a Royal Marine expression describing a long-distance march carrying full kit. It has been suggested that the term is an acronym for *Your Own Marching Pace*. Whereas the army's slang for the same march is a Tab being an abbreviation for Tactical Advance into Battle (the Americans refer to these as *Slogs* or *Humps*).

The most famous Yomp took place following the disembarking from British ships at San Carlos on East Falkland on 21 May 1982 when Royal Marines and members of the Parachute Regiment yomped with their equipment across the island; covering 56 miles in three days each carrying 80 pounds of equipment.

The original battle plan was for a fleet of helicopters to transport the ground troops from the landing sites in preparation for the ground assault on Stanley. On board, the merchant ship Atlantic Conveyor were six Wessex helicopters whose parent squadron was 848 Naval Air Squadron, five RAF HC1 Chinooks from 18 Squadron, eight Fleet Air Arm Sea Harriers and six RAF GR3 Harriers.

When the ship arrived in the South Atlantic, the GR3 jump jets were off-loaded to the aircraft carrier HMS Hermes, whilst the naval jets were divided between HMS Hermes and HMS Invincible. Only one Chinook was flown off before the Atlantic Conveyor was sunk by two Excocet missiles launched from Argentine Super Étendard jet fighters resulting in the deaths of twelve sailors and the loss of the entire cargo.

I received my drafting notification in the spring of 1985 and due to my previous experience on the Sea King helicopter I was posted to RAF Stanley and employed on the Helicopter Servicing Flight (HSF). There was also a Sea King search and rescue contingent based at Navy Point, located across Stanley Sound, directly opposite the town of Stanley.

My tour of duty was for four months and at the time of my notification, personnel were still being flown to Wideawake Airfield on Ascension Island in the mid-Atlantic and then embarking on a ship ready for a two-week *cruise* to the Falklands.

The only airfield in operation at the time was at Stanley Airfield although the new Mount Pleasant Airfield (MPA) was nearing completion. MPA was to be opened by Prince Andrew on 12 May 1985, before becoming fully operational the following year.

I was picked up from Cosford and driven to RAF Innsworth in Gloucester where I was equipped with the necessary cold-weather clothing and my *worm* (sleeping bag) before heading off to Brize Norton. Imagine my surprise on arriving at the airhead to learn that my flight was amongst the first to fly directly to the Falklands.

The scheduled 18-hour flight was on-board a Jumbo that took us from Brize to Wideawake Airfield on Ascension Island. We stopped there for a couple of hours, whilst the aircraft was refuelled and loaded with supplies. In that time, we were fed and managed to get a couple of beers.

It was the first time I'd flown in a 747 and the first time I'd experienced in-flight entertainment, in fact, I watched 'Beverley Hills Cop' which had only recently been released in the UK. The only downside to the trip was the fact that smoking was still allowed!

We arrived at MPA in the late morning (the islands were four hours behind GMT), and once disembarked, we were immediately given a comprehensive brief on the numerous hazards associated with unexploded ordinance located around the island. The Argees assumed that the Brits would launch their attack along the east coast of East Falkland and subsequently heavily mined the entire area.

Apart from the minefields, it was also believed that the Argees had left several booby traps in the surrounding hills and countryside that were potentially still active; the advice given:

Watch where you walk, don't touch anything you're not sure of, and even if you think you're sure the item isn't a bomb, still don't touch it.

Following the briefing, we boarded buses and were driven 30 miles to RAF Stanley. The arrivals process was simplicity in itself and I was taken to the RAF's floating accommodation block commonly referred to as a *Coastel* which was moored in one of the bays close to Stanley Airfield. The Blue Coastel was one of the first floating accommodation blocks to be provided and was occupied by the RAF.

This view is taken from the dirt track road which connected the Coastel to RAF Stanley Airfield. The small dark blue building on the right-hand side, in the foreground, is the Sergeants' mess.

I was met off the bus by a member of HSF who took me to the Sergeant's mess deck where I warned-in and was shown to my room. It really was fortunate that I didn't suffer from claustrophobia. The room was small with very basic amenities comprising four built-in bunk beds, two on one side of the room and two opposite, a table and one chair.

There were four floor-to-ceiling built-in metal wardrobes and a separate combined toilet, shower and washroom. There was one window; unfortunately, there was nothing to see because it looked out onto a solid steel framework.

When I arrived, it was about 14:00 and all four bunks had their individual curtains drawn.

I naturally assumed that three of the bunks were probably occupied by people sleeping off nights and as I hadn't a clue which was mine, rather than disturb anyone, I left my bags and wandered around the Coastel for a while. When I returned there was still no sign of life and so I sat down and waited and waited.

After about half an hour as I couldn't hear signs of breathing or movement, I gingerly pulled back one of the curtains only to find the bunk empty, in fact, all four bunks turned out to be empty! It was an hour or so later, my two roommates arrived from work and following introductions, I was given a guided tour of the facilities and later went to dinner.

That evening, I met up with several of the other SNCOs from HSF in the mess bar and following a few beers, and another comprehensive brief explaining the daily routine, I'd had enough and went to bed.

The next morning, following breakfast I left the Coastel and was met by the SWO who took his position at the top of the gangplank each day. The aim was to make sure that everyone was correctly dressed including ensuring our boots were clean. A bollocking was guaranteed if there was the slightest sign of none compliance!

HSF accommodation comprised of several linked porta cabins which were used for offices and a tea bar. The engineering facility was housed inside two adjacent very large, inflatable *Rubs* (rubberised hangars) that could comfortably house a Sea King, one Chinook, and comprehensive store facilities with all power and heating being provided by portable external units.

There were no shifts associated with HSF. Everyone worked straight days with one day off a week. As there was very little to do in the spare time the *no-shift* pattern was designed to keep everyone occupied.

The beaches surrounding RAF Stanley were absolutely stunning and if it wasn't for the fact that we knew where we were, you could almost imagine that Stanley was situated on a South Seas desert island. The only thing that spoilt the scene was the barbed wire and the DANGER MINES signs.

In a bid to relieve the boredom and monotony of life at RAF Stanley, there were several opportunities to visit some of the more exotic parts of the island. Apart from the military helicopters, there were also a couple of aircraft operated by Bristow's Helicopters affectionately known as *The Erics* (after Eric Bristow, the English darts player).

Whilst I'm unsure now as to the precise purpose of their detachment, they regularly flew passengers on sightseeing and Rest and Recuperation (R&R) trips. I managed to get on one such trip to Saunders Island which is located off the northeast coast of West Falkland.

The main attraction was the abundant wildlife and more especially the Penguins and Albatross', neither of which showed any real fear of humans. We were dropped off at the south-end tip of the island and left to our own devices.

Shortly after the day trip to Saunders Island, I was given the opportunity to spend a couple of days R&R at a sheep farm on the island. The manager had set aside a small cottage so that personnel could *get away* and experience life on a remote small holding.

There were six of us on the jaunt all equipped with our worms and sufficient Compo rations to last the stay. We were picked up from Stanley and flown to the farm on board a Chinook, having earlier landed at Kelly's Garden to drop off supplies for the RAF personnel based there.

As we watched, the Chinook disappear into the distance, we all became acutely aware of the noise—or lack of it! On board the Coastel, in the Sergeants' mess, inside the Rub, HSF Offices or the feeders in fact almost everywhere we went there was noise.

If it wasn't the rumblings from the various power generators or air-conditioning plants, the racket came from aircraft taxying, taking off, landing or overflying—there was never total silence, day or night. It was the first time in several weeks that the senses weren't accosted and as we stood there; I could well imagine what it must be like to be deaf.

We were met by the farm manager and shown to our *accommodation* which comprised of a kitchen, a small living room and a couple of bedrooms. I don't remember what the toilet or washing facilities comprised of but I know we managed. The only heating in the house was being provided by an open fire with the peat *logs* being provided by the farmer and were stacked outside under cover.

I'd never used peat as a heating source and was quite surprised at how much warmth was given off. By the time we awoke in the morning, the fire had more or less died, and as there was no heating in the bedrooms, it was absolutely freezing. Sleeping inside my worm was warm and comfortable. However, on both mornings I awoke to find frost on the inside of the bedroom windows and whenever I breathed out there were dramatic clouds of frosty breath.

I'd never really considered that pigs were carnivorous. I'd always associated their feeding habits with what I'd seen at Cholderton in the fields adjacent to Gran Lewis' house. I had only ever seen pigs eating swill and digging about with their snouts in the mud. That was until I witnessed the feeding of a sow and several of her cute little piglets.

The farmer had shot a couple of upland geese and asked if we wanted to see how quickly they'd be devoured. My God, it was like the piglets had never eaten. They tore the geese to pieces, and within a few short minutes, everything except the goose's beaks was gone, bones and all. I'd later heard that if you wanted to murder someone and cleanly dispose of the body—feed it to the pigs!

The majority of the locals in Stanley were really very friendly and accommodating. Although I suspect that after three years of the armed forces their patience, in some areas, was probably being severely tested. That said, the Argie alternative just didn't bear thinking about it.

One of the traits that members of the armed forces seem to have in abundance is the innate ability to latch on immediately to specific circumstances and events and poke fun. This was highlighted shortly after the Argentineans were expelled and the locals were nicknamed *Bennies* due to the similarity to Benny of *Crossroads* fame (a dreadful 1970s afternoon soap that followed the lives of the staff in a small motel situated close to Birmingham).

Benny, as did some members of the Falkland community, wore a woollen hat, spoke with a slow, droll accent and came across as a simpleton. At first, the locals didn't appreciate the connection. However, when they found out, they complained to the military authorities, and in an effort not to upset the natives, orders were given that the term should not be used.

However, the force's instinctive response was then to re-nickname them *Stills*—the rational is that they're still Bennies.

Whilst I obviously knew that I'd not be Yomping, I had no real idea of what my working environment was likely to be. So, before embarking *down south,* I bought myself a pair of Doc Martins boots; they turned out to be invaluable.

Working on HSF was quiet, and during my time, we only had one Sea King scheduled for a *primary servicing.* It was a pleasure to make small jobs last a lot longer than normal. To supplement the work or lack of it, I occasionally went to Navy Point and helped out on the squadron aircraft. Whilst we were required to be at work for six days there was no real objection if personnel requested additional time off to go for a *Bimble* with other members of the flight.

It was only a half-hour walk into Stanley and once through the town, the entire countryside was available to explore. Although it was three years since the war ended there was still a remarkable amount of intact Argentinean hardware on the various hillsides and walkers had to be ever mindful of the potential for booby-trapped items. I managed a couple of bimbles to Mount Tumbledown and the surrounding areas.

The weather on the Falklands islands could change within an instant from being bright, sunny and calm to gusty heavy rain or snow. In a bid to stop walkers from being caught out, the authorities issued orders that if ever any pedestrians flagged down a military vehicle, the driver was to stop and give them a lift back to the airfield.

The photo, a Squaddies Tribute to Port Stanley, was taken from the top of Mount Tumbledown where Stanley can be viewed between the fingers.

The Gurkhas

Better to die than be a coward, is the motto of the world-famous Nepalese Gurkha soldiers who have been an integral part of the British Army for almost 200 years, but who are these fearsome Nepalese fighters?

The name *Gurkha* comes from the hill town of Gorkha from which the Nepalese kingdom had expanded. The potential of these warriors was first realised by the British at the height of their empire-building in the 19th century. The Victorians identified them as a *Martial Race*, perceiving in them particularly masculine qualities of toughness.

After suffering heavy casualties in the invasion of Nepal, the British East India Company signed a hasty peace deal in 1815; which also allowed it to recruit from the ranks of the former enemy. Following the partition of India in 1947, an agreement between Nepal, India and Britain meant four Gurkha regiments from the Indian army were transferred to the British Army, eventually becoming the Gurkha Brigade.

Since then, the Gurkhas have loyally fought for the British all over the world, receiving 13 Victoria Crosses between them. More than 200,000 fought in the two world wars, and in the past 50 years, they have served in Hong Kong, Malaysia, Borneo, Cyprus, the Falklands, Kosovo, Iraq and Afghanistan. They serve in a variety of roles, mainly in the infantry but with significant numbers of engineers, logisticians and signals specialists.

The ranks have always been dominated by four ethnic groups, the Gurungs and Magars from central Nepal, the Rais and Limbus from the east, who live in villages of impoverished hill farmers. They still carry into battle their traditional weapon; an 18-inch-long curved knife known as the Kukri. In times past, it was said that once a Kukri was drawn in battle, it had to *taste blood,* if not, its owner had to cut himself before returning it to its sheath.

Now, the Gurkhas say, it is used mainly for cooking! It has long been a legend of the Falklands War that the Argentines defending Stanley were so terrified of the Gurkhas, that they ran from their positions before the small but ferocious Gurkhas were able to make contact.

I don't know what truth there was in the story, but I was led to believe that shortly before my arrival the RAF Bomb Disposal officer had discovered an unexploded thousand-pound bomb that had failed to detonate, following the bombing of the airfield by the Vulcan. By all accounts, the discovery was the fulfilment of a personal ambition.

I can't remember whether Trisha sent me a tape for my Walkman or whether she wrote to tell me that she'd heard Jennifer Rush's record 'The Power of Love' and she wanted me to listen to the words. They meant such a lot to her and she believed that those words really epitomised the feelings she had for me.

When I first heard the song, it made me feel so very, very special and even today whenever I hear it, it brings a lump to my throat. Words can mean so many different things to people, however 'The Power of Love' really says it all.

RAF Stanley had a small avionics bay whose personnel carried out repairs to the multitude of aircraft equipment. I was summoned for a meeting with the bay OC and informed that an agreement had been reached with HSF that I was to be internally posted. This was based on the fact that as there were no more aircraft scheduled for servicing, my time would be better spent running the bay.

The bay at the time was being prepared for the impending move from RAF Stanley to MPA and was managed by a Sergeant. Whilst I don't remember how many other personnel were employed there; my job was to take over from him so that he could take over the tasks that were carried out by the Corporal, and so on down the chain, until the little man at the end could carry on copying pornographic films for distribution to the outstations on the island!

I was absolutely stunned, not only was I pissed off that I'd been sent to the Falklands only to be bored out of my skull for two months, but now, I was to move to another section and be party to this seedy operation. Now don't get me wrong, I wasn't a prude and I've seen plenty of pornographic films but there was no way on God's earth that I was staying on the island a moment longer than was absolutely necessary.

I decided to try some bullshit of my own and told the Squadron Leader that my religious beliefs (?) forbade me from taking part in anything that bordered on the obscene; Hallelujah, I've seen the light; and if I was forced to stay then the UK press would find out when I eventually returned home—silence. He gave me a look that could have killed.

The religious element was a total fabrication but it had the desired effect because within three weeks, I was told that my tour was being cut short and I was to return to the UK. The comment was made that I had all the makings of becoming a bolshie chief—I couldn't possibly imagine what they meant!

Whilst I was away, life in Newport for Trisha and the boys carried on in much the same way. Unfortunately, Trisha didn't drive and was obviously restricted as to where she could and couldn't go. Fortunately, Steve and Linda Jackson, Jeff and Jeanette Lloyd and a couple of the other neighbours kept an eye on them and helped out where necessary.

Trisha did tell me a really touching story of how she and Steven were at the end of the cul-de-sac talking with the mother of one of Steven's school friends, when the mother said, "Right, I'd better go and get some tea ready for when Johnnie's dad (not his real name but I don't recall what it was) gets home from work."

To that, Steven replied, "I wish my dad was coming home for tea."

By all accounts, Trisha and the other mother almost choked in tears.

My tour lasted for only 79 days and my only real concern was that the time spent wouldn't be classed as a full four-month tour. I was short of the minimum time required by a couple of weeks and there was a strong possibility that I'd return in the future. However, as there weren't many Chief Technician avionics posts, I decided to take a chance and accepted the early release.

I'd been writing most days to Trisha and she managed to follow suit. The mail generally took four to five days from posting in the UK and getting to Stanley, unfortunately, there were many occasions where there wouldn't be a delivery for several days and then numerous letters would turn up at the same time. We both ensured that each letter was numbered sequentially.

Once I'd been given my return flight details, which were approximately two weeks away, I wanted to surprise Trisha. And rather than both of us writing needlessly or worry her unnecessarily when she didn't receive any letters from me, I hatched a plan. I wrote to her and told her that I was going to another part of the Falklands for a short detachment with the Chinooks and as there were very limited postal facilities available. I suggested that she didn't write for a couple of weeks.

At Tourex, all personnel returning to the UK were required to contact their relevant units and arrange for military transport to be made available at Brize Norton. I contacted Jeff Lloyd who agreed to drive from Cosford with Derek

Whittaker in a service car and pick me up. The flight home was comfortable and the one big bonus was that I didn't suffer from vertigo in the same way that it affected me on the outbound journey.

As planned, Jeff and Derek were waiting for me at Brize and we stopped at a pub for some lunch but unfortunately, it wasn't open. I decided to phone Trisha to let her know that I was back in the UK and would be home within a couple of hours.

When she answered the phone all I said was, "Hello, Sweetheart."

There was a long pause and all she said in reply was, "Is that you, Jonathan?"

She always denied ever calling me that, but she did. My plan to surprise Trisha didn't really work because she somehow guessed what I was up to, but to this day, I still don't understand how she knew—female intuition, maybe.

Jeff dropped me off and the welcome home was fantastic. Trisha really was a very passionate kisser! I can't remember which one of the boys arrived home from school first, I think it was Michael. When I heard the front door opening, I hid in the dining room and when he walked in, I popped my head over the table. He just froze and burst into tears.

I think Linda, our next-door neighbour had brought Steven home from school with her daughter Victoria, a little later, and as usual, when he walked through the front door, he was chattering. He still had his coat on with his school bag on his back and as he walked into the dining room, I did the same again and he burst into tears. Were the tears because they were pleased to see me. I'd like to think so.

During my time away, I'd put on over two stone in weight which was due in no small part to each day having a cooked breakfast, a hot lunch and dinner. This would invariably be followed up later in the evening with a few beers and either a curry or chilli or pasties in the mess bar. Boredom is a terrible thing for the waistline.

I'm assuming that was the reason why I wasn't initially recognised because when Trisha took the boys to school the next morning, one of the more inquisitive members of the Oak Avenue community openly asked her who the man was that they'd seen her with the evening before.

Trisha was quite flabbergasted and all she said was, "It was John, of course." Nosey gits!

Chapter Sixteen
Back to Cosford

(9 October 1985 to 2 December 1986)

Air Radio Techniques Flight

It was too much to hope that I'd be posted back onto Gnat Line or indeed onto the airfield as an instructor in one of the hangars, instead, I was posted into the Air Radio Techniques Flight (ARTF). Of all the places that I really struggled with whilst I was an apprentice, ARTF was the one.

And so, after finishing my brief disembarkation leave, I arrived at ARTF, was welcomed by all and given a brief as to the specific areas I was responsible for. Bloody Hell! I couldn't believe what I was expected to teach. I was subsequently given charge of a syndicate that concentrated on the second half of the radar course.

The only saving grace was that I had just over three months to organise my lessons. However, I was given the course content and time to be spent on each subject. The only printed material available was the relevant pre-printed handouts or booklets that covered the specific course element. The format was such that over a three-month period, I had to teach 284 hours of electronic theory and a certain number of practical lessons.

I was so unfamiliar with the basics that I had to carry out an inordinate amount of studying just to be able to understand what I was supposed to be teaching. I then had to prepare tuition notes and the all-important overhead projector slides (no such luxuries as Microsoft PowerPoint Presentations). A detailed knowledge of each subject was absolutely essential because it wouldn't take long for some of the more astute members of a class to pick up that an instructor was flannelling or waffling.

To overcome this potential embarrassment, there was one aspect of my teaching technique that I passed on to each class at the commencement of the course. I told everyone that I wouldn't waffle and if I didn't know the answer to a question, I'd find out before the start of the next lesson.

I can't remember the number of times I'd go back to the crew room for a tea break or lunch and collar Ron Holland; a very pleasant and capable civilian instructor. He helped me enormously and I can't thank him enough.

The subjects I was expected to teach for the first half of my element of the course included transmission lines, electronic filters and aerials, transmitter principles, power amplifiers, AM and FM principles, pulsed radar and delay lines, modulators and power supplies.

Once these subjects were covered and everyone had passed the various slip tests required, the teaching moved on to the circuit actions associated with laboratory work on the transmitter defect diagnosis chassis. The class was then handed over to the lab SNCO whose job was to teach fault-finding techniques. I was also expected to help with diagnosing faults and assisting in the lab.

On completion of the transmitter phase, it was back to the classroom. The second half of my course covered the receiver theory. This culminated in another session in the lab covering receiver fault-finding.

The final phase covered subjects as linear and digital applications, Doppler and monopulse radars and an introduction to electronic countermeasures (jamming etc.). At the end of the course, the students would sit the 1B2 multi-choice examination. Passing this exam was obviously a must.

When I left RAF Newton, having successfully completed the TIT course, I was awarded a B1 assessment. The evaluation meant that I was considered a capable instructor who could expect to improve with the continued application of the techniques learnt. By way of ensuring that the instructor was improving and not slipping into bad habits, once a year, a member of the training command would sit at the back of a class and assess how well the instructor was performing.

During my two years on Gnat Line, no such continuation assessment was carried out. However, two days before I was due to take my very first class on ARTF, I was told that an assessor from Halton would be sitting in on my course. And so, on 21 March 1986, I introduced myself to the LTech AR, Direct Entry course TAR DE 107. I don't remember ever feeling so nervous, but as it happened, things went well. I was given a detailed breakdown of my faults and strengths and allowed to continue teaching.

Flight Sergeant Bill Preece, the ARTF SNCO, lived near RAF Sealand in Clwyd and commuted daily to Cosford. Shortly after I arrived on the section, Bill was posted to Sealand, which obviously was a great relief to him—no more commuting!

A few short weeks after he began work at Sealand, he received a phone call in the early hours of the morning, informing him that a station generation had been called and that he was to report to his place of work immediately.

As Bill was a primary callout Marshall for RAF Sealand, he proceeded to contact the other marshals, who woke up all of those personnel on their individual lists, directing them to work in exactly the same way as was carried out at RAF Laarbruch. Apparently, almost half of Sealand had reported to work before it was realised that the callout was for RAF Cosford personnel. Cosford's PABX callout list still showed Bill as being based at Cosford.

It was in the summer of that year that my very first ARTF course, TAR DE 107 commenced their airfield work which included the Gnat Line phase. There were several characters on that course and at the end of my time with them I'd actually got to know some of them quite well. The temptation was just too much! I spoke with Harry Chapple, who was running Gnat Line and asked if I could do the taxying phase for my old course, and he agreed.

So as not to raise suspicion, I donned my Denhams and bone dome and went to the aircraft before the class arrived. I sat in the cockpit with the canopy closed and the darkened visor down. The starter crew arrived and hadn't a clue who was sitting in the cockpit. Once the aircraft was started, I contacted ATC and obtained clearance to taxi. When I arrived at the peri-track and went through the pre-planned manoeuvres, there were very few of the course that didn't cock-up in one way or another.

If I was sent the wrong way, I would exaggerate the fact; if I was told to slow down, I would slam on the brakes. If the marshaller's arm motion was slow, I would go painfully slow. Once the session was over and the aircraft shut down, the course was told to stand by the aircraft. When I raised the visor, the look of absolute horror on their faces was a picture. It was exceptionally good fun.

Over a 10-month period in ARTF, I taught three courses: the first two courses comprised 18 students and the last course was only nine-strong. I was very proud to have achieved a 100% pass rate, and dare I say, as each new course started, my confidence grew and I believe I actually enjoyed the work and challenge.

I'd only spent 10 months on ARTF before I was notified that we were once again on the move back to Germany; this time, to RAF Wildenrath in early December. I followed the same ritual regarding applying for married accommodation and was pleased to learn that, subject to a mass influx of postings into Wildenrath, there was nobody on the unfrozen list and there was every chance that housing would be available on the day of our arrival. Sure enough, a notification soon came through that we'd been allocated a four-bedroom flat in the town of Erklenz.

We deliberated as to whether we should sell or rent the house in Newport. I think the decision was more or less made when I recalled the issues that one of my avionics colleagues had when he rented out his house whilst he and his family were abroad.

Apparently, all was going well for the majority of the rental period that was until the renter was notified that his tenancy was not going to be renewed. I believe that he'd asked for council accommodation and when that was denied he simply stopped paying rent and claimed squatter's rights.

The poor owner had nowhere to go once his tour of duty was complete and he ended up living in a caravan at the end of his driveway until the convoluted legal process managed to evict the manipulative renter. Various other stories and scams made the decision for us—we would sell.

The selling process was reasonably straightforward and no sooner had the *For Sale* been planted in the front garden, than we had a visit from a young couple looking for their first home. He worked for Vickers, the tank manufacturer, and they so liked what they saw that they immediately agreed to the asking price—£29,950 which was just below the stamp duty threshold.

They were both paranoid that they'd be *Gazumped* (a despicable process where the vendor, having initially accepted the offer, would then play potential buyers against each other in order to raise the price of the property).

Trisha and I assured them that not only was time against us in order to complete but we both believed it was unethical and downright greedy. Within a very short period, we were visited by a surveyor who told us that the house was in good order with no issues or problems. Imagine our surprise when we were notified that the survey report had picked up a hairline crack that ran through a couple of bricks on the front corner of the house.

The building society surveyor was concerned that the cracks could be indicative of subsidence and recommended that a structural engineer should be called in to assess how serious the *problem* was. The survey cost of £100 or so was to be borne by us and when the report was issued. I was not impressed by what had been recorded.

The cracks were superficial and were not the type of stress cracks associated with subsidence and the engineer believed that they'd probably been there since the house was built. When I challenged the building society and questioned the capability of their surveyor, I was met with the excuse that he was still fairly new at the job and he wasn't sure how serious the problem was. So, it cost us £100 because of his incompetence.

Anne and a friend (?) visited two weeks before we were due to leave and didn't tell Helen she was coming. Helen was really quite upset that she'd not been told. As Ann was leaving, she told us that *we* really must try and keep in touch this time! Cheeky cow, she obviously didn't appreciate that telephones and the mail service were two-way affairs!

Once we found out that we were returning to Germany, we decided to sell the trailer tent and invest in an Elddis Breeze caravan, a little more luxurious. The house sale went without a hitch, and we, once again, found ourselves on the move.

Chapter Seventeen
Royal Air Force Station Wildenrath

(3 December 1986 to 30 November 1990)

The journey to Wildenrath was uneventful and unlike my arrival at Laarbruch, all I had to do was drop off the caravan in the Caravan Park, pop into the family's office, find out where the married quarters were in Erklenz and arrange a march-in time. The whole process was simple in itself. I took Trisha and the boys to *Bauxhof* and after a couple of hours, we were in. I then drove back to Wildenrath and started the arrivals procedure.

Whilst in the general office, I noticed that Christmas raffle tickets were on sale and decided to have a go. The first prize was a Mini. I don't remember what the second prize was but the third prize was an all-inclusive week's holiday in Callela, Spain for two. The tickets cost DM50, about £18 each which I suppose was a little extravagant.

Anyway, I was partway through getting the necessary signatures on my blue card when an announcement came over the station PA that the Christmas draw was about to commence. Imagine my surprise, when my one ticket won the holiday in Spain.

At that stage, I hadn't even shown my face in the Wing Operations Centre (WOC) where I was to work and when I did, I walked down the corridor singing 'Eviva España', much to the amusement of my new work colleagues! I wasn't expected to begin work immediately and was given a couple of days to unpack our boxes at the flat.

I'd only been at work a couple of weeks when I received a phone call from Morley, telling me, that Uncle Tom had died and would we be returning to the UK for the funeral. Under normal circumstances, I would have said yes but Michael and Steven had only just started school and although I was on shift, I perhaps could have got colleagues to cover for me, we decided not to go.

On the evening of 6 March 1987, MS Herald of Free Enterprise, a Townsend Thoresen Roll on Roll off passenger and car ferry owned by European Ferries capsized shortly after sailing. The ferry left the Belgium port of Zeebrugge bound for Dover. At the time the ferry left Zeebrugge, 80% of her crew were embarking upon the return leg of the second Dover-Calais round trip completed during their 24-hour shift. This meant that the majority of the vessel's crew were tired.

Mark Stanley was the bosun's assistant on the vessel and it was his job to close the bow doors. At the time, the vessel sailed from port, he was asleep in his cabin and didn't hear the harbour stations sounding. This was the cue for the bow doors to be closed and all crew members to report to their harbour stations.

Chief Officer Leslie Sabel recalls seeing a man in orange overalls whilst he made his rounds, he assumed this man to be Mark Stanley and therefore that the bow doors had been closed. The Chief Officer returned to the bridge, which was his harbour station, and reported that they were ready to sail.

Captain Lewry could not see the bow doors from the bridge and as there was no other way to substantiate that they were closed, he relied upon the chief officer's report being accurate. Captain Lewry then dismissed the second officer and told Chief Officer Sabel to take his dinner break.

This meant that upon sailing the Herald's bow doors were open. The vessel began to pick up speed and as she hit 15 knots water began to pour in at a rate of 200 tons per minute. As the vessel filled, the bow dropped even further and the water flow increased. The sound of the water gushing onto the vessel was heard by a steward on H deck, the deck on which the engine rooms, stores and passenger accommodations were situated.

He assumed that a pipe had burst and called the assistant purser. The purser then put out a call for the *ship's carpenter* over the ship's public address system. The *ship's carpenter* was a code which was used in the event of a general alarm to avoid alarming the passengers.

At 7:27 the helmsman reported that the vessel wouldn't respond. Captain Lewry immediately put the engines in reverse. Unfortunately, by this point, the vessel was already listing 30 degrees to port and this had no effect.

The vessel righted for a moment before capsizing to port and settling on a sandbar on her side, the sandbank prevented the ferry from completely sinking in deeper water. The water reached the ship's electrical systems and destroyed both the main and emergency power which left the ship in complete darkness.

At the time the Herald capsized, there were 459 passengers and 80 crew members on board and she was carrying 81 cars, 3 buses and 47 lorries. Most of the passengers were relaxing in the passenger lounge or in the cabins below deck. There were also four lorry drivers asleep in their cabs in the bowels of the ship.

When the vessel began listing this alerted the passengers in the lounge that there was a problem, unfortunately, due to the speed of the capsizing there was no time for the passengers to act. The lights went out and water began to pour in.

At this time, Mark Stanley was thrown out of his bunk. Realising what had happened he ran to the lifeboats grabbed an axe and smashed a window of the passenger lounge. Whilst smashing the glass Mark Stanley sustained a deep cut to his right forearm. The passengers were thirty feet below and could not reach the windows to get out.

Mark Stanley therefore lowered a rope through one of the windows and climbed down to reassure passengers that help was on the way and assist in any way he could. He then climbed back up and told two soldiers, who were on leave and on their way home, to get a ladder. Mark Stanley continued to assist until he passed out due to blood loss and exposure to the cold water; he was then covered with an overcoat and taken to safety.

The majority of our shopping was carried out in the local Deutsche shops and supermarkets although we occasionally went to the NAAFI at Rheindahlen to buy certain English goods that we couldn't source locally. The main supermarket in Erklenz had everything we needed and once a week we'd trek off and do the weekly shop.

There was one particularly enduring trait carried out by the shop staff that entailed allowing customers to sample the produce before buying. On one trip, we first went to the delicatessen and the boys were each given a slice of Schinkenwurst (a type of luncheon meat). We then went to the in-store Bakerei where they were given a small brotchen (a crusty roll), and finally, when we bought some fruit and veg, they both received a small banana each.

I do remember the first time we shopped in Tesco's in Ipswich after returning to the UK, and how disconcerted Steven was when he didn't get his expected sample of cooked meat!

We only ever saw milk in cartons which not only tasted good but also froze exceptionally well. Our favourite was a Danish product that showed the picture of a worm sitting amongst long grass on the front of the carton. I guess the picture was meant to depict the fact the cows were fed on fresh grass although I still don't really understand why a worm was shown. Unfortunately, Steven somehow or other got it into his head that it was *worm's milk* and refused point blank to drink it, although he did eventually relent.

Exercises at Wildenrath followed the same tried and trusted format that I'd experienced on my earlier Germany tour. This time as an engineering operations controller, my job entailed assisting the three flying squadrons and all associated engineering departments in dealing with incidents and asset distribution as necessary.

It was a given that something untoward would always happen within the WOC that would test the resource management skills of the boss. I remember one such Mineval where things were getting quite hectic and part way through the second day, Squadron Leader Phil Sperring, OC avionics and a member of the distaff team, tapped me on the shoulder and asked me to follow him into the corridor in a few minutes.

It was standard procedure that whenever you left the console you had to take your complete set of webbing, personal weapon and tin hat in case an incident, evacuation or suchlike was called during your absence. I duly kitted up and told my colleague that I was going to the toilet. Phil then told me that he wanted me to abscond, inconspicuously go home without making too much of a fuss and just play along with whatever happens.

When I returned to my console, I took off my kit and carried on answering the telephones. Questions were asked as to what Phil wanted and whilst I don't remember precisely what I said everyone seemed happy with my answer. I had to choose a time that didn't arouse too much suspicion and also hope that an air raid wasn't called.

After 20 minutes or so, I told the other controller that I needed to go to the loo again, donned my full kit once more, picked up my gun and walked out. The policeman at the entrance asked where I was going and I told him that I was wanted at the standby WOC and he let me out. And that was it; I got into my car and drove home.

Trisha was somewhat surprised when I turned up early and when I told her that I'd deserted I think she thought that I was serious. Half an hour had passed since I got home and I was drinking a cup of tea when there was a knock at the door. I was still dressed in my NBC kit and so, with my machine gun slung over my shoulder, I answered the door. I was met by two armed RAF policeman who told me that I was under arrest, to hand over my weapon and not to do anything stupid.

I did think of running off but decided against it. They took my gun and put me in the back of their Land Rover. Poor Trisha didn't know whether to laugh or cry, whereas the boys found the whole episode highly amusing.

I was driven to the guard room, locked in a cell and after a few minutes, the cell door opened and so the interrogation began. I was asked what I thought I was doing and what did I plan on doing next. I remember Phil telling me to play along with whatever happened and told the police that I'd had enough of the whole war scene and decided that I wanted out.

The scenario was somewhat unreal because, under normal war conditions, the families would have been repatriated to the UK several weeks previously. However, the police also played along and after a few more questions called ENDEX and took me back to the WOC.

Under peacetime operations, there was always one engineering operations controller and maybe two or three Priority Progression Cell (PPC) suppliers in the WOC. However, manning for the engineering element during exercises was such that every desk was occupied and the overall number rose to approximately a dozen people. There were always set scenarios for the exercises insofar as the WOC would be taken out so as to give the standby WOC an opportunity to prove their worth.

Accommodation Challenges, Bauxhof, Erklenz

The RAF flats in Erklenz were absolutely fantastic. There were six flats per block, two per floor and ours was situated on the top floor. Each flat in our block comprised of four bedrooms, a bathroom, a large lounge, a kitchen and a balcony. Situated in the cellar were individually cordoned-off secure areas that could be used to store large items.

When we arrived, there were only three other flats that were occupied, one by a German girl named Ingrid who was married to a soldier, Andy and Kath Walker and their boys Darren and Shayne, who I'm still in contact with today, and another RAF chap and his son (I don't recall his name).

There was a requirement for each block to have an appointed SNCO; the purpose was for the family's office to have a contact in the event of issues or problems. Because everyone got on so well, there was no trouble and the communal areas were always kept clean and tidy, I volunteered for the post—that was to be a big, big mistake.

Unfortunately, shortly after Christmas the single father left for the UK and in early spring an RAF Flight Sergeant and his family moved into the flat opposite us, with the remaining two flats being occupied by army families. That's when the problems really began. Noise in the communal areas increased significantly and became quite unbearable.

One of the army mothers on the ground floor repeatedly allowed her young children to play on the stairs, rather than inside her flat. They were too young to play outside. Not normally a problem you'd think, however, the children regularly sat on the stairs eating their lunch and all too often the rubbish was just left.

There were a number of occasions when I'd arrive home from work to find the bottom stairwell littered with food remains, crisp and sweet packets and spilt sticky drinks, or at least, I *think* that's what the liquid was!

As is the way with the RAF, bullshit was never far away and it was incumbent on everyone to keep the communal areas clean. Before Christmas and shortly after, there hadn't been any issues with keeping those areas hygienic, with only four occupants, we just took it in turns. If someone was away for whatever reason another member would do the business.

That philosophy changed when the new members moved in; there were arguments as to whose turn it was and on many occasions the stairs were left in a mess. Kath and Trisha would invariably sweep the entire block just to keep it presentable.

In an attempt to stop the arguments, as the block SNCO, I posted a notice on each of the three floors detailing who was responsible for the weekly cleaning of the communal areas. All agreed except Ingrid who decided to tear down the notices. I subsequently spoke with her and she eventually relented and the notices went back up.

And it wasn't just the internal elements of the block that were treated irresponsibly. One of the more disgusting aspects of living in Bauxhof was the total disregard that some of the British residents had for cleanliness around the estate. God knows what the locals thought, but there were times when some of the side roads resembled the route to a rubbish tip.

Several parents would send their children to put the rubbish in the large metal flip-top bins; unfortunately, most kids couldn't reach the lid let alone push it open. Instead, the rubbish would be dropped on the ground and left. I can't remember the number of times that I'd picked up bags of rubbish and put them in the proper place.

It was in late May, we decided to take the holiday that I'd won at Christmas. We left Erklenz in the evening, the plan being that we would be in Callela, situated north of Barcelona, by the morning. The German double-decker bus was incredibly comfortable, and it wasn't too long before we crossed the German/French border and headed south.

Although there were toilets on board, we stopped for what we thought was a comfort break, however, we were advised that the autobahn was closed and would remain so for quite a while. It transpired that some French farmers, who objected to the import of Spanish fruit and veg, had set fire to and destroyed several Spanish trucks.

We sat for what seemed like an eternity half expecting news that the French Police had put an end to the protests, but no! Apparently, the police just stood by and watched the destruction being carried out.

The driver, having consulted with their head office, decided to continue with the journey. We had no idea what route we would take. However, it soon became blatantly obvious when we started to ascend some very steep hills, incredibly narrow roads and amazing twisty bends; we were crossing the Pyrenees in a double-decker bus! The driver did a fantastic job and as we passed through Andorra, we were assured that the worst was over.

We eventually arrived in Callela quite late in the evening and were the last to be dropped off at our hotel. Poor Mike, no sooner had he stepped off the bus, than he buried his head in a large bush and threw up. Half an hour later, he was tucking into a McDonalds burger!

The hotel, as far as I can remember was comfortable, included full board and was close to a beautiful, sandy beach. I don't remember what we did for the week but I do remember some of the fantastic, typically Spanish meals we had in the hotel.

There was also in the hotel, a young Scottish couple. They seemed very pleasant but when it came to eating, they turned their noses up at every single meal with the exception of fish and chips. We, however, ate everything that was put in front of us, in fact, several of the staff commented on the last day how impressed they were with Michael and Steven who didn't waste a single meal.

Shortly after returning from holiday, Andy and Kath, a really very lovely couple, were repatriated to the UK and an army family moved in. Events came to a head, when late one evening, we were disturbed by an awful racket coming from the flat below. It sounded like a war zone and we could clearly hear furniture being thrown around the room.

I knocked on the door and was met by a drunken bloke who apologised for the noise. The mess behind him was unimaginable. It was also about that time that the wife of the Flight Sergeant knocked at our door one evening and told me that she'd been watching some British teenagers causing damage in the play park.

Her husband was home and they wanted me, as block SNCO, to go and stop them. I pointed out that if she and he had witnessed the trouble why hadn't he tried to sort it out? Her answer absolutely flabbergasted me. They didn't intervene because they thought that if her husband had told them to stop, the yobs may well have taken their frustrations out on their children!

What a ******* cheek!

This was the same person who believed that he wasn't required to assist with the clean-up prior to a block inspection by the Barrack Warden due to his rank. What a total wassack!

By June of 1987, I'd had enough and spoke with the Family's Officer telling him of the issues. I told him what had happened to me and he commented the same had been experienced by other concerned residents who had also moved out because of the intransigence of certain members of the British community.

It was a perpetual problem and I was thanked for at least trying to make things a little better. We were then offered new accommodation on Wildenrath camp—talk about *out of the frying pan and into the fire.*

June 1987 – The Heron Road Nightmare

The accommodation on Heron Road was made up of eight individual detached blocks and each block comprised of four single-storey units built in the shape of the letter *H*. Each leg of the *H* formed the relevant dwelling. Our leg comprised a standard long lounge/diner, kitchen, bathroom and three bedrooms. We also had an additional room (which formed part of the cross member of the *H*) that was an ideal storage area.

What a difference; compared to Erklenz, it was quite a relief to be able to relax and not have to get involved with how other residents treated the surrounding areas. Unfortunately, that was soon to change. Shortly after Christmas 1987, I sat in the garden on the stairs leading into the kitchen and barbequed some bits and pieces, it wasn't cold and once finished I took the food inside to eat.

The next morning, I went to the kitchen sink and was washing up a cup when I heard one hell of a commotion coming from the garden opposite. I opened the door to be met with a barrage of verbal abuse from our next-door neighbour, Jan Evenden. She was about five foot tall and almost as wide, this coupled with her broad, aggressive, Glaswegian accent gave her quite an intimidating personality.

She was ranting and raving and accused us of spying on her and her family!

She then called me, "F****** mental," for barbequing in the middle of winter before getting on her bike and riding off—what a charmer!

Our two kitchens were directly opposite each other and whenever we were stood at the sink it was the most natural thing in the world to occasionally look out of the window. That in her book constituted spying. I drove off to work shortly afterwards and passed her on her bike.

As I looked in my rearview mirror, I saw her mouthing something and flicking *V* signs at me. That evening, I went to see her and her husband *Compo* a rather dim example of an armourer. I asked why all the abuse and she immediately launched into another tirade of profanities—she really had a way with words. She said that she was tired of being spied on, and then, commented that I couldn't treat people the way I did in Erklenz!

I hadn't the faintest idea what she was talking about. It later transpired that she and Ingrid were friends, and comments had been made about my attempts to clean up the block. I was then lectured by her and told that I should have minded my own business.

That was it, no amount of trying to explain would satisfy her and I left with the parting shot that whatever was done at Erklenz had nothing to do with her, and perhaps, she should mind *her* own business and not listen to pathetic gossip. I left her to it.

One of the advantages of the low-cost endowment scheme we enrolled in while buying our first home in Newport was its flexibility. Even without a mortgage, as long as we maintained the monthly premiums of £25, we would likely have no trouble obtaining another mortgage of up to £25,000.

Unfortunately, during the summer of 1988, we noticed that the general price of houses in the UK had shot up. So much so, that £25,000 wouldn't buy much of anything anywhere on the market. I, therefore, made arrangements with Standard Life to extend our insurance to cover a potential purchase of up to £60,000; the additional premium was £35.

It soon became apparent that prices were accelerating at such a pace that unless we took some drastic action we would be priced out of the market. We managed to get some property brochures for the Chippenham area in Wiltshire and set about deciding which part of the county we could possibly settle in.

It didn't take long before we found a suitable three-bedroom house, spoke with the estate agent and reserved the property. We decided that Trisha and the boys would stay in Germany, whilst I would dash back to the UK, put down a deposit and allow the estate agent to carry out the conveyancing via the post. All that was left for me to do was to book my ferry tickets.

I decided that I should be able to do all that was necessary in about five days and would take place over one of my stand-down periods. Wildenrath had an excellent Personal Service Institute (PSI) travel cell that booked me an outward passage on my selected date. Unfortunately, it was impossible to book a return trip.

In fact, as I remember, there were no return dates available within the following two weeks of my preferred travel dates. I tried several permutations of dates but couldn't secure any that were convenient. In the end, we had to concede defeat and cancel everything.

As far as our lovely neighbour was concerned, the trouble continued, ranging from more verbal abuse not only to Trisha and me but also to Michael and Steven. Her thuggish children would hide in the bushes and call me names as I walked by before running off. On one occasion, as I walked from the kitchen into our garden, I noticed a large placard being held up to the kitchen window directly opposite. Unfortunately, I couldn't make out what was written on it.

Compo was posted to the Falklands in the late summer of 1988, and in an attempt to get to the bottom of her aggression, Trisha and I invited her to sit in the garden and talk. She actually agreed that her attitude wasn't acceptable and that she was almost paranoid about privacy. She also acknowledged that she was obsessive about cleanliness and told us that was why kids' shoes were always on the outside step; they weren't allowed inside the house with shoes on,

Unfortunately, you didn't have to be a spy to notice that the shoes were left outside come rain or shine, frost or snow. We talked for about an hour, and she finally accepted that she wouldn't have lived with the Bauxhof pigs—at least, we agreed on something.

All was going well, until, a few months after Compo came back from the Falklands and things started to get frosty again. Up until then, Trisha and I never went out of our way to ignore Jan and would always say hello and that was as far as the *friendship* went; Trisha really didn't want to get involved.

In an effort to stop the resurrection of the argy-bargy primarily over more spying accusations, we bought a bamboo screen, poles and wires and erected a curtain between the houses.

That seemed to calm things down a little. However, just before we were about to leave for a caravan holiday, I popped into the BP garage to fill up with fuel. On returning, I met Brian Waterall, one of the PPC SNCOs, telling me that everything was all right and not to worry. What on earth had gone on? I went inside and found Trisha in one heck of a state.

Apparently, shortly after I left home, Jan had knocked on the door and accused Trisha of something or other, and then, assaulted her with her handbag. The RAF police were called and when they arrived and listened to what Trisha had to say they suggested that if she wanted to make a formal complaint, she would have to go to the guard room.

My immediate response was to do just that. The evidence was given, statements made and the police advised us to go on holiday and enjoy ourselves. The police were fantastic and even commented (rightly or wrongly) that it wasn't the first time that a complaint had been made against the woman, and that, this incident may well result in the family being repatriated to the UK sooner rather than later.

The news of the assault must have flashed around Wildenrath like wildfire because not long after the incident I was told, and I appreciate that it was only hearsay, by the friend of a girl who also worked in the Malcolm Club that Jan Evenden's violent tendencies and aggression were well known.

Jan's paranoia came to a head one day when the girl stood close by as Jan was telling her cronies about a certain experience. Without warning, Jan accused the girl of being nosy and listening in to a private conversation. She threatened her with a knife. I don't know if that was ever reported. Jan Evenden really was a nasty piece of work.

We arrived back from holiday after three weeks, expecting to find the Evenden house empty but were horrified to see that it was still occupied. The next morning, I went to see the OC Station Services Squadron to find out what was going on. We were told that comment couldn't be made because Jan had been charged with common assault and was awaiting her day in court.

In the meantime, I went to see OC Eng Wing, Wing Commander Dave Case, who listened to the story of events. I also presented a comprehensive diary which went back months. It was decided to call Compo in for a *chat*.

I believe he was told in no uncertain terms that his wife's conduct was totally unacceptable and that it was incumbent on him to keep her under control.

Whilst I'm not a violent person, I seriously considered taking Compo into the woods close by and beating the crap out of him—he was such a useless wimp. Fortunately, common sense prevailed and I dismissed the thought. The last thing I wanted was an assault charge on my service record.

Mrs Evenden's day in the civilian court duly arrived, and fortunately, Trisha wasn't called to give evidence. Jan was given an unconditional discharge which at the time absolutely beggared belief. An unconditional discharge is imposed when the judge doesn't believe that it would be helpful to impose any conditions on the defendant. Why on earth not?

I would have at least expected a condition to be set that would stop her aggressive attitude and force her to just leave us alone. I subsequently spoke with Dave Case and Squadron Leader Geoff Harris who both commented that whilst the outcome wasn't what we would have wanted, it at least, would be *a nail in her coffin* meaning that her violent act was on record.

RAF Wildenrath was situated directly over some of the largest deposits of Anthracite in Western Europe, and there were occasions, during the night when we could hear explosions deep underground as the coal was being mined. Anthracite is a hard, shiny coal that is clean-burning, high in carbon content, and low in volatile matter.

Unfortunately, several houses on Heron Road suffered from subsidence due to the mining and ours was probably one of the worst affected. Most of the doors in the bungalow didn't fit, and the door frames in the two bedrooms had gaps that you could put your fingers in. Following the assault on Trisha, the Family's Officer asked if we would like to move to a three-bedroom house.

The bungalow would then be torn apart and investigations carried out to establish how seriously the property was affected. I think I accepted before the words were out of his mouth. Despite the fact that the house was going to be more or less demolished, we were still required to carry out the full march-out procedure and when we left everything absolutely shone.

Deutsche Wanderung

One of the more pleasant activities we participated in for most of our time at Wildenrath was walking. The German Wandering (Deutsche Wanderung) clubs were scattered throughout and enabled us to explore some of the most beautiful areas of the country.

The rationale behind the walk was that once we registered with a particular club, which was carried out by Wildenrath's booking member (a role I was to later carry out) on arrival at the venue we would sign in, be given a check-off card and follow a pre-defined route. The distances for most walks were either 10 km (6 miles) or 20 km (12 miles) identified by different coloured tapes, flags or arrows.

Periodically, there would be rest areas where refreshments were available and marshalls whose job was to endorse your card thereby ensuring that nobody cheated. Once the walk was finished, the completed card would be handed in, checked and a prize would then be awarded.

There were some pretty naff rewards, but on the other hand, there were some very collectable items. I still have some of the items which include commemorative plates, beer steins, and a small functioning, cuckoo clock to name but a few.

A Mad Chase down the Autobahn

It was during the summer of 1989, that Wendy, Rob and Mum came to visit us at Heron Road. I remember the weather being particularly warm and as a treat, I was suggested that we drive to Cochem, a quaint town on the banks of the River Mosel. We left Wildenrath mid-morning and headed south on the autobahn.

As mentioned earlier, as members of the armed forces in Germany, we were entitled to petrol coupons which saved a small fortune, especially, with the amount of travelling we did. Rob was following us and as we approached a BP petrol station, I indicated that I was pulling in, and instead of Rob following us, he drove on.

I distinctly remember seeing Mum, who was sitting in the rear passenger seat, looking at us as we left the autobahn. I quickly filled up and was soon on our way again. However, Rob wasn't aware that we'd stopped and in the belief that we were still in front of him, drove like a maniac to try and catch up. We, in the meantime, were desperately trying to catch up with him and at one stage we were travelling at 90 mph.

This chase went on for about 30 mins, and we, eventually, caught up with Rob just at the start of the slip road leading to Cochem. I managed to get in front of him and thankfully, guide him off! It later transpired that Rob was following, at break-neck speed, another car that he believed was us and was all set to give up—calling me all the names under the sun for driving so recklessly.

August 1989 – Harrier Way

The house on Harrier Way was superb and the other three houses in the terraced block were occupied by normal people such as Robby and Mary Robinson. I can't recall the names of the other two couples. However, we'd only been in the house for a few weeks when a new couple moved in. I was walking in front of their house when a very tall, good-looking, black guy came towards me.

"Hello, pleased to meet you, I'm John Lewis," I said.

He replied, "Yeah, hello, so am I."

At first, I thought he was taking the pee but he then told me that his Christian name was Roy and his surname was *John Lewis*. His wife, Ali, was white and what a brilliant couple they turned out to be. He was later to tell us that his ancestors were slaves on the island of Martinique in the Caribbean. It was customary at the time for the slaves to take on the Christian name and surname of the plantation owners—hence John Lewis.

Group Captain Alistair McKay the Station Commander, was to join the John Lewis partnership. Despite the rank he achieved in the RAF, he wanted to work his way from the bottom to the top of the organisation. Unfortunately, I never found out if he achieved that ambition.

He was a remarkable officer, very affable, but still exuded an air of authority which was respected by all. As a tribute to the man, arrangements were made prior to his departure to name one of the roads on the station after him—the appointed name—*McKay Alley*.

Exercise Red Flag (Nellis AFB, USA)

Exercise Red Flag is conducted on the Nevada Test and Training Range and involves U.S. and Allied forces from all branches of service. Each Red Flag exercise normally involves a variety of attack, air superiority, defence suppression, airlift, air refuelling and reconnaissance aircraft.

Within a typical 12-month period, more than 1,200 aircraft fly 20,000 plus sorties while training more than 26,750 personnel. Since combat is no place to train aircrews, Red Flag provides a peacetime *battlefield,* within which, our combat Air Forces can train. Inside this battlefield, aircrews train to fight together, survive together and win together. Red Flag-Nellis is held four times annually.

It was in the summer of 1988, the RAF Phantoms were invited to take part in *Red Flag.* Apart from aircraft, air and ground crews from Wildenrath's resident squadrons comprising 19 and 92 Squadrons, there was also a requirement to provide an Eng Ops controller to carry out asset allocation and to liaise with the various USAF agencies.

I was scheduled to go with the squadrons to Red Flag in the summer of 1989 but was asked by a colleague, Nat Rama. He was the SEMA/SAMA (Station Engineering Management Aid and the Station Administration Management Aid) computer manager if he could go in my stead.

As it would be his one and only opportunity to attend, I stood down, and hopefully, would go the following year. Unfortunately, Saddam Hussein invaded Kuwait in 1990 and the entire Red Flag exercise was cancelled! And so, instead of practising destroying enemy aircraft and their assets, it could be done for real.

As an aside, many Westerners believed that Iraq's invasion of Kuwait was largely motivated by its desire to take control of the vast oil reserves. However, the Iraqi government justified the invasion by claiming that Kuwait was a natural part of Iraq which was carved off as a result of British imperialism.

Terrorist Atrocities

Between May 1988 and May 1990, seven people were killed by the Irish Republican Army (IRA) in a campaign of car bombings and shootings aimed at British service personnel based in Germany. The first of the atrocities took place in Roermond, Holland in May 1988 when the IRA opened fire on a vehicle in which three men from the RAF Regiment, based at RAF Wildenrath, were sleeping; one man died.

The most horrific incident happened in October 1989, when Corporal Mick Islania, who worked in the communications centre in the Wing Operations Centre, and his six-month-old baby, Nivruti, were shot dead as they left a restaurant in Wildenrath village; his wife Smita, who was driving the car was uninjured but was treated for shock.

I worked with Mick in the WOC and had only recently helped him to fit rear fog lights to the VW Jetta which he was later to die in. Michael was playing on the sports field close to where the shooting took place and heard the automatic gunfire. It was reported that following the shooting, the gunmen then stopped at the entrance to the station and waved their guns at the RAF police checkpoint before disappearing across the Dutch border near Roermond.

The IRA reported that they'd shot Mick but expressed *profound regret* for killing the child. The campaign in Germany ended shortly after two Australian tourists, mistaken for British servicemen because of their short hair, were gunned down, once again in Roermond.

The attack was deeply unpopular even with IRA sympathisers in Australia which led to the Australian Prime Minister, John Howard, refusing to meet Gerry Adams from Sinn Fein who was visiting.

All private vehicles used by BFG personnel had to be registered with the military authorities. Once registered, the vehicle would be allocated a specific BFG number plate, the format was the letter *B* prefix followed by white alpha/numeric characters on a black background, for example, B123 ABC. The plate immediately identified the vehicle as being owned by a British serviceman.

We were required to carry out vehicle searches whenever and wherever the vehicle had been left unattended. In an effort to make the cars a little less conspicuous, the authorities abandoned the BFG plates and instigated a change to the standard UK-style plates.

However, because the plates were produced on army and RAF stations in Germany, they were very plain and didn't show the traditional garage advertisement details which were commonplace on plates produced in the UK.

We were also still required to carry out searches which, to a lot of people's minds, merely drew attention to the possibility that the vehicle was owned by a serviceman; the rationale being that a normal UK holidaymaker wouldn't go through the checking process.

We didn't use the Elddis caravan too much but decided on upgrading to a Burstner caravan, a huge van with an enclosed shower, kitchen, and dining area, where the table folded down into two single beds and a permanent double bed. What a contrast to our earlier exploits. Because of the size of our new toy, we needed to buy a new car and settled on a Mazda 626.

It was on one of our many trips down to southern Germany that we decided to visit the Dachau Nazi Concentration camp, located northwest of Munich. Unfortunately, as we approached a set of traffic lights not far from Dachau, I realised, I should have taken a filter road to the right which was designed to make life a lot easier. Rather than try and negotiate a very tight turn at the lights, I decided to reverse the car and caravan just a very short distance.

I looked in both of the extended caravan mirrors and as I couldn't see any other vehicle started to reverse. I hadn't gone more than a few inches or so when there was a loud bang, and on getting out of the car, found that I'd reversed into a poxy Fiat 500 car. It was obviously my fault, fortunately, the only damage was two creases on either side of his bonnet where the caravan light cluster had hit.

We passed insurance details and the driver then said that it was a good job he wasn't driving his father's BMW. I said that perhaps he should have been driving it, then at least I would have seen him in my mirrors. The driver didn't have an explanation as to why he had stopped so close to the back of our caravan.

Dachau camp was opened in 1933, shortly after Hitler came to power and served as a model for all later concentration camps. It was also used as a *school of violence* training centre for the SS men; under whose command it stood.

In the 12 years of its existence, over 200,000 people from all over Europe were imprisoned there; many suffering inhumane treatment from the medical experiments performed on them by German physicians. Our actual visit was a sobering experience and one that I'll not forget for a long time.

It was in the spring of 1989 that Trisha received the horrendous news that her darling mother Helen had been diagnosed with lung cancer and was to start chemotherapy. Helen had smoked for several years, and in all the time that I'd known her, she'd always had a cough; nothing raspy or phlegmy. Helen never thought it was serious.

Unfortunately, the seeds had obviously been sown. Trisha, quite naturally, was absolutely devastated, as were we all. We discussed going to Southport to see Helen and try to be a comfort to Morley but Helen insisted that we should wait. No sooner had Trisha had that conversation with Helen, than she received a phone call late one evening (Germany time) from Anne, telling her that it wasn't fair on her brother John that he should suffer the distress on his own.

She suggested that we visit. What a typically selfish statement from her. She had no idea how upset we all were. The fact that Trisha was in constant contact with Helen wasn't taken into account.

Anne didn't consider the fact that we couldn't just jump into the car and pop down the road, it was a 1600-mile round trip. I had to arrange shift cover, book ferries and take the boys out of school—not necessarily difficult tasks but nevertheless needed to be coordinated. That probably was one of the most selfish things that Anne had ever said.

The shift pattern in the Wing Operations Centre (WOC) was such that as long as somebody was on duty, the five Chief Techs between us could arrange or swap cover as necessary. I arranged for one of my colleagues to stand in for me and booked a return ferry trip from Rotterdam to Hull with North Sea Ferries.

The beauty of that particular route was that, we would have an overnight cabin, arrive reasonably refreshed and once in the UK drive from Hull to Liverpool on the M62. The ferry was comfortable with the ticket including an evening meal and breakfast where you could eat as much as you wished.

The food choice was pretty good and Michael couldn't resist trying as big a variety as possible, he was subsequently sick—very, very sick!

It was the one and only time in our married life that Trisha wasn't particularly looking forward to seeing Helen. They'd spoken on the phone many times with Helen always gasping for breath with only a couple of words passing her lips for each short breath she took.

I think we'd built up a mental image of what Helen looked like and when we saw her, I'm so sorry to say but she looked dreadful. She'd lost a lot of her hair and was wearing a wig; this coupled with her gaunt appearance deeply upset us all but more so Trisha.

I don't remember how long we stayed, but Edith put us up at Coronation Avenue. We spent the majority of the time just trying to help Morley cope. After a few days, we left Southport, and sadly and very reluctantly, headed back to Germany. That was to be the last time that we'd see dear Helen alive.

Over the next few months, Trisha was in constant contact with Helen. She felt totally useless at not being able to do anything and we never gave up hope that Helen may get better. However, I think in the back of our minds we knew that because the cancer was in such an advanced state and inoperable, the future was not looking good—we prayed an awful lot.

It was during the summer of that year, that we decided to explore the eastern side of Germany, very close to the Czechoslovakian border. Trisha spoke with Helen asking if that was okay. Helen said that as her treatment was ongoing and as there was nothing we could do; we were to go and enjoy ourselves. Enjoyment really was the last thing on our minds.

Helen really was a lovely lady, an exceptional mother-in-law and a fantastic grandmother to Mike and Steven—she was loved by everyone.

The Soviet Block Dissolves and the Wall Comes Down

The Berlin Wall was officially referred to by the GDR authorities as the *Anti-Fascist Rampart*, implying that neighbouring West Germany had not been fully de-Nazified. The West Berlin city government sometimes referred to it as the *Wall of Shame*; a term coined by Mayor Willi Brandt while condemning the Wall's restriction on freedom of movement.

The socialist economies in Eastern Europe had been suffering along with that of the Soviet Union, with Gorbachev looking toward *glasnost* (openness) and *Perestroika* (reconstruction) as a remedy for their economic troubles. It was during the summer of 1989 that thousands of East Germans loaded their Trabants with as much as they could carry, and drove to either Hungary or Czechoslovakia én route to West Germany—the so-called *Trabi Trail*.

Our time spent holidaying on the Czech border was a real eye-opener. Everywhere we went, we came across Trabis loaded to the gunnels with consumer goods. Even if they were accessible to the inhabitants of East Germany, they were probably financially out of reach.

Despite the abuse aimed at the iconic Trabi, there was no getting away from the fact the little car could really motor. There was one occasion where we were following a rather dilapidated Trabi on the autobahn, and whilst it wasn't difficult keeping up with it in the Mazda, he certainly wasn't hanging about.

The look of absolute astonishment on the face of a Mercedes driver, as the Trabi, with smoke billowing from its exhaust, flashed past him was a real picture.

Later in 1989, a series of radical political changes occurred in the Eastern Bloc's authoritarian systems and the erosion of political power in the pro-Soviet governments in nearby Poland and Hungary accelerated the final demise of what was a thoroughly corrupt system.

After several weeks of civil unrest, the East German government announced on 9 November 1989 that all GDR citizens could visit West Germany and West Berlin. Crowds of East Germans crossed and climbed onto the wall, joined by West Germans on the other side in a celebratory atmosphere.

Gulf War One – The Invasion of Kuwait

The Iraq/Kuwait war was a major conflict between the Republic of Iraq and the State of Kuwait which resulted in the seven-month-long Iraqi occupation of Kuwait. This subsequently led to direct military intervention by the USA-led forces in the Gulf War. Kuwait was a close ally of Iraq during the Iraq-Iran war and functioned as the country's major port once Basra was shut down by the fighting.

However, after the war ended, the friendly relations between the two neighbouring Arab countries turned sour for several economic and diplomatic reasons that culminated in an Iraqi invasion of Kuwait.

Kuwait had heavily funded the eight-year-long Iraqi war against Iran and Kuwait's large-scale economic assistance often triggered hostile Iranian actions against it. Iran repeatedly targeted Kuwaiti oil tankers in 1984 and fired weapons at Kuwaiti security personnel stationed on the island of Bubiyan in 1988.

By the time the Iran-Iraq war ended, Iraq was not in a financial position to repay the US $14 billion it had borrowed from Kuwait to finance its war, and requested Kuwait to forgive the debt. Iraq argued that the war had prevented the rise of Persian influence in the Arab World.

However, Kuwait's reluctance to pardon the debt created strains in the relationship between the two Arab countries. During late 1989, several official meetings were held between the Kuwaiti and Iraqi leaders but they were unable to break the deadlock between the two.

The Iraqi invasion and occupation of Kuwait was unanimously condemned by all major world powers, even countries traditionally considered to be close Iraqi allies, such as France and India, called for immediate withdrawal of all Iraqi forces from Kuwait. Several countries, including the USSR and China, placed an arms embargo on Iraq.

NATO members were particularly critical of the Iraqi occupation and by late 1990, the USA had issued an ultimatum to Iraq to withdraw its forces from

Kuwait by 15 January 1991 or face war. However, on 3 August 1990, the UN Security Council passed Resolution 660, condemning the Iraqi invasion of Kuwait and demanding that Iraq, unconditionally, withdraw all forces deployed in Kuwait.

After a series of failed negotiations between major world powers and Iraq, the USA-led coalition forces launched a massive military assault on Iraq, and Iraqi forces stationed in Kuwait in mid-January 1991.

Elements of the two Phantom flying squadrons based at Wildenrath were sent to Cyprus to give air defence support to the many Allied aircraft that were transiting the Mediterranean. As one would expect, the operational and support elements at Wildenrath picked up considerably. This was more noticeable for the ops staff and the volume of signal traffic associated with the Gulf War.

One specific element was the number of NOTAMs (Notice to Airmen) we received. A NOTAM is filed with an aviation authority to alert pilots of any hazards én route or at a specific location. As an Eng Ops controller, we were routinely copied on all NOTAMS and although we weren't required to act on the information, it nevertheless kept us informed of potential difficulties.

During the build-up to the Gulf War, I received several NOTAMs concerning one particular Hercules flight from the UK. Over a period of several hours, the flight plan kept changing and each time there was a revision, a new NOTAM was transmitted.

The guy in the UK who was coordinating the signal traffic had quite obviously had enough of the constant amendments, because, on his last transmission, he concluded the signal with the following: *John 11:35.* The text is the shortest verse in the Bible and merely reads:

Jesus wept.

At least he had a sense of humour!

Hostilities continued and on 25 February, Kuwait was officially liberated from Iraq forces. On 15 March 1991, the Emir of Kuwait returned to the country after spending more than eight months in exile. During the Iraqi occupation, about 1,000 Kuwaiti civilians were killed and more than 300,000 residents fled the country.

11 August 1990

We'd known that Helen was seriously ill for some time and was not expected to recover. Nevertheless, it was still a tremendous shock to hear that she had passed away. Time now, really was of the essence and we had to make urgent plans to get back to Southport for the funeral. As usual, my colleagues in the WOC stepped in and offered to cover my shift. As it transpired, I still owed them shift time when I eventually left Germany, but never had the opportunity to repay them.

The trip to the UK was a little more complicated than previous. We managed to get tickets for the trip from Rotterdam to Hull but were unable to secure return tickets on our chosen dates. Instead, we had to use the Dover to Calais crossing.

The day of the funeral arrived and we were all full of trepidation and under the circumstances, Morley coped extremely well. It was to be held in the Roman Catholic Church a short walk from Sandbrook Road. Protocol normally dictates that immediate family should be sat on the front row.

However, dear Anne had other plans. As we arrived at the church, Anne took Michel and Steven and plonked herself next to Morley and John, leaving no room for Trisha. We subsequently had to sit several rows behind. Anne should have sat with me in the row behind the family—Trisha never forgave her for that little stunt!

When I received my posting notice from PMC, I was somewhat surprised to find that I'd been posted to the Phantom Aircraft Engineering Development and Investigation Team (PAEDIT) responsible for the Missile Control System (MCS) element of the aircraft.

My drafter at PMC had decided that, because I was an avionics Chief Technician and had been employed on a Phantom unit; I must know everything that needed to be known about the Phantom MCS—how wrong could he have been.

I was aware of the various acronyms, expressions and what the kit was capable of doing. I learnt enough about the system to be able to brief the OC engineering wing each morning as to the various faults, problems and fixes. But there was no way in a million years that I could carry out detailed fault investigations and the like.

I subsequently spoke with my Flight Commander and pointed out the problem and, in turn, got in touch with PMC at Innsworth. After a short discussion, it was agreed that I would still go to Wattisham but join 74 (F) Squadron as the MCS trade manager. It was still a daunting task but a little more manageable than what I'd earlier been offered.

Clean-up in preparation for the march-out from Harrier Way was no different from any of the previous married quarters we'd occupied. We began a few weeks before the handover, and as one room was finished it was closed off and by the time we got downstairs the whole of the upper floor was more or less prepared.

There were one or two scuff marks on the walls in the living room and when I tried to remove them, I was horrified to notice that the top quarter of the walls were covered in a very thin film of soot—not really noticeable until I'd started to clean.

At first, we couldn't understand where it had come from. It then dawned on us that we'd burnt a lot of candles over the previous few months and the soot had built up slowly over time. We ended up having to wash the walls in the entire room from top to bottom.

We were also advised that the particular barrack warden made a point of checking *under* the carpets for dirt and to ensure that the floor had been polished.

Come the day of the march-out everything was in order, the removal van had collected our bits and pieces and the caravan was loaded up with what was left of our possessions. The house was ready. Trisha then went to Ali and Roy's for a cup of tea, whilst I met with the families officer and barrack warden.

The handover went without a glitch (including a check under the carpets) and once complete, the Family's Officer asked to speak with Trisha. I knew that things had gone well and I went to get her. I told her, with quite a stern expression on my face, that she was wanted next door. The look of horror on her face was memorable.

However, the Family's Officer then went on to say how impressed he was with the cleanliness of the house and that it was a shame that all married quarters weren't handed over in the same condition. He sincerely thanked her for her efforts. Nothing else needed to be said—well done, sweetheart!

Having spent the previous night on the living room floor in sleeping bags, by the time we said our goodbyes to the various friends and finished loading up the car and caravan we were all absolutely knackered. We left Wildenrath late in the evening and drove through the night passing through Luxembourg and onto Calais; ready to board the ferry for Felixstowe.

Chapter Eighteen
Royal Air Force Station Wattisham

(30 November 1990 to 12 November 1992)

We arrived at Felixstowe docks in the early hours. After going through the normal registration procedures with HM Customs for the duty-free car and the caravan, we had only a short drive to RAF Wattisham. There was a huge shortage of married quarters at Wattisham and we were to be temporarily housed in an unfurnished house on the base.

Unfortunately, it hadn't been occupied for several months. Our removal van duly arrived from Germany and no sooner had that been unloaded than the van containing those household items that had been kept in storage for the last four years also turned up—it was a total nightmare!

We were informed that we'd be moving to another house in Stowupland shortly into 1991 and for that reason, it wasn't worth unpacking everything—only the very basic commodities. Bearing that fact in mind, we decided that it wasn't worth registering the boys at the local school and they had an extended Christmas break. Wattisham was situated in the Suffolk countryside a short distance from the town of Ipswich and was home to two Phantom air defence squadrons.

Number 56 Squadron

56 Squadron was one of the oldest and most successful squadrons of the RAF with battle honours from many significant air campaigns of both world wars. The squadron moved to RAF Wattisham in 1957 with the Hawker Hunter where it would spend the next 35 years defending the UK airspace. They converted to the English Electric Lightning in 1960 but briefly left Wattisham in 1967 deploying to RAF Akrotiri in Cyprus before returning once again to Wattisham in 1975.

In 1976, the squadron exchanged their Lightnings for the McDonnell Douglas Phantom FGR2 aircraft, initially sharing the base with a sister Phantom operator, 23 Squadron. However, following the Falklands conflict, 23 Squadron was dispatched to the South Atlantic and was replaced at Wattisham by 74 (F) Squadron. 56 Squadron operated the Phantom until the aircraft was finally retired from service in 1992.

Number 74 (F) Squadron – The Fighting Tigers

74 (F) Squadron was formed at Colney, a village and civil parish in Hertfordshire on 1 July 1917. It initially operated the Avro 405K, a biplane used in the training role and its first operational fighters were SE5As which were flown in France from March 1918 until the squadron returned to Britain where it disbanded on 3 July 1919.

Since the First World War, the squadron has discharged itself honourably under the formidable lead of such men as Mannock VC, *Sailor* Malan and Mungo-Park, all aces and outstanding fighter leaders. The squadron motto *I Fear no Man* utilises a tiger's face which was approved by King George VI in February 1937 and was developed from an unofficial emblem used during the First World War.

During the squadron's distinguished career, it has flown a variety of aircraft including the Hawker Demon, the Gloster Gauntlet, the Hawker Hurricane, the Gloster Meteor, the Hawker Hunter and the English Electric Lightning.

In the wake of the Falklands War, and the subsequent deployment of 23 Squadron and their Phantoms to the islands on a permanent basis, it was decided to purchase another Phantom Squadron to fill the gap in the UK air defence system.

To do this 74 (F) Squadron reformed at RAF Wattisham on 31 July 1984 and was equipped with ex-US Navy/Marine F-4Js (designated as the F-4J (UK) in RAF service). The aircraft's armament consisted of four Sky Flash or Sparrow Radar-guided missiles, four AIM 9L Sidewinder heat-seeking missiles and one SUU 23A, 20 mm, Vulcan cannon.

My First Fighter Squadron

Before long, my disembarkation leave was over. I duly arrived at the squadron and was met at the entrance to the Pilot's Briefing Facility (PBF) by

Chief Tech Sandy Sanderson, one of the engineering rectification controllers. Sandy's job was to run the engineering element in the PBF ensuring that there was always sufficient aircraft to meet the flying programme.

I was immediately aware of several aircraft overflying the airfield and was more than a little curious to find out what was going on. All Sandy said was that the squadron always flew a *Diamond-Nine* formation at the end of every week. What! Nine aircraft each Friday morning, you really must be kidding.

Thankfully, he told it was because that formation was to be the final flight of the fabled Phantom F4-J and in Jan 1991, the squadron gave up their F4J variant and received several surplus Phantom FGR2s.

As is the case for any new arrival, the majority of my time, prior to the Christmas break, was spent shadowing my work colleagues and learning about the operational and engineering requirements as a member of the squadron. Although I'd spent the previous four years on a Phantom aircraft unit there really was no comparison between my role then, as an engineer operations controller, and what I was expected to do as the Phantom Missile Control System (MCS) Trade Manager.

Meanwhile, Trisha wanted Morley to spend the festive season with us, which, in itself wasn't an issue. After all, we had sufficient bedrooms for everyone, the main problem was space. The house was full of our furniture and every available space was taken up with unpacked boxes.

I wasn't particularly looking forward to a 500-mile return journey to pick up Morley from Southport. But by way of consolation, John agreed to bring Morley to a service station near Leicester, where I would meet him and bring him back to Wattisham. Under the circumstances, we had a pleasant break even though we celebrated Christmas 1990 living out of boxes!

Christmas came and went and as we entered the New Year of 1991, I was informed that the AMQ at Wattisham was to be refurbished and we were to move to Hornbeam Road in Stowupland; a satellite estate comprising a small number of married accommodation properties. This was to be our sixth house in five years! Fortunately, we'd unpacked very little since arriving only six weeks previously, and the move went without a hitch.

In the meantime, arrangements had been made for me to attend the month-long MCS *short course* at RAF Coningsby, Lincolnshire. Whilst I was familiar with the entire concept of radar systems fitted to aircraft whether used for navigation, weather detection or Electronic Counter Measures (ECM); the MCS philosophy was somewhat alien to me.

Aircraft radar and intercept theories have always been considered to be more of a black art. Most people understand the idea of sending out a pulse of radio energy in a known direction and measuring the time an echo takes to return from a target. This is basic pulse radar (ping-pong divided by two).

In other words, the distance to an object is calculated by measuring the time a pulse of radio energy takes to travel to the object and to be reflected back (ping-pong—transmission and echo). Then, divide it by two (to get the distance one way), and then, multiply that time by the speed of light (3×10^8 ms^{-1}).

The problem with this is that, it only works where there are no other big radar reflectors around to confuse the signals. The earth, for example, is very, very big and forms a huge radar target. However, scientists and engineers solved the problem of detecting targets moving at low levels in the ground radar clutter (the multitude of large echoes from the earth and things upon it).

The MCS radar pack for the Phantom was carried in the nose of the aircraft behind the *Radome* and produced a nominal transmitter power of 1,525 watts; that's one big microwave oven! The antenna was hydraulically driven, slewable from 60° left to 60° right (azimuth) and 60° up and down (elevation).

The antenna could be operated *gyros in* where the scan pattern was stabilised in space regardless of the aircraft's pitch or bank angles (attitude) or *gyros out* where the scan pattern was relative to the aircraft's orientation. All the radar controls were in the rear cockpit, operated by the navigator. The exception was the Pilot Lock Mode (PLM) button, which allowed the pilot to lock onto a visual target at close range. The MCS comprised several innovative features such as:

Pulse Doppler (PD)—It was very powerful and with a good *look-down* performance as it measures the closing velocity of a target rather than its range. All ground returns were compressed into a single, curved band across the scope, referred to as the main beam clutter. While this removed the ground clutter from the scope, it also meant that targets closing on the fighter at the same speed as the ground (side-on to the fighter) couldn't be detected.

As an aside, the Doppler Principle is one that everyone is aware of but very few will understand. Most people will have stood on a railway platform and heard the horn or whistle from an approaching train. When the train is stationary and the horn is sounded, the frequency heard is constant. However, the frequency heard as the train approaches appears to change and continues to change as the train moves away. This is called the *Doppler Shift*.

A better analogy can be likened to standing stationary in the sea and noting how many waves wash over you. Providing the frequency of the waves remains constant, and you start to walk forwards, you will experience an increase in wave frequency. Conversely, if you then walk backwards, fewer waves will hit you indicating a decrease in wave frequency.

And so, regarding the use of the Doppler Shift in the MCS (and with the equipment used by the police when monitoring a motorist's speed,) with some electronic wizardry, the equipment can detect whether a target is closing in on or moving away from the aircraft.

Short pulse—short-range detection of a target of up to approximately 10 nautical miles, very accurate, and used to visually identify a target at night or in poor weather.

Chirp—a longer range mode using pulse-expansion/pulse-compression—a clever bit of signal processing that greatly improves radar performance. Chirp was very good for detecting targets that were side-on to the aircraft and, therefore not visible in PD.

Mapping—*high map* and *low map* were air-to-ground modes used for navigation and weapons aiming.

Air-to-ground ranging—used Doppler beam sharpening to produce a very narrow beam capable of very accurate distance measurement with the antenna locked to the aircraft's boresight (the centre line), often used to strafe during air-to-ground gunnery.

I must admit, I struggled with the course at Coningsby partly due to its complexity but also due to the somewhat indifferent attitude of one or two of the instructors. Their general attitude was, I believe, more designed to stage manage how knowledgeable and clever they wanted to be perceived.

When I was an apprentice, I'd noticed a similar attitude with some of the instructors—very cock sure of themselves. Nothing wrong with that you might think, but under certain circumstances it can come across as sheer arrogance.

Coningsby was about 110 miles from Stowupland and driving home for weekends wasn't a big issue. That was until the middle weekend of the month. Heavy snow had been forecast and rather than spend time in the Sergeants' mess I decided to tempt fate and risk the journey home. The A1(M) and the A14 were both clear and everyone seemed to be taking heed of the poor driving conditions.

That was until I approached Bury St Edmunds. The outside lane of the dual carriageway was thick with snow. However, that didn't stop one impatient dunderhead, who decided not to travel sedately in convoy, and instead, he overtook everyone. He'd only gone about 100 yards or so ahead of me when I saw a huge flurry of snow, brake lights and then headlights pointing towards me. The moron had only crashed into the central reservation and surprise, surprise, nobody stopped!

I'd only driven on the A14 once before and unfortunately, that evening, I took the Stowmarket turning, instead of continuing to the Stowupland exit.

No problem, I thought.

However, the roads in town hadn't been cleared and there was at least 3" of lying snow. 50 yards ahead of me was another car also taking it very gingerly, behind which I kept my distance. He indicated right to turn up Violet Hill Road, I braked very gently still maintaining my distance behind him and as he pulled off, I took my foot off the brake. The driver then stalled his car and in a flash, I slowly slid into the back of him.

He jumped out, apologised, and admitted that it was his fault and that I was in no way to blame. A fat lot of good that admission did. As far as his insurance company was concerned; because I'd driven into the back of him, I was driven without due care and attention! The bonnet and grill of my beautiful one-year-old Mazda 626 was crumpled but still drivable.

Anyway, after making all the necessary arrangements for the car to be repaired, I didn't venture home again until the course had finished.

The married quarter at Stowupland was habitable but small compared with the AMQs we'd lived in whilst in Germany. It was in March of 1991 that we decided enough was enough and put in a bid for 70 Lowery Way on the Chilton Hall estate in Stowmarket, a modest three-bedroom semi.

The house was being built by Lawrence Homes and we'd put aside a small deposit for house purchase. Despite the fact that the house was still a shell, we went ahead and applied for a mortgage. The building society sent valuers who assessed that the property, once complete, was worth £52,000. Unfortunately, the builders would accept nothing less than £54,000 and despite ours and the estate agent's protestations, they would not back down.

Whilst we had sufficient funds to buy, with an approved 95% mortgage, we were still short of £2,000. Trisha and I discussed the options, and there weren't many! The location of the house was perfect with only a short walk to school for the boys and close to the town centre.

If we wanted 70 Lowery Way, the only real option was to ask Aunt Edith to help us out with a short-term loan to bridge the gap. Without any hesitation, she agreed.

And so, in April we moved out of our 10th married quarter and despite the rigours of life associated with living in public accommodation, we were only ever charged for the loss of one teaspoon and two pillowcases (in fact, those items weren't lost but merely accidentally packed prior to posting).

Life on 74 (F) Squadron was fantastic. I got a real buzz from working with some very talented people, some who had spent a considerable time associated with the mighty Phantom and more or less knew the radar system inside out. Although there were some system faults that were mind-blowingly complex. For my part, whilst classed as a comparative novice, my MCS colleagues helped enormously.

Fred Page

During my time in the RAF, I've been in the privileged position of meeting and working with some real characters. It was on 74 (F) Squadron that I came across a gentleman who, without a doubt, was a real *diamond geezer*.

I first met Fred Page, the squadron cleaner, when I was being given a guided tour of the various facilities. He was busy in the PBF and I remember him as if was only yesterday. He bore a remarkable facial resemblance to that of Field Marshall Montgomery, of El Alamein fame, with quite a wiry frame.

I was introduced to him and we immediately hit it off. He referred to almost everyone, with the exception of the aircrew, with his characteristic London accent as *mate*. However, he always called the officers *sir*.

Fred would often recite stories of his life, his marriage to the lovely Paula and on many occasions his time as a Bevin Boy.

The Bevin Boys

In 1943, four years into the war, the British Government faced a terrible predicament—it was estimated that there were only three weeks' stocks of vital coal supplies left. With an urgent need for more coal to support the war effort, and unable to attract enough workers to meet this demand, a large workforce was conscripted to work in the coal mines, they became known as the *Bevin Boys*.

Their fate had been decided by the then wartime Minister of Labour and National Service, Ernest Bevin. The names of those young men of call-up age were drawn from a hat. If a name came out of the hat that man was destined not for the glamour of a uniform but to go down the pit.

The conditions in which they were employed were dangerous and potentially deadly, yet many of them were branded as cowards for not going off to fight. In fact, of the 50,000 Bevin Boys employed during the 2nd World War and up until 1948, only 47 were conscientious objectors.

Trisha and I became very close friends with Fred and Paula and would regularly visit them just for a chat. Unfortunately, Paula passed away during my time on the squadron and poor Fred, as you can imagine, was devastated. Paula was cremated but Fred didn't really know what to do with her ashes, he thought that she may have liked them to be scattered at a beauty spot overlooking Needham Market.

And so, Trisha and I took Fred to *their special place* and stayed with him whilst he scattered Paula's ashes. Unfortunately, Fred was in such a state and as he emptied the urn, he didn't notice that the wind had changed direction and blew the ashes all over his trousers. In his normal, casual, nonchalant way he just brushed them off and wiped away a tear.

As evidence of the popularity of the man, prior to the squadron disbanding, Fred was invited to a *Top Table* dining-in event in the Sergeant's mess. Now, during my time as an SNCO, I've attended several dining-in nights, but never have I attended one where the squadron cleaner was afforded the privilege of being seated with the honorary guests on the Top Table.

Following the meal and once all the traditional thanks and speeches had been carried out, Fred asked if he could say a few words. I don't remember precisely what he said, but he truly humbled us all, he was magnificent!

Unfortunately, Fred passed away a short while later. Trisha and I, along with other ex-squadron members, attended his funeral in Needham Market. Once again, due to Fred's popularity and pure charisma, what happened at the end of the service was pure magic. We were told to gather on the pavement, outside of the church and in a mark of respect to this amazing man, a Hawk Jet from RAF Valley did a fly past in his honour—what a way to go Fred!

Squadron Detachments

The Royal International Air Tattoo (RIAT)

My first detachment was to the RIAT based at RAF Fairford in Gloucestershire. RIAT is held annually over the third weekend in July. As far as I can remember, we took four aircraft and a team of approximately 20 ground crew. Not only were we there to partake in the IAT, but there were several other *Tiger* squadrons from other participating Air Forces; all celebrating the 70th anniversary of the formation of the Tiger Association.

The NATO Tiger Association or the Association of Tiger Squadrons was established in 1961 and promoted by the French Defence Minister Pierre Messmer. Its role was to promote solidarity between NATO Air Forces.

One of the participating nations was the newly formed Czech Republic which came into being following the fall of the Berlin Wall and the break-up of the Soviet Union. Their contribution to the Tiger meet was a MiG 29 Fulcrum.

When the aircraft arrived on the flight line, the Czech groundcrew, who'd earlier arrived in a giant Antonov transport aircraft; immediately fitted engine intake blanks, exhaust blanks and cockpit canopy covers in place with the intention of stopping anyone snooping.

By the end of the detachment, the canopy covers had been removed allowing all and sundry to view the cockpit and dozens of *Zaps* (squadron sticky badges) had been stuck all over the aircraft.

Apart from the groundcrew and the associated spares for the MiG that arrived in the Antonov, there were several huge casks of *Budvar* beer, ready to be consumed as part of the anniversary celebrations.

Beer brewing in the city of *Ceske Budejovice*, which in German means *Budweis* dates back to the 13th century. During the time when both Czech and German were official languages in the kingdom, two breweries were founded in the city. Both breweries made beer which they called *Budweiser*, similar to how brewers in the city of Pilsen made a beer generically called Pilsner.

The beer from Budweis began to be exported to the United States in 1872–73 and then again in 1933. In 1876, the American brewer Anheuser-Busch began making a beer which they also called *Budweiser*, motivated in part, by a desire to brew a beer similar in quality, colour, flavour and taste to the beer then made at Budweis.

Unfortunately, the Budweiser Budvar Brewery and the American Brewery, Anheuser-Busch have been in an ongoing trademark dispute over the name Budweiser since the start of the 20th century.

I do remember several friendly disputes at RIAT, as to which was the *true* Budweiser but I can say without doubt that the Czech Budvar was far superior to the gassy, chemical American version.

Air Combat Manoeuvring Instrumentation (ACMI)

The ACMI detachment was carried out at Decimomannu, an Italian Air Force base situated in the southern reaches of Sardinia. Deci was used by various NATO nations to carry out detailed recordings of airborne engagements. Using a unique in-flight recording system, each engagement could be analysed by computer during post-flight debriefs.

The computer's frame-by-frame evaluation would determine whether a missile had been launched, and whether or not the missile had found its target.

The work ethic was such that as long as the aircraft were serviceable and fit for the following day sorties, then anything goes.

I spent my 40th birthday in the sun and by way of celebration, Dave and Al arranged for a cake to be made by the Italian catering staff and presented to me at dinner that evening. In fact, come to think of it, I spent three significant birthday events away from home—my 18th at Cosford and my 21st at Masirah.

One of the more memorable escapades took place with Dave *Knobby* Harris (now sadly departed) and Al *Cooperman* Cooper. We decided to borrow some bikes and cycle to one of the local Italian restaurants. We'd only gone a short distance when Al decided that he wanted to sample one of the Prickly Pears that grew in abundance alongside the road.

Now, whilst I'd seen the fruit-bearing shrubs when I'd visited other Mediterranean countries, I knew very little about the fruit and certainly wouldn't have launched myself at them with the same fervour that Al did. He grabbed a small item, about the same size and texture as a kiwi fruit and bit into it. No sooner had his lips touched the skin than he let out a loud cry accompanied by some very course expletives.

What nobody knew was that the fruit was covered in a million tiny hairs that had embedded themselves in his lips and fingers. And so, there we were, three whiter than white Brits standing at the roadside: Al with his upturned hands and mouth wide open, whilst Dave and I tried to remove the offending barbs.

To make matters worse, most of the passing locals realising what was going on, couldn't resist honking their horns as they passed.

Unfortunately, the detachment was initially planned to last for two weeks. However, due to technical problems with the range, the detachment was terminated after only one week.

Armament Practice Camp (APC)

My final major detachment with the squadron was to RAF Akrotiri in Cyprus in April 1992, taking part in a four-week APC. The purpose of APC was to ensure that the crews were combat-ready should their skills be required in defence of the skies over the United Kingdom.

APC allowed the aircrew to practice their gunnery skills on towed banner targets, the size of a football goalmouth, with more or less perfect flying conditions. Their weapon, the formidable 20 mm M61 Vulcan 6-barrel Gatling cannon housed within the SUU-23 gun pod, was capable of firing 3000 rounds per minute with each round tipped with ink to show up on the target.

The long banners were towed behind Hawk aircraft belonging to 100 Squadron, affectionately known as the *Tatty ton*.

We left Wattisham on Thursday, 16 April, the Maundy Thursday, and arrived at Akrotiri to find that the base was closed for Easter. It later transpired that we had to leave the UK earlier, otherwise, we'd have had to wait several weeks for passenger aircraft to take the entire groundcrew to Akrotiri, unless, we left the UK before Easter. As it turned out, things could not have worked out better.

Several of us went to Limassol and booked a three-day trip; leaving Limassol on a Saturday morning, sailing to Haifa in Israel and visiting all of the religious sites in and around Bethlehem and Jerusalem. That night, we set sail for Egypt arriving in Port Said on a Sunday morning.

We boarded coaches and the entire convoy, comprising some 13 vehicles, was escorted by armed Egyptian military for the three-hour journey to Cairo. As we were driven through Port Said, each road junction or intersection was closed to local traffic by the police and the convoy just sped through. There were fears that if the coaches had to join the normal congested traffic there was the possibility that we could be attacked by militants.

The journey through the desert was quite boring, we passed through small insignificant villages with nothing but sand for as far as the eye could see. However, what I failed to appreciate at the time was the fact that the route took us very close to the Suez Canal which was made blatantly clear when all of a sudden, a huge container ship came into view little more than 100 yards from the convoy.

Whilst I've seen many travel shows which cover the region, believe me, there is absolutely nothing to compare with seeing firsthand the marvels of the ancient world. I of course refer to the Pyramids and the Sphinx—absolutely wonderful.

One of the pilots, Squadron Leader John McGarry, who'd recently returned from an exchange tour with the USAF having spent 16 years with the RAF, was shortly to retire, wanted to give a demonstration of the firepower of the cannon. He also wanted to carry out a high-speed pass by way of a final goodbye as a Phantom pilot.

Before he took off, he was adamant that all of our aircraft on the dispersal were to have their canopies closed—the reason was to become apparent later. Once he'd taken off, we piled into whatever squadron transport was available and made our way to the cliffs overlooking the sea. By the time we got to the best vantage point, John was on the final approach to his firing point and we were not to be disappointed!

The sound of the gun letting rip was absolutely amazing. Eager to get back to the line, once again we jumped into the Land Rover and John spent several minutes circling the airfield so as to give us time to get back. I managed to climb to the top of the airfield lighting tower and watch with astonishment as John flew *hell-for-leather* adjacent to the flight line where the remaining aircraft were parked.

As this detachment was to be one of the last for the Tigers, journalists from the Bury Free Press were invited to attend. Their coverage, which appeared in the newspaper on 22 May 1991, was extensive and was accompanied by a plethora of photographs. However, one of the most awe-inspiring was one showing John *beating up* the flight line; flying at close to 500 mph at approximately 30 feet,

The press was requested not to print the photograph, but, unfortunately, they did, and I believe the squadron boss, Wing Commander Nick Spiller, got quite the bollocking on his return to Wattisham.

Missile Practice Camp (MPC)

The MPC was carried out at the Strike Command Air-to-Air Guided Weapons Operational Evaluation Unit (STCAAME). It was later to be renamed the Air Guided Weapons Operational Evaluation Unit (AGWOEU). RAF Valley in Anglesey, an event that I'd heard talked about numerous times but never once did I appreciate the amount of work involved, especially for those of us of the aircraft Missile Control System persuasion.

The purpose of MPC was to give aircrew the opportunity to fire live missiles during simulated air-to-air combat. As far as memory serves, the weather was good which our aircrew made the most of.

I can't remember how long the detachment lasted, but suffice it to say, that we had a huge number of faults on the MCS system. This was despite the fact that the allocated aircraft were given the *once-over* prior to leaving Wattisham. We were always the last trade to finish at cease flying, that was apart from the *bomb heads* who spent an inordinate amount of time fitting ejection seat pans and prepping for the next day's sorties.

The detachment was brought to an abrupt end when a potentially life-threatening event took place. One of the aircraft took off with a full complement of Skyflash air-to-air radar-guided missiles. When the time came to launch a missile from the starboard pylon, the pilot pressed the fire trigger but didn't see the missile streak off into the distance.

Instead, he heard a very loud bang and noticed one of the missile's guidance fins stuck in the starboard engine cowling. Apparently, it was almost beating itself to death before detaching itself and spiralling towards the ground. The crew were incredibly lucky, to say the least!

By all accounts, when the missile launched from one of the rear, starboard stations, it hit the forward AIM 9L heat-seeking missile launcher which deflected it towards the engine intake. It was decided to leave the aircraft at RAF Valley until a decision could be made as to its future. As it happened, the cost involved really wasn't worth it and everything that could be salvaged was removed. The aircraft frame finished its days being used by Valley's RAF firemen to practice on.

The Demise of the Mighty Phantom

Ludicrously despite being partly manufactured by UK firms, and bought with UK taxpayer's money, the USA had stipulated that the aircraft could not be disposed of to any non-government organisations. Thus, an important part of the UK's aviation history has, for the most part, been reduced to scrap, despite museums across the country crying out for a chance to exhibit an example of this powerful aircraft.

A few have somehow escaped the bureaucratic edicts from above, but it is a small number. Most that were not immediately scrapped on retirement have succumbed to the scrapman's attentions in the years since, the final mean-spirited act in the story of the UK's Phantoms.

After 25 years of service, the Phantoms ended their illustrious RAF career and as a result of the Options for Change military budget reduction in 1990, it was decided to phase out the Phantom. In October 1992, 74 (F) Squadron was finally disbanded.

On 5 October 1990, a press conference was held outside number 10 Downing Street where Prime Minister Margaret Thatcher announced that the UK would join the Exchange Rate Mechanism (ERM). Her chancellor, at the time, was John Major, who did little more than stand alongside her and say nothing. That was a relief because he had one of the most boring, monotonous, Dalek-sounding voices imaginable.

The object of the ERM was based on the concept of fixed currency exchange rate margins. However, there was variability of the exchange rates within the confines of the upper and lower end of the margins. The overall aim of the ERM was to reduce exchange rate variability and achieve monetary stability in Europe prior to the introduction of the Euro.

Maggie predicted that the ERM would enable the building societies to reduce mortgage interest rates. Unfortunately, in an effort to maintain the pound's parity with the Deutsche Mark, interest rates were kept at much higher rate levels that were good for the UK economy.

By 16 September 1992, as speculators placed even larger bets against the pound, John Major, who by then was Prime Minister, authorised the Bank of England to increase its base rate from an already punitive 10% to 12%. At this point, the chancellor, Norman Lamont, urged the UK to pull out of the ERM and let Sterling float.

However, Cabinet colleagues Michael Heseltine and Kenneth Clarke both were obsessed with the idea that the UK should later join the Euro, persuaded Major to ramp up interest rates to a staggering 15%.

Both of these men were quite content to see the cost of mortgages increase by 50% in a single day; in pursuit of their own ideological commitment to further this country's integration into the European project. Major went along with it.

By the end of the day, even the 50% increase couldn't keep the pound at the mandated level against the Deutsche Mark, and the UK exited the ERM. That day was known as Black Wednesday.

Anyway, the reason I mentioned the ERM was the frightening fact that our house was in negative equity (worth a lot less than the price we paid for it) and we would not be able to pay the proposed increase in mortgage repayments.

We could move back into married quarters but would be heavily in debt with nothing to show for it. Fortunately, the chancellor made the correct decision and we left the ERM, and not a moment too soon in my humble opinion.

It was about this time that Trisha decided to apply for a job. I believe she would have liked to go back to telephonist-oriented employment. However, she came across an advertisement in a local newspaper with Atco-Qualcast, a thriving lawn mower/garden machinery manufacturer based in Stowmarket.

The requirement was for a purchase ledger clerk whose prime role was to issue credit notes to companies that had returned defective equipment. Trisha always had a confident disposition. However, she admitted that she knew little or nothing about that particular vocation, but was prepared to give it a go.

I don't remember how many applicants there were for the post but Trisha attended the interview and was subsequently offered the job. The only downside was the fact that she didn't drive and the factory was located approximately two miles from home. We only had one car, which I needed for work. So, she resorted to riding her bike until such time as she passed her driving test.

Chapter Nineteen
Royal Air Force Station Honington

(12 November 1992 to 13 September 1993)

RAF Honington was situated a few miles north of Bury St Edmunds in Suffolk. When I left Wattisham, I had no real idea what type of employment I would be undertaking. All I knew was that it was not on the resident Tornado Weapons Conversion Unit (TWCU) which really only left one option—avionics bay work!

As it turned out, the job was straightforward enough. I was to be the avionics bay chief, responsible for the Tornado Ground Attack radar system, and once again, I knew absolutely nothing about the equipment and was unfamiliar with bay protocols.

However, the team in the bay were exceptional and helped enormously in easing me into the job. My Flight Sergeant Woody was a real star; he was laid back and taught me a lot about the requirements associated with working in a bay environment.

I'd only been on the squadron for a couple of months and had got quite used to my surroundings when I was summoned to the office of another Flight Sergeant, Barry Turner. Apparently, he'd picked up a Junior Tech who was walking from the car park and not wearing his beret.

When questioned as to why; all the lad could say in his defence was, he regularly sees a Chief (me) who didn't bother wearing his headdress and it if was okay for me, then, it must be okay for him to do it—Twat!

I was then told in no uncertain terms that I was setting a bad example and asked why I was incorrectly dressed. Honington was the only unit that I ever served where I had my own parking slot—designated *SNCO I/C Radar Bay*. When I told him that my parking slot was literally only a few yards from the entrance, I couldn't see the point of putting on a hat to walk the short distance, he almost blew a gasket!

He also commented that I should be wearing a hat whilst driving on the station. I couldn't be bothered arguing, and anyway, I really didn't give a monkey's shit!

At the time there were still several issues associated with drawing attention to yourself by travelling in private cars whilst wearing a military uniform. Most people would put on a civilian jacket or jumper to hide the fact. However, I decided that I would leave my uniform trousers, tie, jumper and shoes in my office and travel to work in civilian clothes, taking in a clean work shirt each day. That worked absolutely fine, and at least, I didn't have to wear a bloody beret and mess up my hair!

Work in the bay wasn't particularly challenging because everyone knew exactly what to do, there was a Sergeant in charge of each of the two shifts. My only real job was to administer the teams, carry out their annual assessments and appraisals and try to protect them from any crap that was dished out by the flying squadrons.

I was only just beginning to get my feet under the table when the news came through that TWCU was being moved to RAF Lossiemouth in Scotland and all operational flying at Honington would cease. I couldn't believe it. I was asked by Woody if I had any preferences as to where I would like to go (I think that some of the bay personnel would end up going to Scotland).

Michael and Steven were both settled in school and as far as Mike was concerned, he was 16 years old and in a crucial part of his education. Trisha was going from strength to strength working for Atco-Qualcast and had really made a name for herself as being a reliable, conscientious, exceptionally talented and well-liked individual.

We certainly couldn't afford to move again, even with the help of the various financial schemes available for individuals who were posted. To make matters worse, we were still in the unenviable position of being stuck in the *negative equity* trap. I told Woody that I didn't want to go *north of the border* and was subsequently offered a post at RAF Swanton Morley in Norfolk. I decided that I would commute the 100-mile return journey on a daily basis.

So, in September 1993, I said goodbye to the team whom I'd become very fond of. At my going away *do,* I was presented with a small model of a Golden Retriever that was standing upright, wearing trousers, a green jumper and holding a golfing putter—I was quite touched! As is normal, whenever anyone leaves, I was also given a large *sorry, you're leaving* card that had been signed by almost everyone in the avionics building.

However, there was one signatory whose comment showed what a pathetic individual he really was. It was the plonker of a Flight Sergeant who had torn a strip off me for not wearing a hat!

His comment inside the card said, "That was a bit extreme coming to work in civvies just so you don't have to wear a hat."

What a total tosser!

Chapter Twenty
Royal Air Force Station Swanton Morley

(13 September 1993 to 18 January 1995)

I arrived at RAF Swanton Morley on the 13 September 1993. The station was located three miles north of the Norfolk town of East Dereham and was home to the Central Servicing and Development Establishment (CSDE), a very specialist unit that concentrated on developing innovative and specialist systems and solutions for the RAF and Fleet Air Arm aircraft.

For my part, I was to be employed on the Helicopter and Vibration Flight (HVF) as the aero engine vibration analysis specialist. I never liked to use the term e*xpert* in any of the jobs I'd ever done. I do remember being told once upon a time, that an expert can be looked on as a *has been* as in *Ex* and a *drip under pressure* as in *Spurt*.

The HVF team comprised Flight Lieutenant Andy Marsh, Flight Sergeant Chris Pink, Chief Techs Chris Ray, Ivor Linnington, Danny Glen, Steve Jackson and Sergeant Paul Spencer-White, a Data Analyst. Attached to HVF was the School of Vibration Control, run by Sergeant Ronnie Blurton.

I was tasked with introducing the very latest computerised system aptly named Vibration Monitoring Equipment (VME) into service. The VME was a Condition Monitoring (CM) system, manufactured by Stewart Hughes Limited (SHL), a company based at Chandlers Ford near Eastleigh in Hampshire.

The equipment was primarily concerned with the early detection of failure of any of the rotating components of an aircraft jet engine. It was capable of measuring, monitoring, diagnosing and offering vibration trend analysis for the Ardour 104 and 151 jet engines fitted to the Jaguar and Hawk aircraft respectively. Also, the RB199 engines fitted to the ground attack and air defence variants of the Tornado (GR4 and F3 respectively), the Spey engines, fitted to the Nimrod reconnaissance aircraft and the Pegasus engines fitted to the Harrier.

The equipment was also required to be fitted into all relevant Uninstalled Engine Test Facilities (UETFs) for each of the aircraft types. Once again, I knew absolutely nothing about the job and was thrown in at the deep end. Nevertheless, I was given ample time to study what I was required to do. I spent the first three months reading every single enclosure on file that was associated with the new equipment that I was to introduce into service.

I'd experienced some real challenges throughout my career but this job really did stretch my mind. Unfortunately, my predecessor Colin Musket who'd been on the project for several years, was to be discharged from the RAF a mere two weeks after I joined the team. Once he was gone, there would be nobody else to quiz or question.

To some, including me, Swanton Morley was considered a graveyard; somewhere where only the *old and past-it* and those who wanted an easy life were posted and once there it would be impossible to escape. However, despite my initial reluctance to be *put out to grass* at the Norfolk base, my tour turned out to be one of the most enjoyable. The HVF team really was an exceptional bunch of characters, each a specialist in their own particular area.

My leader, Flight Sergeant Chris Pink was one of those personalities who was totally unflappable and seemed to take everything in his stride. He hadn't been in the job very long either.

The computer age hadn't really taken off when I arrived at Swanton in 1993, and whilst the remainder of the team had desktop 486 processor computers, for my part, I was stuck with a laptop with no hard drive, a 286 processor and all documents were held on a floppy disc. Windows to me, then, was something that was in a wall of a building.

I must admit, that I was a complete illiterate novice when it came to word processing. I would spend many an hour reading documents held on file, extracting what I thought were relevant facts and compiling spreadsheets. I also spent many hours complaining that my system was not only slow but incredibly unreliable. It was about that time that Mal Davies arrived, a very switched-on cookey who really was computer-literate.

I went on leave and on my return found that my old 286 had been replaced by a new 486 model. A version of Windows had been installed and the whole system made life too much easier for me.

However, several weeks later, at a lunchtime *goodbye* function once all of the traditional presentations were complete, Chris stood up and asked Ronnie

Blurton to make one final presentation. At the time, Noel Edmunds was the presenter of a particular Saturday night extravaganza, whereby, he would deliberately lead someone up the garden path and culminate the spoof with a *Gotcha*.

I was handed a small parcel, neatly wrapped and asked to unwrap it in front of everyone. Once open, to say I was speechless really would be an understatement—it was a small sports trophy with a crude sticker saying *Gotcha*.

The only word I can really remember saying was *Bastards*. Ronnie was almost wetting himself and much to everyone's amusement, Mal explained that all he had done was to install windows onto the system and replace the 286 sticker with a 486 one—Bastards!

There was a lot of very serious work undertaken by the HVF team, but on the other hand, there were plenty of occasions where we could let our hair down and enjoy some exceptional social functions. Every now and then, I'd book a room in the mess, stay overnight and take part in some outrageous partying.

On one particular session, rather than drive to Dereham, for obvious reasons, we decided to book two taxis and meet in one of the local pubs. The first taxi arrived and quickly departed with half of the team on board. Chris, Ronnie and I were waiting inside the mess porch when a car pulled up outside.

Ronnie, in his normal exuberant self, launched himself into the front seat of the taxi to be met with a, "What are you doing," from the female driver.

Ronnie was most put out when she explained that she had only come to pick up her husband!

One of the less pleasant activities at Swanton was *guarding*. Unfortunately, the majority of personnel at Swanton were SNCOs, predominately Sergeants and Chief Techs. So, even as a chief, I wasn't exempt from the trials and tribulations of doing my bit; trying to keep the unit secure! I spent many a miserable night in the sangar whiling away the hours peering out of the slits in the sangar wall.

It was decided that Chris and I would take the new Stewart Hughes Project Manager, Andy Dolin an ex-Fleet Air Arm Lieutenant to RAF Marham, introduce him to the UETF personnel and give him an idea of how the equipment was configured and used within that environment. Andy booked himself into one of the hotels in Swaffham and I was to stop the night with Chris and Sue.

That evening we met in the restaurant and later on retired to the bar. I don't know where the evening went but all of a sudden, the barman was calling *last orders* and he asked if we were residents.

Pinkie immediately responded with an emphatic *yes*. The doors were locked and so we carried on drinking. After a while, the barman asked if we wanted any more drinks, Andy told us that he had some drinks in his room and we decided to leave. When we got there, it transpired that he had none.

So, there we were, in Andy's room, with no drinks and the front door to the hotel locked and barred. I really don't know how Pinkie thought we would get out of the hotel once we'd told the barman that we were residents. But as a *leader of men,* he assured me that it would be okay. Naively, I accepted what he said.

Pinkie asked me to have a look out of the window and see if we could jump from there to the ground. It was pitch black, I couldn't see a thing and had no idea how high up we were.

The next minute, all I heard was, "Stop f****** about you tart and get out."

I felt a very sharp push, and the next minute, I found myself in the bushes. Talk about being a *leader of men*!

Things seemed to be going well and I was managing the commuting, that was until the decision was taken to close Swanton Morley under the *Options for Change* scenario. The option entailed the restructuring of the armed forces and was primarily aimed at cutting defence spending following the end of the Cold War.

The UK military strategy had until this point been almost entirely focused on defending the UK against the Soviet military; whether by the Royal Marines in Scandinavia, the RAF in West Germany or over the North Sea, the Royal Navy in the Norwegian Sea and North Atlantic or the British Army of the Rhine in Germany.

With the collapse of the Soviet Union and the Warsaw Pact, these scenarios were no longer relevant. While criticised both before and after, it was an exercise mirrored by governments of almost every major western military power, the so-called *peace dividend.* Among the changes implemented was the cutting of total manpower by approximately 18% to around 255,000 (120,000 Army, 60,000 Royal Navy and 75,000 RAF).

Closing the unit meant that the entire workforce had to move to RAF Wyton in Cambridgeshire. Once again, I really couldn't believe what was happening. And so, after only 16 months at Swanton, we had to up-stick, move to RAF Wyton and become part of the newly formed *Logistic Support Services 2* (LSS2) organisation.

Whilst it was only a short hop from Swanton Morley to Wyton, the journey from Stowmarket was considerably longer. When I arrived back in the UK from Wildenrath, the commute to Wattisham was about seven miles and the drive to Honington was approximately 16 miles. I thought the journey to Swanton of 50 miles was bad enough but the drive to Wyton was now 65 miles, a daily commute of 130 miles!

Chapter Twenty-One
Royal Air Force Station Wyton

(18 January 1995 to 23 September 1997)

The area around Wyton has been associated with aviation since 1912; a period that embraces almost the entire history of aviation. On 1 April 1918, the Royal Air Force was formed, the oldest independent Air Force in the world. Wyton continued to train units for overseas operations as it had done previously for the Royal Flying Corps.

Several aviation milestones have been recorded from Royal Air Force Wyton. The first sortie of WW2 took off from the unit as well as the first aircraft of the 1000 bomber raids on Germany. The legendary Pathfinder Force was formed at Wyton and Wyton aircraft took part in the last Bomber Command raid on Germany.

When I first joined the RAF in 1968, there were approximately 104,000 personnel in the service and throughout my career (and up to the present day), that number has been steadily reducing. I think it was midway through 1996 that the Ministry asked for volunteer redundees and by that stage of my career (!) I'd more or less had enough.

Following a careers brief, where I was told that my overall assessment scores weren't high enough to be considered for promotion to Flight Sergeant, I decided to apply for redundancy. My most recent assessment was good and included a Special Recommendation for promotion.

Once upon a time, a *Spec-Rec* was sufficient to get you onto the promotion board, but that dispensation had only recently been withdrawn, and with the draw-down of several units there were very few vacancies available for my rank and trade. Iain Davitt, who I'd worked with on the Phantoms, was also at Wyton and he too was bored with the lack of promotion prospects and also put in his papers.

I don't remember how many people had applied for redundancy, but a few days before the names of the successful applicants were announced, I had a phone call from Iain. He told me that he'd just had a conversation with someone from the admin section who confirmed that he had been successful with his application. I asked if any other names had been leaked—unfortunately not.

A few days later, I received notification that I was to go to the general office where I and all other applicants would be notified of the outcome. As I entered the admin section, I was asked my name and told to stand on the left-hand side of the door to the Chief Clerk's office. As others arrived some were told to join my queue whilst others were told to join the queue to the right of the office.

Imagine my surprise, when I saw Iain at the head of my queue. Word soon passed down the line that if you were in Iain Davitt's line—bingo, you'd cracked it, because after all he had already been told that he was one of the successful applicants. Redundancy and a nice pay-off, here we come, or so we thought!

Iain was the first to be called into the Chief Clerk's office and he was soon out again. The look of horror on his face was an absolute picture and one that I'll not forget.

All he said to me in his Scottish accent was, "I didn't f******* well get it."

His confidante had got it completely wrong. Well, talk about deflated and pissed off and word of the faux pas went down our line even faster. It was shortly after that episode that Iain decided he wanted out and applied for Premature Voluntary Redundancy (PVR). The PVR process was fairly rapid and it wasn't too long before he had secured work with Ionica, a Cambridge-based microwave telecommunications company.

For my part, I'd spent the previous two years attending Ipswich College studying Parts 1 and 2 of the City and Guilds Electrical Installation course but still had a full year to go before the programme was complete. I also intended to study the Inspection and Testing and the Electrical Regulations modules. The intention was that I'd at least be capable of doing something apart from aircraft work come the day of my retirement from the services.

Work continued on the VME programme and I seemed to be spending more and more time with a car strapped to my arse. Apart from the ridiculous amount of travelling I was doing just getting to and from work, I also spent many hours driving around the UK; visiting the numerous Tornado squadrons—RAF Marham in Norfolk, RAF Coningsby in Lincolnshire, RAF Lossiemouth and RAF Leuchars both in Scotland. I also covered RAF Kinloss, home of the

Nimrod, also in Scotland, RAF Valley on the isle of Anglesey and RAF Coltishall in Norfolk. On top of those units, I also visited RAF Brüggen in Germany.

Following a request from the UETF at RAF Brüggen to help out with a VME issue that was holding up *passing off* the RB199 engines. I contacted the MT office requesting a vehicle to drive to Germany. My ulterior motive was to be able to bring back an abundance of goodies for the rest of the team.

I was told in no uncertain terms that much more notification would be required and I'd have to fly to Dusseldorf. The booking of flights was simple, so too was organising transport for when I arrived in Germany.

UK airport security, whilst quite stringent, nevertheless still left a lot to be desired. It was whilst I was boarding the flight that I witnessed two passengers in a heated argument concerning seat allocation. The chap who was seated was adamant that it was his seat whilst the man standing was equally resolute that the seat was his.

The issue was quickly resolved when the stewardess checked the boarding pass of the man standing and then requested the same of the seated man. What happened next was priceless. The stewardess calmly said that his ticket was for Barcelona. However, we were travelling to Dusseldorf. Without a second's hesitation, he was off; very amusing.

But the question on everyone's lips was, "How on earth did he manage to get on board our flight in the first place?"

It was in the spring of 1997, as I approached my 46th birthday, that I began seriously thinking about what direction I wanted my life to go. I became acutely tired due to the excessive travelling I was doing but also became disillusioned with the lack of promotion prospects. I'd been a Chief Tech for 13 years and RAF units were closing down like they were going out of fashion.

My terms of service meant that I would be discharged on my 47th birthday, a mere 12 months away. The only way I could extend my service until the age of 55 was to get promoted to Flight Sergeant, and that wasn't going to happen. And so, after serving Queen and country for almost 29 years, Trisha and I decided that I should call it a day and look elsewhere for work.

I was discharged on 24 September 1997.

Chapter Twenty-Two
A New Beginning

I had anticipated that I probably wouldn't continue in the aviation industry and decided in the summer of 1995 to do *day-release* in Ipswich College and train to become an electrician and one day maybe have my own business. The city and guilds training was very good however, I found the attitude of some of the students very frustrating. I wanted to learn, not because I had to, but more because I wanted to.

There were two characters, who sat at the back of the classroom and treated the course as a joke. They were disruptive, often late for class and took very little notice of what the instructor had to say. The instructor, in some respects, didn't handle their behaviour well at all, and after one particular occasion, I asked them to stop being unruly because it was getting tedious.

It transpired that their company was paying for their two-year course and they'd still have a job regardless of whether they passed or not, although I found that hard to believe! When I mentioned that the cost of the course was coming out of my own pocket (a little lie) they calmed down a lot. To this day, I don't know how they fared. For my part, I achieved passes in all areas of the course at the college.

Following my discharge, I spent several months doing all of the things I was unable to do whilst serving and felt a little apprehensive about going into business. I did, however, spend quite a while with my brother-in-law Rob, who had a fledgling electrical installation business in Andover, learning the ropes and helping out with jobs.

Michael was just finishing his second year at De-Montfort University and was preparing to go to Germany for a year and work with BMW as part of his engineering degree course. He'd struggled towards the end of that year and had to take several re-sits. He and his partner Julie, travelled down from Leicester with the aim of having a few days with us before Michael left the country.

Whilst they were on the train, I received a phone call from the university asking me to let Michael know that he'd passed all of the re-sits. They duly arrived and I said nothing! We took them for a meal in Needham Market, and towards the end of the evening, I broke the news; he was absolutely ecstatic and rightly so.

I had to attend Cambridge Hospital the next morning to have an operation on my ear and remove a Basal cell carcinoma that had been bothering me for quite a while. When we eventually arrived home, we were met with the sight of Michael hosing down the front of the house. He'd been sick out of his bedroom window during the night. It can't have been anything he ate! Anyway, Julie went back to Leicester. Trisha and I took Michael to Stansted Airport a day or so later.

As mentioned in the prologue, Steven, having qualified at Ipswich collage as a tree surgeon, was preparing to move to West Yorkshire to take up employment with *Air Valley*, a tree surgeon company.

Non-Destructive Testing (NDT)

During my time on HVF, I'd spent a lot of time with personnel from the NDT flight based at Swanton Morley. The team, comprising three civil service technicians, were responsible for repairing and calibrating all elements of the NDT equipment portfolio. The actual NDT squadron was manned by a mix of RAF and Fleet Air Arm SNCOs as well as some civil service engineers.

When RAF Swanton Morley closed down, the entire NDT squadron was moved to RAF St Athan in South Wales. As it transpired, only two of the technicians transferred from Swanton thereby leaving the section seriously undermanned.

Non-destructive testing is a valuable technique used by many industries which blends quality assurance and material science to evaluate the properties of a material, component, structure or system without causing any damage which is especially beneficial when associated with aircraft. There are various types of NDT which include visual inspection, radiography, ultrasonic testing, magnetic particle testing and penetrant dye testing.

It was in the early summer of 1998 that I learnt that a vacancy had arisen on the servicing team. As I'd visited the unit several times whilst based at Wyton, I was well aware of the type of work that was carried out. I also knew the bay manager, so, I decided to apply for the job. There are many who, after leaving the armed forces, pursue a career in the MoD.

In my case, because I'd spent several hours on front-line aircraft, I was well aware that unless proper logistical practices were in place, the aircraft would be going nowhere. Come the day of my interview, and bearing in mind that I'd be repairing equipment and not designing circuits, I was somewhat surprised at some of the questions posed by the first of the three interviewers:

"John, how would you increase the effective range of radar equipment?"

"How would you increase the dynamic range of an ammeter and a voltmeter?"

What!

These were the first two questions asked and although I knew the answers to both and all subsequent questions, they really weren't what I was expecting. Anyway, once the torture was over, I was told that all candidates would be notified of the outcome later that afternoon.

Stowmarket was at least 270 miles away, and as I didn't have a mobile, I gave Ange and Ian's home telephone number in Martock which was only a couple of hours away. Sure enough, shortly before 17:00, the phone rang.

"You're in!" was the message from Ed and after a brief chat, that was it!

I was to join the MoD as a PTO (Professional and Technology Officer) in October 1998.

As soon as I got home, Trisha and I started to make plans as to where we were going to live and although the house in Stowmarket was worth marginally more than we paid for it, it went on the market more or less straight away. We drove to the Vale of Glamorgan and spent a few days in a Travel Lodge near Cardiff airport and spent a considerable amount of time *house hunting*.

We eventually found the perfect place—a four-bedroom house with a large garden front and rear. It was absolutely beautiful, so beautiful in fact we put in an offer of £92,000 which was accepted straight away. We drove back to Stowmarket and arranged the mortgage. Trisha gave her notice with Atco-Qualcast and we started to make all of the necessary arrangements.

Unfortunately, as usual, things moved slowly with the mortgage application and as I had to start work in October 1998, I would have to stay at Saints in rented accommodation until such time as all the ends were tied up. I spent two months travelling home on a Friday and returning to work on Monday morning—it was absolutely knackering!

We eventually moved into our home in Rhoose shortly after New Year's Day, 1999.

Chapter Twenty-Three
St Athan

Work in the lab was interesting and quite challenging, to begin with, however, it didn't take too long to realise that, despite the fact that I'd known the bay manager for several years, he turned out to be nothing more than a bully, a hypocrite and a drunkard. I'll say no more apart from the fact that, I had a miserable time for a large part of my time there.

Trisha was a *trier* and whenever she set her mind to doing something, she invariably succeeded. Once we'd sorted out the house and settled in, we discussed her return to work, not because she was bored but because it had more to do with our newly acquired mortgage and the associated costs. We visited some of the job shops in Llantwitt Major and Barry and also looked for relevant employment in the local papers.

Customer services was her forte and she eventually joined British Gas in Cardiff where she began training as a *dual fuel executive*, responsible for dealing with issues and complaints from customers. I don't remember there being a requirement for her to *cold call* people.

She worked some very odd shift hours though, some days going to work at midday and not returning until 10:30 at night having not eaten much all day. She would drive to Barry Island railway station and catch the train into Cardiff. She'd only been working for two months or so when she contracted a viral infection that affected both of her inner ears.

A lot of people in her department had also been sick with the complaint. The infection caused her to feel dizzy and sick when she stood up and she quite obviously couldn't drive, let alone work on a switchboard. She was in constant contact with the company and produced periodic sick notes. However, after two months, she received her P45, with no covering letter or explanation as to why she'd been dismissed.

The sickness and dizziness eventually wore off in September, by which time, she began to feel exceptionally tired and spent the next few months in bed seldom awake for more than a few hours each day. She saw the doctor on many occasions and he initially believed the tiredness was related to the virus. Over the next year, she saw several specialists in the hospitals in and around Cardiff and nobody could offer a rational diagnosis.

She had countless blood tests and at one stage it was thought by the specialists that she may have liver cancer and when that was discounted it was suggested that she may have Lupus. Lupus is also referred to as autoimmune syndrome where the immune system produces antibodies that attack and destroy the body's healthy cells and tissues. That too was discounted.

She was then referred to another consultant, Doctor Evans, who was about as much use as an ashtray on a motorbike. He checked her over, asked her lots of questions and admitted that he didn't really know what the problem was. Trisha mentioned in passing, that she was having trouble losing weight and instead of the buffoon doctor being sympathetic he merely commented that there weren't many fat people in Biafra!

We were both shocked and stunned and I wrote to the medical council and complained about his totally unprofessional and crass attitude. The reply wasn't worth the paper it was printed on and merely stated that Doctor Evans hadn't meant to offend—that was it—no apology!

What he obviously hadn't taken into account or even considered was that whilst Trisha spent a lot of time in bed, she still needed to eat and it didn't take a brain surgeon to realise that if her daily intake was 1000 calories but only expended 500 calories she would put on weight.

Trisha's GP, Doctor Penrose said from day one that he would get to the bottom of the problem and sure enough he did—he never gave up on Trisha eventually diagnosing her complaint as ME. Once upon a time, ME was dismissed as being *all in the mind*. But the illness that sceptics called Yuppie Flu, is more than just a figment of the imagination.

Researchers have suggested that those suffering from chronic fatigue syndrome which causes extreme weakness, inability to think straight, disrupted sleep patterns and headaches have biological abnormalities. The symptoms, Trisha explained so explicitly one day, could be likened to having not slept for several days and running a marathon with a severe hangover.

It is believed that the underlying problem is almost certainly associated with a viral infection such as glandular fever, which can hide in the body for months even years and stop the process in which omega-3 and omega-6 essential fats are converted into fatty acids. Without these essential acids, a number of symptoms manifest themselves, the most obvious is fatigue. Trisha suffered extensively from glandular fever in her late teens and early 20s!

Dr Penrose advised that whilst there was no real cure it could be controlled not through drugs but by pacing oneself and trying not to overexert herself. Unfortunately, Trisha was a *doer* and couldn't bear to be sat around. Over the course of the following years, on those days that she felt well she would invariably drain herself which resulted in her suffering.

In April 2000, which was our 25th wedding anniversary year, we planned on going around the world with John and Carol Owen, the couple we first met whilst camping beneath the Eagles Nest near Berchtesgaden. We thought the trip would be a great tonic for Trisha although living out of a suitcase is hard work for the most able-bodied of people.

I asked the bay manager if I could take leave, unpaid, if necessary, to cover the period where I didn't have sufficient days available. But he wouldn't make the decision; instead, I'd have to speak with HR—their response was an immediate-yes!

We deliberated as to whether Trisha could really manage the five-week trip and eventually decided that the journey shouldn't be too physical and she could probably relax. We spent the evening of 14 April in a hotel close to Heathrow, ready for an early start the next morning. The shuttle bus arrived at the hotel and there was the traditional mad panic to get on board. Unfortunately, we were amongst the last to embark and our terminal was the last stop on the route.

We stood, with our suitcases, at the front of the bus which wasn't really a problem until we arrived at the first stop. There were several passengers who were seated at the rear of the bus and we had to haul our bags and suitcases off before they could retrieve theirs. We then had to drag our bags back on again. This scenario was repeated again at the next two stops. By the time we arrived at our terminal, I was knackered.

Wendy, Rob and Annie managed to get to the terminal in time to see us off having endured heavy snow on the M3 and M25. Getting through security then was straightforward enough and little did we know that the process would take on a whole new path following the 9/11 atrocities that would take place later the next year.

Once I and my carry-on luggage had been scanned, I gathered my stuff together. Trisha, unfortunately, was pulled to one side and had her handbag searched. Whilst I was waiting for her, I took my bag off my shoulder, bent forward to drop it onto the ground, and as I did, I felt a terrible searing pain across the small of my back.

For the next nine hours én route to Singapore, I was in utter agony and the pain didn't really subside for the next 10 days when we left Australia. The tour was an amazing experience and something that will live with me forever. Our itinerary included three days in Singapore, and four days in Cairns, Australia. Then, we flew to Brisbane and spent the next five days driving from Brisbane to Sydney where we explored the city for the next five days.

We then flew to New Zealand where we spent three days with friends of John and Carol in Wellington and caught up with the washing, etc. The highlight of the trip was the seven days we spent in Fiji—it was absolutely beautiful! Following a flight across the international date line, we arrived in L.A. and spent three days there before continuing to London. By the time we arrived home, we were both worn out.

Having been away on such a fantastic holiday, I expected a little more interest from my co-workers than I got.

Instead, all I got from the bay manager was, "Did you have a good time?"

To which I obviously replied that we did, and he just walked away; there were no other questions, and that was it, nothing else! Nobody, absolutely nobody, asked about the trip—smacks of jealousy I reckon!

In 2003, following a chat with PJ, our next-door neighbour, who was the senior avionics engineer with British Airways at Rhoose airport, I applied for a job in the same role as that which I'd filled in the RAF. I attended an aptitude test and a week later was invited for an interview; which I felt went really well. Shortly after that, I received a letter inviting me to attend a medical.

I was asked, on the day of the medical, if had any medical conditions that they needed to be made aware of. I told them that I was awaiting surgery for an inguinal hernia but I knew the doctors didn't anticipate any problems. That, apparently was enough to stop me from being employed by BA! When I told my manager that I'd applied for the job, he went berserk, insisting that I should have consulted with him before applying.

After that episode of ranting and raving from him, I decided that enough was enough, and made a point of telling him that I was applying for a promotion. I had one interview with an Integrated Project Team (IPT) in Andover and to be quite honest, I wouldn't have employed me—I was useless!

Anyway, a few months later, a job came up at the Royal Naval Air Station (RNAS), Yeovilton which sounded great and I did a lot more preparation than I did before my last interview.

The post was for a project manager responsible for covering obsolescence issues for the Merlin Helicopter Avionics Test Equipment. I duly attended the interview, was accepted and left St Athan, not before time, on promotion to an HPTO (Higher Professional and Technology Officer).

For the six years, we were at St Athan, the poor darling struggled on and there was many a time when I'd come home from work to find she'd been crying with pure frustration at not being able to carry out normal, basic household chores.

If she tried, she was left feeling totally wrecked and had to go to bed sometimes for days on end. The one saving grace was Amrita (PJ's wife), she was a real friend in the true sense of the word, and I honestly don't know what we would have done if it wasn't for her.

Chapter Twenty-Four
Our Last Move

As I remember, I was given time by the civil service to find a home and remarkedly they would pay for hotel accommodation for 3 days whilst we hunted for somewhere to live. One of the idiosyncrasies associated with this offer was that we'd be obliged to allow the civil service to sell our house in Rhoose, not a problem I mistakenly thought. Unfortunately, I hadn't realised how constraining that would turn out to be.

Our house, a detached four-bedroom property was valued at £218,000 and we were entitled to move into a like-for-like home in and around Yeovilton; the rationale being that we should not be disadvantaged because we had to move with the job. If a similar house at Yeovilton was more expensive, then we could claim the difference in value.

If, however, the value of the property was lower, then that was it. According to the civil service area valuations, a four-bedroom property was substantially lower in Somerset than in the Vale of Glamorgan—what a load of absolute rubbish! No matter how many four-bedroom properties we viewed, we couldn't find one that even remotely matched the one we were leaving.

Time moved on, and I arrived at the Merlin IPT to be met with acute surprise by my boss, a RN Lieutenant Commander. He asked me why I'd volunteered for a TUPE post, my response surprised him even more—I had not the faintest idea what TUPE was. It transpired that TUPE (Transfer of Undertaking for the Protection of Employment) was not advertised in the jobs bulletin and the plan was that the job would eventually move to AgustaWestland, the helicopter manufacturer based in Yeovil.

As Westlands already had an obsolescence manager, there was a very good chance that I'd be made redundant—bloody marvellous and without a moment's hesitation, HR became involved!

Whilst HR launched into why this monumental cock-up had occurred, I started to get to grips with the job. Trisha was still living in Rhoose and I was accommodated in the Ilchester Arms Hotel until such times as I found a suitable home. Our Rhoose property had been valued at £219,950 but every four-bedroom house I saw advertised, was completely out of our price range, and on one occasion, the difference was about £40,000.

For almost six weeks, after work, I visited numerous estate agents. I did look at a few houses but I wasn't prepared to pay the extortionate prices that were being asked. After much fruitless searching, it became obvious that to buy a comparable house was not going to happen. Instead, I started to look for a large three-bedroom house which in itself wasn't an easy task.

However, I eventually found a nice property in Somerton, arranged a viewing and decided that that was, potentially, where we might settle. I picked up Trisha and arranged another viewing. She agreed it was perfect. The asking price was £218,500, however, the house needed considerable work to be carried out and although it was only five years old, it was very, very dirty.

The cooker was caked in grease, there was grease dripping from the light fittings in the kitchen, the én was disgusting and the carpets were stained beyond belief. Whilst I appreciate that most of the dirt was only cosmetic, it needed totally redecorating. We eventually negotiated a price of £212,000.

The Rhoose property was put onto the market with an asking price of £219,500 and the normal conveyancing process for both properties began. Things were going swimmingly well until I received a call from the civil service rep who was dealing with the sale of our house.

One of the vagaries of house sales with the civil service is that negotiating a sale price just doesn't really happen. As it transpired, no sooner had the *For Sale* sign gone up than an offer was put to the local estate agent. The lady who eventually bought the house knew about the civil service scheme and offered £210,000. She was well aware that the offer would be accepted without question and the estate agent was obliged to pass that offer on.

So, we ended up moving into a house that was infinitely smaller and more expensive than the one we were leaving—we were not happy bunnies! We were also very tempted to leave the property without cleaning it. However, having never left a property in any other condition other than immaculate, we scrubbed everything from top to bottom.

We arrived in Somerton, closely followed by the removal van, and set about the arduous task of settling in. The removals guys were brilliant and worked like the proverbial Trojans. Come the evening, they decided that they were going to one of the local pubs for some well-deserved libation.

Before they left, I told them that they were more than welcome to have a shower and freshen up—an offer they quickly accepted. However, before they did, I (jokingly) asked that they sign a waiver abdicating us from responsibility for any disease that they may contract due to the filthy state of the on-suite shower!

I never did find out why TUPE hadn't been mentioned when the job was advertised. However, I spent three months on the IPT before I was offered a job on the Health and Usage Monitoring (HUMS) IPT also based at Yeovilton.

A HUMS records the status of critical systems on helicopters, including cockpit voice in the case of an accident, so that the early detection of progressive defects, or indications of them is possible. Therefore, rectification can be achieved before they have an immediate effect on operational safety.

The on-board equipment stores data on a PCMCIA Card. For analysis, the card is downloaded after the flight and maintenance analysis can then be performed on a ground-based computer. HUMS is also colloquially referred to as the *Black Box,* although it is actually coloured bright orange. The team were tasked with the fitting of HUMS to the Fleet Air Arm and RAF Sea King Helicopters, there was also a future requirement to equip all Fleet Air Arm and Army Lynx helicopters.

The post I was to be employed in was as the IPT's HUMS Project risk Manager, responsible for identifying and assessing those risks that could impede the safety, security or financial success of the program. There was no alternative, I either accepted the job or I'd be moved to Westlands. Needless to say, I very reluctantly accepted the post.

The personnel on the team were great, but the job itself absolutely sucked! I was to spend the next three years on the HUMS team before that was closed down once the modification to the Sea King fleet was complete. I moved on to the Lynx, and then the Wildcat IPT, where I was to spend the remainder of my time in the MoD.

Chapter Twenty-Five
The End of My World

Trisha and I first holidayed on the Greek Islands in 1997, the year I left the RAF when we bought a cheap last-minute week-long room-only holiday on the island of Lesbos. The only reason we decided on that particular break was because of the dreadful August week Gill, Pete, Grahame, Trisha and I had spent in a Devon cottage—it rained incessantly.

It was then in 2004 that we started regularly holidaying with Gillian and Pete when we visited Cyprus, we revisited the next year. Then, Kefalonia followed by Crete and in 2008, we went to Zakynthos (Zante). Whilst Trisha had suffered minor backache in the past, she was in acute pain for the majority of the holiday spending some afternoons in bed instead of relaxing by the pool.

I believe she initially damaged herself whilst pulling a suitcase over rough ground as we arrived at the hotel. She really did put on a brave face and always came out with us in the evenings. Halfway through the holiday, Gillian was taken seriously ill and ended up being admitted to the hospital in Zante with a serious stomach problem where she was kept overnight in some of the worst conditions imaginable.

The holiday was a great disappointment to both Gillian and Trisha because of the individual pain they both suffered. When we eventually arrived home, there was a message on the answering phone from Ken Twist telling us that Kath, Trisha's friend since they were young children, had died. Ken was quite distraught at not being able to contact us and advise us that the funeral was scheduled for the next day.

I asked Trisha if she wanted to leave immediately but her back was still very sore and she really didn't think she could make it. She contacted Ken and passed on her deepest, sincerest condolences—Kath had been ill for a few years and was on medication and oxygen for an enlarged heart condition. She and Trisha were the absolute best of friends.

Trisha's back didn't really get much better, and by the end of that week, the whites of her eyes and skin had started to turn yellow. She saw the doctor the following Monday who advised her that if the condition didn't improve by the end of the week, she was to contact him and he would have her admitted to A&E in Yeovil as a matter of urgency.

We assumed that she may have picked up hepatitis bearing in mind where we'd been holidaying. The condition got worse and, on Monday, I took her to Yeovil Hospital where she was booked into the A&E department. As we sat outside the ward, we heard a real commotion coming from the other end of the corridor and looked around to see a chap trying to hold up and support a young woman who was screaming her head off.

We initially didn't know what was going on but it soon became blatantly obvious that she'd just received some devastating news. Within a short time, Trisha was having blood tests and an ultrasound scan on her stomach. Whilst I was waiting, I heard one of the doctors on the ward mention something about the lady who had just had a scan but I couldn't make out precisely what he'd said.

The next minute, Trisha was back with me accompanied by her normal, beautiful, smile—a smile as wide as the world! Arrangements were made to admit her and keep her in overnight. The next day, the 9 September 2008, Trisha called me at work at about 10:00.

All she said was, "You'd better get in here straight away, things are not looking good."

She was in good spirits when I'd left her the previous night and I still believed the problem to be hepatitis. My mind was racing and I really couldn't think what could be wrong. As I pulled out of the car park at Yeovilton, a sudden terrible, terrible uneasy feeling came over me but I quickly dismissed it—I really didn't think anything untoward was going to happen to Trisha.

Parking at the hospital was a nightmare but I managed to find a slot just outside the main entrance. Unfortunately, I was restricted to only two hours of waiting. When I arrived at the ward, Trisha was in a side room, and at the time, she wasn't aware of what was wrong but had been told earlier that a doctor wanted to speak with us together.

The doctor was busy with other patients and we'd been waiting for almost two hours, by which time, I had to leave and move the car or risk being clamped.

The car parks and the local roads were chock-a-block and I had to drive so far away from the hospital it took me 20 minutes to walk back.

When I returned, I met the doctor who told us that the yellowing of Trisha's eyes and skin was caused by a build-up of bile from a blocked bile duct and that the blockage was caused by cancerous tumours.

He then went on to tell us that the ultrasound and subsequent Magnetic Resonance Imaging (MRI) scan showed that the head of the pancreas, the liver and the duodenum were all heavily tumoured and that she was suffering from advanced, stage V pancreatic cancer.

The most devastating revelation was then delivered—it was inoperable. Although, he went on to say that it was treatable. By then, my mind was moving at a million miles an hour and for a brief moment, I thought that the treatment may actually offer a cure. But no, there is a big difference between treating a disease and actually curing it.

Trisha and I knew so little about pancreatic cancer that it really didn't mean that much to us and I think that's probably the case with a large proportion of the population. We were to find out much later on that every year, in the UK alone; approximately 7000 people are diagnosed with this cruelly aggressive type of cancer of which less than 3% live past the five-year point, with the remaining sufferers dying within six months.

We were both stunned and didn't know what to say. A couple of nurses came in over the next few hours to talk to and comfort Trisha. I considered not telling the family until later that day but really couldn't contain myself and phoned Gillian and Wendy. Trisha sat in bed completely emotionless, just staring at me—no tears, no conversation, she was completely and utterly stunned into silence.

I, however, cannot ever remember crying so much. I never really thought of myself as a particularly emotional person but the tears just went on and on and to this day, under certain conditions, just the thought of her or the very mention of her name brings a lump to my throat and tears soon follow.

Within a relatively short period of time, Trisha was being prepared for surgery. I accompanied her to the operating theatre and waited outside. As she was taken away, the surgeon came and sat next to me. He explained that the surgical procedure was very straightforward and would involve putting a stent (a small tube) inside the bile duct effectively opening it up and allowing the bile from the liver to naturally drain away.

I went back to the sideward and waited. The operation was soon over, and before long, Trisha was back with me. I don't remember much of what happened after that, it really was a blur.

I do, however, remember both of us being asked by a doctor what Trisha's wishes were in the event that her heart should stop beating at any time during her treatment. Neither of us knew what that question actually meant until it was explained that if she suffered from heart failure, provided she had previously consented, then an attempt would be made to resuscitate her.

If, however, she had declined, then the doctors would not attempt to restart her heart. It was pointed out that the resuscitation procedure was complicated and would invariably cause severe damage to her body and ribcage. What a terrible question; how on earth could we be asked to effectively consign Trisha to a certain death?

We weren't asked again, thankfully, and I don't know what I would have done if I'd been asked to decide on my own.

By now she was very tired and tried to rest. What must have been going through her mind I really can't contemplate and only God would know. I do remember struggling to come to terms with what was happening. For a brief while, instead of showing concern for my darling Trisha, I actually started to feel sorry for *myself*.

How on earth would *I* manage when she was gone? How will her death affect *me*? There were some truly selfish, uncontrollable thoughts going through my head and it took real effort to dismiss them—self-pity is a terrible emotion.

I called in to see Ange and Ian that evening and phoned Michael and Steven. Both of them wanted to come immediately to see her, but I put them off until we had a better idea as to what we were going to do.

We'd seriously considered moving abroad to a warmer climate and I don't know if it was merely physiological or whether there were any real health benefits but Trisha always felt better when in the warmth. Whilst we may have talked about emigrating, we decided that we wouldn't leave whilst Morley was still alive and probably not whilst Pattie was still with us either.

I fell in love with Kefalonia and whilst Trisha was quite taken with the place, I think she preferred Cyprus. We discussed on many occasions how we would fund the move and sustain our lifestyle. Trisha was keen to let our property in Somerton and rent wherever we settled.

Her rationale was that if something were to happen to one of us, the surviving partner would, at least, have somewhere to return to. I, on the other hand, wanted to sell up and buy in the new country. As things turned out, I'll never know, but I think Trisha's scheme would probably have been the best.

Trisha's backache never improved and she was in constant pain both day and night. She spent a great deal of time in bed and at night would wake me and sometimes frighten me as she screamed in pain whenever she tried to move. I did say to her on more than one occasion that if she carried on like that, she'd probably give me a heart attack.

But as a martyr to back pain, I knew precisely how she was suffering. She had various visits from the doctor; who prescribed more and more painkillers and muscle relaxants all of which seemed to do very little to ease her suffering.

She had her first consultation with her oncologist, Dr Faulk in mid-October, who told her that there was a clinical trial in progress whereby a certain number of patients suffering from advanced pancreatic cancer would be given only the chemotherapy drug Gemcitabine. Whilst another group would be given Gemcitabine with an additional chemotherapy drug (no patient was told which group they fell into and I later found out that Trisha was not one of the later patients).

Doctor Faulk was very good; he explained the problems and issues associated with the treatment and didn't pull any punches. He told us that it would be difficult. Trisha told him that she didn't want to know how long she had to live. She only wanted to know how to recognise the symptoms which might show that her time was close.

He told her there would be a general malaise and deterioration in her health which made her laugh because the ME had given her those same conditions for the previous nine years.

We were visited a few days later by a palliative care nurse who explained her role and how she could help. Palliative care (from the Latin *palliare* meaning to cloak) focuses on the relief of pain and other symptoms for people facing death. The goal of the care is to improve quality of life by increasing comfort, promoting dignity and providing a support system to the person who is ill or dying as well as those close to them.

Facing death can be a time of real crisis, which gives rise to profound questions about the meaning of life and may challenge one's sense of self-belief.

Before the chemo treatment started, we decided to go to Yorkshire to visit Steven in his new home at the cottage and also invite Michael, Julie and the grandchildren with the aim of celebrating Mike's 32nd birthday with a BBQ. Wendy, Rob and Annie were also in Scotland and decided to call in on their way home and join in.

The journey was quite uncomfortable for Trisha and she later confided in me that she had seriously considered asking me to go back home shortly after passing Newbury but didn't say anything at the time because she so wanted to see everyone. Steven's home was brilliant, unfortunately, it was also incredibly cold and Trisha was unable to sit on the low settee instead opting to lie in bed for the majority of the time. (Even Wendy found it cold and climbed into bed with Trisha to get warm!)

We had only been with Steven for two days, but Trisha was in so much pain that we drove home on Sunday, and on our return, she visited the doctors again who prescribed more drugs.

Trisha began her chemo treatment the following week in the Macmillan Centre at Yeovil Hospital. The staff were absolutely fantastic and so caring. I don't want to single out any particular individual (more so because I can't remember everyone's name) but the one name that I do remember is Nita.

Nita was the senior staff nurse and she had such a reassuring and calming influence in everything she said or did. The day began with a blood test that would determine the level of white blood cells present and whether they were sufficient in quantity to defend the body against infectious disease (the chemo drug depletes white blood cells).

Once confirmation was received from the lab, the treatment started. That same routine was followed before each treatment session. Trisha always had problems giving blood and the administration of the chemo drug was no different. The intravenous route into her body was via a vein on top of her hand and on those occasions that a suitable vein couldn't be found a vein in the wrist was used which was acutely painful if the rate of flow was too high.

The treatment was carried out once a week for three weeks followed by a week off to allow the blood to regenerate. As well as the visits to the hospital, Gemcitabine was also taken in tablet form—seven tablets a day for three weeks. Prior to the commencement of the next three-week session, Trisha would have an MRI scan which would indicate whether the chemo was having any effect on the tumours.

The results were recorded on the computer enabling the doctor to view the results almost immediately, and at her first appointment all Doctor Faulk said was, "The results are good, the tumours are shrinking and the treatment will continue."

It was one of the very few occasions that I saw my darling smile.

Halfway through the first week-off, Trisha had to visit the local doctors again because of the back pain which seemed to be getting worse and, on that occasion, she was prescribed liquid morphine. The following week, we arrived at the radiography department but she was in so much pain that she had to take a couple of swigs of morphine prior to going for the MRI scan. I had to stay in the waiting room, and at the end of the treatment, I heard her screaming as several assistants tried to get her off the scanner bed.

It took almost 15 minutes to put her onto a trolley and take her to a quiet area where she was eventually given a jab in the small of her back which dulled the pain such that she could at least walk. By the time we got home, she was absolutely worn out and the painkiller was beginning to wear off.

I called our doctor, who, by then, had been contacted by the hospital. He informed me that a bed had been reserved at St Margaret's Hospice in Yeovil and on hearing the word *hospice* I had some serious reservations. However, the doctor was quick to tell me that the hospice wasn't only somewhere where the terminally ill were sent to end their days but the staff were also experts in pain control techniques.

We drove to the hospice, and within a very short time, Trisha was booked in and made comfortable. I went home and returned later that evening to find her in bed with an intravenous drip in her arm. I sat down and for several minutes, she didn't initially acknowledge that I was there.

When she did, she opened her eyes, looked at me and all she said was, "I think you'd better go," before closing her eyes again.

I was gutted and extremely upset.

I went to see her the following evening and was pleased to see that she was a lot more comfortable. She'd been fitted with a battery-powered syringe driver that continuously delivered a controlled dose of painkiller and muscle relaxant. Over the next few days, she continued to improve and for the first time in three months, her pain was under control. She even managed to put on some makeup, which really cheered up both of us.

She spent 10 days or so in the hospice, and in that time, she became very friendly with Judy, the daughter of an elderly lady who was nearing the end of her days. It was just so typical of Trisha; there she was in pain and dying from cancer herself and she still had time to think of someone else by befriending Judy and offering support.

On Trisha's last weekend in the hospice Michael, Julie, Jacob, Charlotte and Millie spent a really enjoyable afternoon with us. That evening Ange and Ian joined us at Tarentino's, the Italian restaurant in Ilchester where I told the staff, who knew us both very well; that Trisha was terminally ill—they were all mortified.

It was shortly after coming out of the hospice towards the end of November 2008, whilst watching TV we learnt that Patrick Swayze had been diagnosed in January with stage IV Pancreatic Cancer, the same as Trisha. He undertook chemotherapy and treatment with an experimental drug, Vatalanib which the doctors hoped would cut off the blood supply to the tumours.

Despite repeated tabloid claims that his death was imminent, Swayze continued to pursue his career. Unfortunately, during the interview, it was mentioned that most advanced pancreatic cancer patients live no longer than six months.

Until then, I hadn't tried to find out how long Trisha had left, but now she knew. As she was diagnosed two and a half months earlier, it didn't take a brilliant mathematician to work out that she had potentially three and a half months to live. Patrick Swayze was to die on 14 September 2009, aged 57.

Trisha continued to wear the driver and over the following few weeks, she was visited daily at home by a district nurse who would refill the syringe. It was for the first time in quite a while that she wasn't in pain, managed to sleep and went shopping together. On a couple of occasions, we had lunch in the Lime Kiln Inn near Somerton.

Trisha had been on the driver for about a month when it was decided that the time was right for her to come off it and any subsequent pain relief would be provided by pills. The driver restricted Trisha's movement but seemed to effectively control the pain and I believe its removal was a profound mistake.

Once the driver was removed, at the peak, she was taking 17 pills a day, comprising various painkillers, muscle relaxants, anti-sickness, enzymes, vitamins and the like. On top of that, she was also taking eight chemo tablets each day (for three weeks each month). As time progressed, she would dread the daily pill-taking ritual.

Early in January, she began to have acute difficulty in holding a normal conversation, became confused and forgetful and I put down the ridiculous cocktail of drugs she was taking. The pills also had a catastrophic effect on her mind because she became absolutely paranoid whenever I left the house and asked me to turn off all electrical appliances that were plugged in—they didn't even have to be switched on.

She would invariably fall asleep and wake up in a panic not knowing where she was and would phone me wanting to know where I was. The problem was also compounded by the fact that my mobile provider, T Mobile, didn't give coverage for the Street and Glastonbury areas.

This issue only came to light when I returned home, having been shopping, to find Sue comforting Trisha who was in a real state having tried to phone me but couldn't get a connection. I changed providers immediately.

One of the more frightening aspects of living with someone who has a terminal illness is the alarming prospect of them dying during their sleep. There were occasions when I'd wake up in the night and couldn't hear Trisha breathing or sense any movement from her. My immediate response would be to put on the light and jump out of bed only to be welcomed with a surprised look on her face. That scenario was repeated many times.

I was desperate to continue with my area of work on the Lynx Project Team and was given dispensation to work from home. Unfortunately, due to crap internet connectivity, there were many occasions when I could do nothing and opted to go to Yeovilton. Trisha sometimes would beg me not to leave her alone and I invariably stayed at home but there were a couple of times where I just couldn't afford not to go to work.

The main focus of my work at the time was centred on the earlier capture of several Royal Navy sailors on 23 March 2007. The RN personnel, from HMS Cornwall, were searching a merchant vessel in shallow international waters off the Iraqi coast, and were subsequently surrounded by members of the Navy of the Iranian Revolutionary Guards.

They were accused of being inside Iran's territorial waters and were detained off the Iran-Iraq coast for a total of 13 days. Their capture was put down to the fact that whilst the Warship, HMS Cornwall was in contact with the boarding party on the Rigid Hull Inflatable Boat (RHIB) via secure communications, the ship's Lynx Helicopter had no such compatible secure system and contact was lost.

Consequently, I was tasked by Navy Command with project managing the fitting of a *walk-on* secure communication network to the helicopter, thus, enabling the Warship, the RHIB and the Lynx Mk 8 to be able to securely talk to each other.

The complexity of carrying out a service modification of that nature meant that I couldn't always work from home, and I was required to liaise with the Navy engineers and QinetiQ. Also, on occasion chair meetings throughout the various phases of the modification programme.

Things came to a head when I went to cuddle her one morning and she started shaking, cringing and cowering away from me, telling me that she couldn't bear me to touch her. She apologised but couldn't explain why she felt the way she did. I accepted what she said and reassured her that I knew it wasn't in her nature to be like that and put it all down to the drugs.

Whatever the reason, it was a further devastating and depressing blow to my already sagging morale. I was at my wits end; it was about as much as I could stand and contacted the palliative care nurse who came to visit us. I listed the drugs that Trisha was taking and *told* the nurse that *I* was going to gradually reduce the amount she was taking. She agreed. It couldn't have come at a better time.

I then remembered something that had come to light shortly after Helen had died. Morley had confided in Trisha telling her that Helen was suffering considerably with the pain and she was also on a cocktail of drugs. For no apparent reason, Helen rounded on poor Morley telling him not to touch her and that she hated him. I then appreciated exactly what the poor fellow had gone through.

Over the next couple of weeks, I managed to reduce Trisha's dependency on painkillers and muscle relaxants to such a level that, whilst it didn't compromise her pain relief, it gave her poor body time to recover. I successfully reduced the daily pill count from 17 to only 3.

Within a very short period of time, she became less confused, much more coherent and started to look more with it. She even let me briefly touch her by allowing me to put my hand on her shoulder when we were in bed. Unfortunately, any physical contact would never be the same again. It was about that time that she had a fall.

She'd dropped something on the dining room carpet and had fallen backwards as she bent down which resulted in banging her back against the door frame. Within a couple of days, she noticed a small lump close to her breast bone and because it wasn't painful she wasn't too concerned.

It wasn't too long after that she once again began to show signs of jaundice and an appointment was made for her to go back into hospital. I believe the lump was caused by the dislodging of the stent which in turn caused the closure of the bile duct.

The only prescriptions that Trisha didn't pay for were those that were prescribed and administered whilst she was in hospital. Everything else I had to stump up for. However, I was advised by the doctors to apply for a payment exemption certificate which, because of Trisha's terminal illness, would enable her to be prescribed free medicines.

Until that chit arrived, I still had to pay but was advised by the pharmacy that all I had to do was to hang onto the receipts. By the time the certificate arrived, I had spent over £100 on the ever-burgeoning list of drugs that Trisha was prescribed—some worked and gave relief whilst others had no effect.

When I received the exemption certificate, I duly presented the receipts to the pharmacy only to be told that they were the wrong type of receipt. It transpired that each time I bought the drugs I should have mentioned that I needed a specific receipt—the till receipt on its own wasn't good enough.

The chemo pills and intravenous drugs still made her feel sick and it was obvious that the prescribed anti-sickness drugs weren't helping. I read somewhere that ginger is widely used as a digestive aid for mild stomach upset and is commonly recommended by healthcare professionals to help prevent or treat nausea and vomiting associated with motion sickness, morning sickness and chemotherapy.

Nothing to lose, we thought.

So, she tried a liquid ginger supplement. Unfortunately, the ginger caused Trisha's urinary tract to swell and close preventing her from passing water. Once again, the medical centre was contacted and a nurse came and fitted a catheter.

Trisha was taken into Yeovil Hospital on a Monday and told that she would have the stent replaced on the next scheduled operating day—stents were only fitted on a Tuesday! Come the next day, it was decided that there were more urgent cases and controversially Trisha would have to wait a further week.

The stent was eventually replaced and by the following Monday, the jaundice had started to diminish. She decided that come what may, she was leaving that afternoon after having spent two weeks in the hospital. When Trisha was admitted she weighed 11 stone and during that fortnight for some obscure reason, which we didn't understand at the time, her arms, legs and stomach had become severely distended and she had put on two stone—two stone for God's sake on hospital food!

Getting her dressed was a real challenge, none of her clothes would fit and she squeezed herself into a blouse and trousers. I had the feeling that the doctors were reluctant to discharge her, but she was so determined to go home. Just before we left, we were visited by a lady who told us that she would make arrangements for an orthopaedic bed, a Portaloo and various other pieces of equipment to be delivered and placed in a downstairs room.

I tried to reason with her telling her that there was nowhere for the items to go and anyway I wanted Trisha to sleep in our own bed. She wouldn't accept the fact that Trisha would be sleeping downstairs on her own and I might not hear her if she wanted help. She persisted and on more than one occasion would totally ignore my protestations and speak over me.

She just wouldn't let it rest and I ended up telling her in no uncertain terms that I would not accept the items if they were delivered—she wasn't a happy bunny. However, she reluctantly accepted our wishes. To this day, I haven't had a clue who the devil she was, but whatever her vocation was, she really didn't have much of a clue on how to deal with people who didn't want that particular type of help.

I considered complaining to the hospital at her unsympathetic and ridiculous intransigence, but with everything else that was going on, I decided not to take it any further.

We eventually arrived home on Monday, 3 March, and fortunately, Steven was waiting. We struggled to get Trisha upstairs in her wheelchair and into bed. By the time she was undressed and in her night clothes, she was not only totally knackered but in pain due to the swelling of her legs. I spent a while gently rubbing talcum powder onto her feet and ankles which offered some relief but decided to call the doctor who came almost immediately.

I know the National Health Service has had some pretty bad publicity over the years, but for our part, the doctors and nurses at Somerton Medical Centre reacted admirably, and I really couldn't fault the care bestowed on Trisha. Doctor

Leake prescribed water tablets but in retrospect, I believe he knew that it wasn't just water retention that was causing the problem.

For the remainder of the week, Trisha struggled. She didn't eat a great deal but did drink normally, however, she was having real difficulty in carrying out her normal ablution activities and I invariably did what I could to help. I hadn't realised until then how demanding it was to care for someone who is more or less totally infirm.

On those occasions that Trisha was resting, Steven and I would be downstairs and if we were wanted, rather than shouting, she would ring a small bell that she kept on the bedside table. In the early hours of Sunday morning, she was having acute difficulty breathing, she was trying to clear her throat but just couldn't get enough breath to cough, and this coupled with her severely distended stomach drove her to ask me to call the doctor.

I was very reluctant telling her that if I did, she would probably be taken back into the hospital which neither of us wanted. But by then she'd had enough. The paramedics duly arrived and immediately administered oxygen, and over the next couple of hours, they and a doctor assessed her and decided to take her back into hospital.

I can still see her being strapped into the wheelchair and watching her being wheeled into the back of the ambulance—she didn't look back. It still brings a lump to my throat and the tears soon follow whenever I think of it. I suggested to Steven that, perhaps, he should go back to Yorkshire as there was nothing more that he could do. Once again, I was on my own in the house.

I packed some clean clothes for Trisha and left for Yeovil a few moments later. By the time I got to the hospital, she had been assessed at A&E and was being booked into a ward. One of the first actions the doctor took was to draw off the liquid that was causing Trisha so much distress and over the next few hours a total of five litres of a vile, brown liquid was drained from her body—five litres, for heaven's sake!

That equates to almost seven bottles of wine! By the end of the afternoon, her breathing had eased a little and she was a lot more comfortable. It was later explained to me that the tumours were producing the liquid which had subsequently built up in the body cavities and was pushing against Trisha's diaphragm, which in turn, was reducing her lung capacity causing the shallowness in her breathing.

The duty doctor again asked whether Trisha wanted to be resuscitated if her heart failed. This time, she said that she did, but we never signed any papers confirming her decision. I left the hospital in the evening and went home feeling utterly and completely depressed.

The next morning, I again visited Trisha who had been moved to another ward and I found her in reasonable spirits. I'd only been with her for a short while when I received a message from the Macmillan unit telling me that Doctor Faulk wanted to speak with us. Trisha was far too tired and I went on my own.

He was quite honest, telling me that Trisha was very weak and her chemo treatment would not continue unless she made a significant improvement. I knew exactly what was being said and asked Nita how long until the end. She believed it was weeks rather than months. I then mentioned that it was going to be very difficult telling Trisha that her time was close.

Nita asked why I had to tell her the exact details. I said that I'd never lied or kept secrets from her throughout our 34 years of married life, and I wasn't about to start now. The response was that I should suggest that treatment would only start again once her strength had improved and nothing more.

Okay, that wasn't lying, I thought and it seemed to offer a fairly reasonable compromise.

By the time I got back to the ward, I was in a pretty inconsolable state and when Trisha asked me what had been said, I immediately broke down. I told her that the treatment was being stopped.

However, judging by the state I was in she guessed that things weren't right and said, "Something else has been mentioned, hasn't it?"

I remember looking up and noticed that some visitors to other patients in the ward were looking at me but the tears just wouldn't stop. My only response was to reiterate what I'd said—I just couldn't bring myself to tell her anything else. She had eaten and drunk a little but really fancied some ice cream, so I walked into town and bought a few small tubs of Haggen Daz ice cream.

As I walked, I remember thinking that after all we'd been through together and worked, for since we first met, everything was about to come crashing down. I'd like to think that throughout the majority of our life together, in most instances, we were in control of our own destiny, but now, there was absolutely nothing either of us could do about our circumstances.

Trisha particularly enjoyed the ice cream and I sat with her not really knowing what to say. After all, what sort of a conversation can you have with someone, let alone the love of your life who is nearing the end of their time on the earth? She still had the tube in her tummy and the catheter fitted, both of which were draining. I spent a few more hours with her and left when she started to feel tired; by which time, I was both physically and severely mentally worn out.

Chapter Twenty-Six
The Saddest Day of My Life

As I remember, I had a very disturbed night's sleep having contemplated long and hard about what was about to happen and coupled with a cold that had been developing over the previous few days, I felt pretty shitty. I was about to leave for the hospital on Tuesday morning when I had a phone call telling me that Trisha was being moved to St Margaret Hospice that afternoon.

So, this is it, I thought.

I, once again packed some clothes and headed off. By the time I'd booked in with the hospice reception, Trisha was in bed and was looking and feeling a little better. She even managed a smile for me as I walked in. I didn't get too close to her because of my damned cold and repeatedly had to wash my hands so as not to contaminate her, or indeed, anyone else in the ward.

She was hooked up to oxygen which was being dispensed through a small tube that had been placed into each nostril. Unfortunately, her breathing was still very shallow and she couldn't speak many words without having to constantly gasp for breath. It was so upsetting because her condition reminded me so much of Helen's last days. Despite her obvious weakness and the misgivings that I'd had the previous day, regarding what to say to Trisha, we sat and talked.

By now, I sincerely believe that Trisha knew that things were on a downward spiral and it was only a matter of time before she was to meet her maker. We continued talking and she told me she wanted me to make a donation to the Hospice and the McMillan charity. Whilst my combined MoD wage, RAF pension, savings and Pattie's inheritance were quite reasonable we were trying to be frugal with what money we had.

We'd always assumed that I would be the first to go in which case Trisha would be dependent on a small RAF and MoD widow's pension. Therefore, any additional savings we could put away would add to her disposable income. Trisha wanted me to give £5000 to the hospice and a smaller sum to McMillan.

I told her that I thought the figures to be a little excessive but agreed that I'd make a donation once my finances and more especially, Probate, had been sorted out. As it transpired, I gave £2500 and £1500 respectively having previously donated £1500 and £1000 to the two charities.

We also discussed what music should be played at the crematorium. I suggested either Barry White's 'You're My First, My Last, My Everything' or The Three Degrees' 'When Will I See You Again'.

They were chosen because they were two of our favourite courting songs from 1974.

All Trisha said was, "Why not have both?"

Sorted!

We said many things that afternoon, and today there is still one particular conversation that disturbs me. I can't remember how the subject was broached but I said that whilst I wasn't afraid of dying, I was, however, frightened at the thought of spending the rest of my life without her.

She didn't say much, although a few weeks earlier, she had told me that I was still young enough to re-marry and she didn't want me to be lonely.

When her dinner was delivered, I offered to help her. It was the first time I'd fed another person since Steven was a baby, some 28 years earlier, only this time it was my beautiful wife whom I was feeding. By the time she'd eaten, she was starting to feel tired and I decided to leave and let her rest. I washed my hands for the umpteenth time and went to say goodbye.

As I bent over to kiss her on the forehead, she let out a massive scream just as two carers were walking past. Trisha didn't want me to kiss her whilst I was suffering from the cold which I suppose, due to weakened immune system, was to be expected.

As I walked out of the ward, I looked back at her, she winked at me and quietly said, "I'm okay, I'm okay."

I bumped into Doctor Raff Salleh and asked whether it was worth asking Michael to return from Finland where he was working at the time. Raff told me not to bother for the time being because he believed that Trisha's time wasn't quite nigh.

The telephone woke me at 6:50 on the morning of Wednesday 11 March. When I answered, the person at the other end asked me to confirm who I was and then told me that Trisha had passed away earlier that morning. They didn't know the precise time but told me that they'd given her some water at 6:00 and when they next checked at about 6:40, she'd gone.

I tried to speak but my throat was sore and all I could manage was to croak, "Oh no, please no."

The nurse asked if I was on my own and if I was all right. There wasn't anything that could be done and I thanked her for calling. I remember pacing up and down the landing for several minutes, absolutely crying my eyes out and trying to get my thoughts together. I decided to call everyone once my throat had eased a little.

I obviously hadn't appreciated it at the time but the previous evening was to be the last time that I'd seen my love alive. She was wearing an old pair of my glasses, and even today, I can still see her face looking at me.

By the time I'd notified Ange and Ian, Wendy and Rob and Pete and Gill it was about 8:00 and they all agreed to meet at Somerton at around 10:00. Steven was in his work's van in Leeds when I called and he decided, without a moment's hesitation, that he would come straight away.

But before he left, rather than travel in the van, he went straight to a Mercedes garage and bought himself a car that he'd recently been eyeing up, a Mercedes 180 Kompressor.

I contacted Michael last of all because of the time difference and caught him just before he was about to go out on an ice test drive in the Bentley. I assumed that his mind would not be on the job and asked him not to drive. He agreed and made arrangements to fly home.

We arrived at the hospice at about 11:00 and I wanted to see Trisha on my own. As I was walking past one of the wards, Raff saw me and he quite literally flew off his chair, ran towards me and profoundly apologised for what he'd said the previous evening. Even he was surprised at the rapidity of Trisha's demise.

She'd been moved to a side ward and when I walked into the darkened room and saw her, I felt a real sense of foreboding. She was lying on her side in bed and I immediately knelt down and cuddled her—she was still warm and it was the first time I'd been that close to her for months and months. Unfortunately, her eyes had opened slightly which really spooked me and I asked the nurse to close them.

The nurse did so and left us alone. I just sat and talked. The strange thing was that I felt a certain degree of relief seeing Trisha, knowing that her suffering was at last at an end, although mine was about to begin. I stayed with her for a while and then went back to the waiting room.

Everyone except Ian then went to see her; Ian wanted to remember her as she once was and not as a corpse. My darling now looked peaceful (the nurse had in the meantime smeared a little Vaseline onto Trisha's eyelids which helped to keep them closed). She'd lost a lot of hair over the previous few months and what was left looked very thin and patchy. Her skin was still quite yellow.

I very much regret not being with her during the last moments of her life and it fills me with deep remorse when I think that although she was in a ward with a couple of other patients, she was ultimately on her own at the end. Did she suffer, was she in pain, or did she just close her eyes and quietly go to sleep? I'll never know.

At what point in one's life do things stop being given, and instead be taken away; friends, relatives, family, health, there's got to be a point.

Whilst Trisha wasn't a practising Catholic, she nevertheless was a believer and had asked a few weeks previously that when the time was right, I was to contact a priest and arrange for her to be given the last rites. The last rites form part of the Catholic seven sacraments: Baptism, Confirmation, Holy Communion, Confession, Marriage, Holy Orders and Anointing of the Sick.

The last of which is administered to the sick and dying in order to give spiritual strength. These sacraments are the life of the Catholic church. Unfortunately, because of the swiftness with which everything happened I never had a chance to arrange the last rites for her.

However, I could see nothing wrong with administering the rites even though Trisha was no longer with us. The hospice made the necessary arrangements and a priest came from Sherborne who carried out the solemn ceremony. And that was it; Trisha's soul then belonged to God Almighty and I know the Lord would be with her, ready to take her on her next adventure.

Doctor Raff told me that he wouldn't be carrying out a post-mortem as he knew exactly the cause of death which was a great relief to me. I had earlier thought about Trisha's already broken and ruined body being cut open which filled me with absolute dread. Trisha and I had spoken in the dim and distant past about donating organs, she was happy to do it but had set one condition; if something did happen to her, she didn't want her eyes to be donated (she had such beautiful eyes), everything else however was fair game.

I know that a cornea transplant from donated eyes is a very simple and successful procedure. In Trisha's case though, I assume the medical profession would never use any body parts that could be potentially riddled with cancer cells which thankfully absolved me from having to make that decision.

Raff gave me the death certificate which showed the cause of death as *Metastatic Carcinoma of the Pancreas*. The noun *metastatic* refers to the spread of cancer from the original tumour to other parts of the body by means of tiny clumps of cells transported by the blood or lymph glands.

Gillian and Pete then took me to the registrar to record Trisha's passing. By the time I got home, my emotions were all over the place, but strangely I think I felt a certain degree of relief and associated calm. I then realised that after almost 34 years of having a companion to love, who loved me in return, having a shoulder to cry on and share each other's problems and who was always there for me…I was very suddenly on my own.

One of the first things I did was to return the unused drugs. I just wanted them out of my sight. I took a huge carrier bag to the pharmacy and mentioned that many of the boxes or cartons hadn't been opened and could still be used only to be told that they would all be destroyed.

Goodbye, My Darling

The following few days were surreal. I think I'd more or less mentally prepared myself for what needed to be done weeks earlier but when the time actually came to sit down and plan the procedures, it was a different story—I found the whole scenario difficult. I first went to the undertakers in Somerton to set in motion the necessary chain of events.

They were naturally sympathetic and not only covered the immediate aspects of what needed to be done but also what should be done at a slower pace. The very first question: did I want Trisha to be buried or cremated?

If I'd told the undertaker that her body was to be buried, I know I'd have been haunted forevermore; Trisha absolutely hated the idea of being put into the ground. She had told me many moons ago that she wanted to be cremated as she had a morbid fear of being buried alive.

Various forms were filled in covering press announcements, cremation dates, priest attendance, music to be played during the funeral, flowers and donations, what type of cask were Trisha's ashes to be placed in, and finally, the eventual interment of her ashes. Arrangements were then made to have her body brought home to Somerton.

I visited the undertakers on the day she arrived. I was shown to the small room and for the second time in less than a week, I found myself absolutely full of apprehension and trepidation. Those feelings turned out to be unnecessary because once inside, and I saw Trisha lying in the open coffin all of my fears subsided.

She was dressed in a white, plainly patterned, one-piece cotton dress and despite her thinning hair, it had been arranged in such a way that it hid the severity of the loss. The yellowing jaundice had abated and with her hands gently crossed and positioned on her tummy, she looked the absolute picture of loveliness and serenity.

Trisha always had the perfect, English rose complexion, and now, as she lay there, there were no signs of wrinkles or any evidence of the inner bodily turmoil that had preceded her death—she was at last truly at peace. I just stood and stared at her. She was quite obviously cold but I bent down to say goodbye and softly kissed her lips which in itself felt strange because it was the first time that I'd ever kissed her and she had not reciprocated. And as I left, I felt a certain degree of inner calm.

When I registered Trisha's death, I was given several pamphlets which covered most aspects of dealing with bereavement both financially and emotionally. A day or so before the funeral, I tentatively looked at all possible options on how to deal with the tricky subject of probate. As I remember there were four options open to me.

The first was to put the entire business in the hands of solicitors, the second was to allow my bank to sort things out, and the third involved appointing a specialist company or I could deal with the whole issue myself.

I quickly dismissed the first two options due to the ridiculous costs involved; charges worked out to be approximately £8000. I considered dealing with probate myself but shied away due to the potential complexity which left me only one option. I contacted a company that had advertised their wares in the information pack; the initial advice would be impartial, free and without obligation.

A few days before the funeral, I was visited by a rep from the company. She was obviously dressed to thrill or kill, but either way, she looked quite attractive. We talked generally for quite a while before getting down to the nitty-gritty subject of probate and precisely what the company had to offer. Their costs were substantially cheaper than the first two options, about £2000 in all and it was pointed out that they would do absolutely everything; all I had to do was to initially furnish all of the relevant documents and information.

I'd never really been the impulsive sort and that day was no different. I told her that I was leaving for Rawden after the funeral and would make a decision on my return to Somerset. She understood and suggested that to save time, should I decide on using her company, she would be happy to collate all of my documents including the house deeds, insurance policies, wills, savings, bank details and full personal information.

She went on to tell me that if I decided not to continue then all documents would be returned and there would be a nominal fee of only a few pounds to cover the basic admin costs. I agreed and she then recorded the necessary details on her laptop and left with all of my documents.

A few days later, I received confirmation that all of the necessary arrangements, from the undertaker's perspective, were in order. All that remained for me to do was to arrange for a priest to carry out the service, sort out where the wake was to take place, and send out invites to the various friends and relatives.

It was decided that the funeral would take place on 19 March at Yeovil crematorium, a mere eight days after Trisha's passing. Over the next few days, I received many letters and cards from friends and relatives; all offering their love, sympathy and condolences. One of the most touching was a hand-designed letter I received from Gillian, it read:

My Dearest Pat

Never had the chance to say goodbye to you, you spared us all that awful pain, bless you, no words can say how much I am going to miss you, you really were the most dearest and loveliest person I had the privilege to know, you were simply the best Pat, you are going to leave a massive hole, but I will always keep a very special place in my heart for you..

We all have some lovely memories of you, and will treasure them for ever, we can look back on them and smile, and be comforted by them.

We all loved you so much, God has taken such a lovely special Angel. Rest in peace my dearest. See you in a while.

All my Love, love you for ever

Gillian
xxxxxxxxxxxx

There was also one card that really touched me. I was so taken aback by the text that I decided to reproduce the words and made some laminated copies. The poignant text read:

The Rose Beyond the Wall

A Rose once grew where all could see,
Sheltered beside a garden wall,
And as the days passed swiftly by,
It spread its branches, straight and tall.

One day a beam of light shone through,
A crevice that had opened wide,
The Rose bent gently towards its warmth,
Then passed beyond to the other side.

Now you who deeply feel its loss,
Be comforted, the Rose blooms there,
Its beauty is even greater now,
Nurtured by God's own loving care.

The morning of the 19 dawned, and it was time to say my final goodbye to the one person in the universe whom I truly loved. I asked Michael and Steven if they wanted to see Trisha for the last time. They both agreed. Up until then, neither of them had seen a dead body; let alone the body of the woman who had given them life and brought them into this world, who nurtured and cared for them for the majority of their time on earth.

As before, Trisha looked the absolute portrait of tranquillity. Neither of us spoke, and for several minutes we just looked at her. The boys said their goodbyes and as they left, I lay a hand on hers and kissed her forehead. I don't remember shedding any tears; they were to come later on.

By the time we got back to *Cornerstone,* Amy, Steve's ex-girlfriend and Matt, one of Steve's friends had arrived from Leeds. Amy didn't have to say anything; the expression on her face and the tears she shed said it all. Amy was beautiful and she and Trisha got on fantastically well. I'm still in touch with Amy's parents, Steve and Chris—they're an absolutely fabulous couple.

By 10:00, all members of the family had arrived and we waited for the hearse to arrive. When I initially viewed the house on my own in 2004 and later decided to buy the property, never in my wildest dreams did I ever contemplate that Trisha's last journey to the house would be in a coffin. The ride to the crematorium was unhurried and dignified and as we arrived, I was taken aback at the number of people who had decided to attend.

We'd only been living in Somerton for five years and had made friends with only a few people. Apart from family, relations and some of our lovely neighbours there were also friends and work colleagues from the Lynx IPT, the HUMS IPT and also St Athan—I was really quite touched.

I'd also earlier received a card from Jeff and Jeanette, our dear friends in Cyprus, who told me that they'd be in church in Polemi at the precise time that the service started and would say a prayer for Trisha.

The hearse arrived and John, Michael, Steven and I, as pallbearers, arranged ourselves to accept the coffin. As we entered the crematorium Barry White's 'You're My First, My Last, My Everything' was playing.

When I first met the priest to make arrangements, we'd agreed that the service was to be a relatively simple affair and that I'd read the eulogy. During my time in the RAF and MoD, I'd chaired meetings, taught students, and given presentations without really batting an eyelid and I was never awe-inspired by rank.

However, I certainly wasn't prepared for that day in the crematorium when I stood at the lectern in front of the congregation, I was absolutely petrified. I started by giving a background as to how and where Trisha and I met and how she'd followed the flag etc. I then told the reason why we'd chosen the two songs. It was then that I began to choke and tried to continue, but the words just wouldn't come. I looked at the priest in the hope that he would finish off the reading but he shook his head. I just couldn't go on.

It was then that Steven casually stood up from the pew, walked behind me and took the unfinished script from me. By the time I got back to my seat, the curtain had been drawn around the coffin, and I never got the chance to say my final, final goodbyes.

In an instant, the coffin and my beautiful, darling wife and companion of 34 years were gone. Trisha was my whole life for all of that time and despite the fact I'd tried to prepare myself for what was going to happen, it was incredibly difficult to believe that she was no longer with me.

Roy Lee, one of the Lynx team's real characters, later commented that Steven was a big man not only in the physical sense but it took a big man to do what he did and take over the reading of the eulogy—thanks a million Steve! The rest of the day was somewhat of an anti-climax. I decided to take some time off and went back to Rawden with Steve with the aim of helping out with his business.

I think the two weeks away was enough, I really needed to try and get back into the swing of things and concentrate on work. As I pulled up outside *Cornerstone* I can remember thinking that things would never be the same again. Despite the fact that I had plenty of people who obviously cared for me, for all intents and purposes, as of then, I was on my own.

There were several bereavement cards and letters awaiting my return and one was an appointment for Trisha to attend Taunton hospital—they'd eventually got around to sorting out her back problem. I contacted the appointments department and when I told the receptionist that Trisha was no longer with us, the nurse couldn't apologise enough.

These things happen I suppose, and I quickly dismissed the faux pas. Another more annoying letter was from the probate company. Whilst with Steve, I'd spent several hours on the internet looking at the possibility of the do-it-yourself scheme—I downloaded the forms and the whole process looked straightforward enough.

After all, our finances were in pretty good shape, we had no mortgage, no debts and nothing to hide such as offshore bank accounts or dubious financial undertakings. And so, just before leaving Rawden, I emailed the company telling them of my decision and asked that all documents be returned.

Their letter acknowledged receipt of my email and wanted me to pay them £100 for the privilege of doing virtually nothing. The letter also stated that my documents would only be returned upon receipt of payment for the services rendered—I was not happy.

I subsequently wrote to the company and in no uncertain terms told them that when I'd passed the various documents to their rep, I had stipulated that no work was to be carried out until I'd decided on the way forward. I also pointed out that I felt I was being taken advantage of during a particularly difficult time and that the fee was extortionate. A week or so later, I received a recorded delivery envelope containing all of my documents and a letter cancelling the charges.

One of the first things I had to do was to sort out the interment of Trisha's ashes. By the time I'd returned home, the local undertakers had received the ornate wooden casket containing her remains.

I made arrangements for a plot to be set aside in Somerton cemetery and the only criterion I set was that Trisha's casket was to be buried at double depth; this was to enable my ashes to be one day be buried with hers. I hadn't decided on the precise date of the interment—there were still things that needed to be finalised. I then took Trisha home.

That done, I set about the task of transferring all of our savings accounts, ISAs and premium bonds into my name, deleting Trisha's details from our bank account and notifying the council that I was a single occupant of Cornerstone which entitled me to a reduction in my council tax.

The probate forms presented no real challenges and it didn't take long to draw up a comprehensive list of my entire financial position. The completed forms, will and death certificate were posted to the probate office in Bristol and within a very short time, I was notified of the hearing date. The process was simplicity itself.

I drove to Bristol, met with the probate officer, confirmed my details and swore on the Bible that the evidence provided was, to the best of my knowledge, a true and accurate reflection of my circumstances, and that was it. The whole procedure had cost me £90 for the probate licence, a couple of pounds for the recorded delivery of the documents, plus the price of petrol for a return trip from Somerton to Bristol. A total of approximately £110, a far cry from what I potentially could have been charged—the moral to that story is, DIY.

Over the next five months, I threw myself into work and spent a lot of time contemplating what to do next. I found it very difficult to get my head around what direction I wanted my life to move in. In the meantime, Gillian and Pete had booked their annual holiday opting once again for two weeks on the island of Crete at the Dias apartments, situated in Agia Marina, a small town west of Chania.

Trisha and I had stayed at the Dias with them only two years previously and thoroughly enjoyed the area. Unfortunately, Gill was very upset at the thought of Trisha and me not being with them for what had more or less been an annual event. I had considered tagging along but quickly dismissed it.

Gill and Pete were scheduled to leave during the first week of August and when I mentioned to Steve that I'd really like to go but would find it difficult to travel on my own, all he said was, "You don't have to go on your own, I'll go with you."

And so, I set things in motion, unfortunately, I didn't know any of the holiday details but getting that info from Gill was easy. All it took was some idle conversation with her and I got all of the information I needed. I subsequently logged onto the First Choice website, and booked Steve and me onto the same flight and venue as Gill and Pete—but details were kept a secret from everyone.

I then arranged for the interment of Trisha's ashes to take place on the afternoon of 3 August, which was the day before the start of the holiday. For all previous holidays, Trisha and I would always leave Somerton at about 01:00 in the morning, drive to Durrington and we'd all go to Gatwick in a minibus. That holiday was to follow the same format only Gill and Pete wouldn't know about my plans until Steve and I turned up at their door.

Come the day of the interment ceremony everyone met at Cornerstone apart from Amrita and PJ, our dear Sikh friends from Rhoose who went straight to the cemetery. I went into the dining room to find Gill in an absolute flood of tears and almost inconsolable. She sobbed that she wasn't looking forward to the holiday as she believed that it just wouldn't be the same without Trisha.

Despite the fact that, unbeknown to her, Steve and I would be joining her later that evening, I really couldn't prolong the agony and took her into the lounge and in front of everyone announced that Steve and I would be holidaying with them in Crete—she cried even more. However, I didn't tell her that we'd also be in the same Dias apartment complex, I merely told them that we were close by—they'd only find out when we were dropped off with them.

Chapter Twenty-Seven
And Where to Now?

Towards the end of Trisha's time, we discussed many things and the most difficult was what I would do once she was gone. Whilst I hadn't given it too much thought, I did suggest that I might move to Yorkshire and maybe help Steven with his business. Trisha thought it a good idea, but if I did leave Somerset, then she wanted her ashes scattered at Southport along with Helen and Morley's and Tom and Edith's.

I wasn't particularly happy with that because not only was the cemetery not particularly well maintained but the distance involved if I wanted to visit, wherever I lived, was not convenient. We came to a compromise—her ashes would be interred in Somerton's cemetery if I promised never to leave the market town and my ashes would be eventually interred with hers. A promise that I will not break come what may.

She always put on a brave face and never gave up hoping that a miracle would happen and always tried to look her best whenever we went out. I unintentionally upset her when I told her that I would find it difficult to have pictures of her around the house because I knew it would cause me real heartache. She started crying and begged me not to forget her.

I answered, "How on earth could I ever forget someone who'd been the centre of my universe for over 34 years?"

She was happy with that reply.

Trisha's dear Aunt Pattie, died on 3 March 2008, after a short illness. Soon afterwards, we went to Pattie's home at Fairhaven in Churchtown along with John to clear out the house ready for sale. Who'd have thought then that just one dreadful year later Trisha would also be nearing the end of her life.

Throughout most of 2010, I contemplated what to do with the rest of my life, and whilst I never dismissed the fact that I might one day find another soulmate, lover or companion, I wasn't actively looking. My attitude was that if it was meant to happen then I'd happily let fate play its hand. But on the other hand, I began to miss the companionship.

I really couldn't see myself continuing in the MoD, but on the other hand, I still wanted to keep myself active not only physically but also mentally—decisions, decisions. Once I'd decided that I was going to leave the MoD, I applied for a one-day *retirement* course. The course was oriented around those aspects associated with finishing full-time employment and covered a multitude of areas and subjects in the hope that the transition would be straightforward and organised.

There were 15 or so other attendees on the course and we each in turn had to introduce ourselves, give a brief explanation as to the type of work we were currently involved in and whether or not we had drawn up any specific retirement plans. Because I'd already made up my mind that I was going to retire come what may, I'd more or less decided the avenue that I wanted to concentrate on.

Due to my project management experience, my background in the building industry, DIY and my organisational propensity I fancied getting involved with charity work abroad. I searched the internet and came across a local charity that quite simply fitted the bill.

Just a Drop

The *Just-a-Drop* charity specialised in providing clean drinking water and sanitation to villages situated in remote areas across Africa and India. The president was a gentleman named John Blashford Snell, an ex-Army Colonel who was extremely well known within the world of exploration. I believe it was him and his team that were the first to successfully navigate the Blue Nile.

I contacted John via email; telling him of my interest and arranged a meeting to discuss what I might have to offer. The *Just-a-Drop* charity shared John's expedition headquarters in the village of Motcombe in Dorset.

John believed that I potentially had a lot to offer to the charity and put me in touch with the relatively newly appointed project coordinator, John Purefoy (JP), who lived in South Petherton, another pretty little Somerset village. I first met JP in February of 2011. He explained his role within the charity and spoke enthusiastically about how people's lives can be totally transformed just by providing something, that we, in the developed, take so much for granted.

He was at pains to point out that the charity carried out similar work to the Water Aid Charity only on a much smaller scale, and finances, as one would expect, were tight. I was told that if I did join the charity the only element that would be paid for would be the flights to and from the country of interest.

Everything else including relevant accommodation, food and subsistence would have to be self-funded. That presented no problems at all for me. He earnestly believed that my attributes could be put to good use and JP asked for a copy of my CV.

It was in March of that year that the MoD decided that there were to be more redundancies and I decided to put my name on the list of volunteers. As time progressed, I kept in touch with JP and in the late summer I was informed that I was one of the successful applicants and I was to be made redundant on 10 October 2011.

I immediately informed JP and met with him and Melissa, his newly appointed deputy project manager and arrangements were made for me to start work with the charity on 13 October, a mere three days after leaving the MoD. I was told that initially I would be reviewing old projects and going through all the documentation associated with those projects which would culminate in a trip to Uganda just before or soon after Christmas 2011.

I celebrated my 60th birthday on the 24 September with family and friends and was very proud to announce that the charity had accepted me.

A few days before my retirement day I received a call from JP asking to reschedule my start date to 20 October, which was fine, at least it would give me a little more time to get used to the fact that paid employment was at an end. The 10th dawned and after 43 years of a working life, that was to be my final day.

Tradition dictates that the team leader carries out a presentation, listing achievements, thank-yous and the like to the rest of the team. And so, just before lunch, the project team were called to the floorplate where Captain Richard McAlwain carried out the solemn duty of getting rid of me. After the routine slander and giving of gifts I was asked to say a few words.

Apart from the standard expressions of gratitude, I then told everyone how very pleased I was to be able to announce that I was soon to start work with the charity and would be leaving for Uganda within a few months. I received a tumultuous round of applause and best wishes—and that was it. I'd been looking forward to leaving for so long but when the moment actually arrived and I handed in my I.D. card to security, it dawned on me that I was once again at a crossroads in my life.

I was keen to start with the charity and arrived at Motcombe just before 10:00 on the morning of 20 October, as agreed. I met Melissa, who offered me a cup of tea and she told me that since our meeting only a few weeks previously they'd had a change of mind. As of then, the charity was looking for a civil engineer who was experienced in the water and sanitation discipline to carry out the work. WHAT!

I didn't say much, I was gutted and struggled to come to terms with what I was being told. Instant repartee was never been one of my strong points and I couldn't think of a quick reply apart from *why*?

What really pissed me off was that JP didn't have the decency to be there and tell me himself. After all, it was he who I'd negotiated with and it was he who had asked for my start date to be rescheduled, but instead, he left it to his side-kick to do the dirty work.

I was then told that there was still plenty of work that needed to be done which I could help out with—the main one being to set up a new database and file the masses of documents held in the office—Filing? Filing?

She couldn't be Fu**ing serious, could she?

To think, I'd given up a £36,000 salary to become nothing more than an unpaid filing clerk! She then went on to add that she didn't believe that I'd want to do that. How bloody right she was. I finished my tea and walked out.

As I drove back to Somerton my mind was in a real mess. After all of the anticipation and the preparation that I'd carried out ready to tell people of my pride and pleasure at being able to help those a lot less fortunate than most people in the UK. I was incredibly pissed off. How could circumstances change so quickly in such a short space of time?

Whilst I had JP's telephone number, I was in no mood to talk with him, instead, I emailed him and asked for an explanation. The main thrust of my anger was centred on the fact that if there was ever the slightest hint of doubt as to my suitability, why was I kept hanging on? If my attributes were not quite what the charity wanted, why wasn't I told much earlier?

I could have handled the rejection but to have to wait for almost seven months to be told on my first day that I wasn't what they wanted was a real slap in the face. It was at least a week before I received a reply from JP and its content didn't surprise me. It was full of all sorts of *bullshit* which seemed to concentrate on his relative newness to the project, the changes that were going on within the charity world and how much reliance there was on financial accountability.

Fine, all of the projects I'd been involved with whilst at Yeovilton were centred on accountability. My first project was valued at some £36M, the next £10M and if I could handle some of the crap that went on in that world, I know that I was more than capable of handling what was required in the charity world.

There was no mention of my technical ability or competence (or lack of it) and he apologised for what had happened. What a load of cock and bollocks! His reply still didn't explain why I wasn't told earlier.

Chapter Twenty-Eight
Being Widowed

"In this world, nothing can be said to be certain, except death and taxes"

Unfortunately, unless a couple die together, being widowed is the inevitable outcome of all partnerships or marriages that don't end up with either separation or divorce. It will happen to each and every one of us sooner or later. When one partner dies, the love of your life is lost—the person on whom you've relied for physical and emotional support.

There's no right or wrong way to grieve and there's no telling how long it may take. Bereavement affects different people in many different ways. Everyone is unique but healing takes time and uses up an awful lot of energy.

The adage 'Time is a great healer' is true. And, in my case, the first year to 18 months was probably the worst. I spent a great deal of time at work and found it difficult and upsetting coming home on a dark, cold, winter night to an empty house—the best recourse after eating dinner and tidying up was to go to bed early and sleep. After the first year, I'd accumulated several hours of flexi time and a couple of weeks of unused leave, neither of which I managed to use.

For months after Trisha had gone, I had real difficulty when visiting somewhere that we'd previously visited together. It didn't matter where it was, it could have been somewhere as innocuous as shopping in a particular store, visiting a pub or restaurant or driving along a specific road. I felt absolutely wretched.

The first time I went on my own to Lidl and Sainsbury's in Street was heartbreaking; the reason, I'd been into those stores with Trisha who was in a wheelchair. But the time ultimately came when I had no choice and had to go to all of those different places and as it happened, I began to feel comfortable.

The day after Valentine's Day 2012, I was dreaming of Trisha. In the dream, she bent over me and gave me such a passionate kiss that I awoke with quite a start—it felt so real I was absolutely convinced that she was in the bedroom.

Throughout our married life, we never had a will, it really was a case of *we must do it* and always putting it off until tomorrow. Thank God, nothing happened to either of us. However, one of the very first things we did once Trisha was diagnosed was to arrange a visit to a Solicitor.

We'd heard that there was a legal scheme whereby if one partner dies the survivor cannot be forced to sell the home to cover care fees in the future. The principal requirement was that the house had to be registered as *tenants-in-common*.

In this situation, each person owns their share of their home outright, which means they can bequeath it to whoever they wish on their death. Assuming that the first person to die hasn't left their share to the surviving spouse, then this half of the property has to be discounted and the council cannot force the sale and count the whole property towards the survivor's assets for means testing.

However, if the home is registered as *joint tenants,* then on the first death that person's share goes automatically to the other person and the entire property will count towards a means testing assessment. The will was very quickly drawn up and signed by all parties.

I told the boys that they jointly owned half of the value of the house and half of the value of our joint savings. Their response was excellent. They were both thankful that Trisha had bequeathed her half of the house but they weren't interested in the money.

Trisha and I had planned on buying a Mazda MX5 Roadster sports car when the time and finances were right and it was Steven who suggested that I go ahead and buy the car anyway. I didn't need much more of an excuse and bought a new top-of-the-range model in the summer of 2009. Throughout all of our married life, apart from the first few years, we were never really strapped for cash.

However, we never squandered what spare money we had, and as mentioned earlier we tried to save for Trisha's benefit should I die first. One of the most difficult phases I went through following Trisha's death was spending money on items that once upon a time if I'd bought them, I would have considered as extravagant.

The very first item was an *iPod* music system, which months earlier, I wouldn't have dreamed of buying. I spent a small fortune on clothes and shoes for work and leisure and generally, if I saw something I fancied, then I would buy it. Neither of us were extravagant, but reflecting on it now, I'm torn between believing that my urge to spend stemmed from years of frugality or that I was simply embracing a carefree attitude, fully aware that from that moment onward, I only needed to look out for myself.

The sad thing was that just two short months before Trisha's devastating diagnosis we had made the final payment on our 25-year-old mortgage; it was a real kick in the teeth. We had so many plans. Two years earlier, I was promoted to a Senior PTO, and at last, I was on a pretty reasonable wage.

I had a good index-linked RAF pension and Trisha was to later receive a substantial sum of money in Aunt Pattie's will. For the first time in all of our married life, we had money to spend and enjoy but alas, fate stepped in to deny us that pleasure—isn't life a real bummer?

I'd fancied a shotgun for a while having been introduced to the sport when I arrived at Yeovilton and spent an afternoon at Podimore Clay Pigeon Club with some work colleagues. Pete and I subsequently went to Southern Counties Club and I bought a gun which he looked after whilst my licence was being processed. Before the licence could be approved, protocol dictated that a firearms police officer was required to meet with and assess the proposed licence holder.

A very pleasant police officer came from Yeovil and quizzed me as to why I wanted a gun and so on. He then asked who else lived with me. When I told him that I'd recently been widowed he stopped in his tracks and for a moment I thought that may well be an excuse for the licence to be denied.

He was obviously thinking that I wanted the gun to kill myself and did ask if I'd had any thoughts of self-harming. All I said was that in the very early days, those thoughts had entered my mind, but I soon dismissed them when I realised that I'd only cause more distress to the family.

He went on to suggest that once I'd got my gun, if ever I should get suicidal thoughts, then I should phone Pete and ask him to come take the gun off me. Now, I'm obviously not a physiologist but surely if I wanted to kill myself, the last thing that I would contemplate would be to try and get someone to stop me, especially as Pete lived 45 miles away!

On a practical level, there was an assortment of tasks which needed to be sorted and not left unattended—probate being the main one. I guess that fulfilling these roles, alone and unsupported, may well be an overwhelming task for some. Fortunately, it didn't bother me.

From day one of our marriage, I had always managed our finances, we'd always had a joint bank account and whatever we had was shared and nothing *whatsoever* was hidden. The majority of our savings were held in Trisha's name—a method of ensuring that her personal tax allowance was utilised to the full.

Quite bizarrely, Trisha had mentioned only a few months before being diagnosed that she knew very little about internet banking and commented that if something happened to me, she wouldn't have a clue where to start; I promised to show her! I don't think she would have struggled; she wasn't stupid and she had a good, sound head on her shoulders.

Towards the end of the first year, the intensity of my grief did ease a little but, I still felt uneasy.

The thought of starting a new relationship was never far away but Trisha's immortal words, "Watch out for Slappers and Gold diggers," soon reined them in.

Even in my youth, I'd only ever had a couple of girlfriends, nothing serious, because I was always quite shy, although I never seemed to have much difficulty in talking with the opposite sex. I've always thought of myself as a sincere sort of person and wouldn't dream of taking advantage of anyone either emotionally or otherwise. I certainly wasn't into one-night stands. Many people enter a new relationship just for companionship, although some may feel guilty about this. Others may choose to stay alone.

In all of our 34 years together, I never strayed or went with another woman, although, there certainly was every opportunity to *play away* considering my many detachments and overnight trips. Trisha once told me, she didn't mind me looking at other women but I wasn't to pass comment and never, ever, ever was I to touch.

And anyway, after all the matchmaking that Tom and Edith had carried out, if I had strayed, I'm sure they would have haunted me for all eternity. Apart from that, the wedding vows "till death do us part" actually meant something to both of us. Even now, Trisha and I may be bodily parted but, in my heart, soul and mind she will always be there—no matter who else comes along.

I cannot possibly fault the love, concern and support shown to me by Ange and Ian, Wendy and Rob, Gillian and Pete, Mike and Julie, Steven and Francesca, neighbours and my many work colleagues. As mentioned earlier, Trisha did say to me only a week or so before she died that when she was gone, she didn't want me to be lonely.

To date, I haven't felt particularly lonely. However, loneliness is a strange beast insofar as I have lots going on in my life. But on occasions, I do feel isolated. The analogy that best explains that feeling can be summarised by what Ester Ransom said following the death of her husband, Desmond Wilcox. She said:

"I have some people to do something with, but I have nobody to do nothing with."

Chapter Twenty-Nine
A New Beginning?

"A time will come when you believe that everything is over—not so, it's just the beginning."

And so, as I finish this journal, I'm reflecting on my life, I don't think it's been too bad, there have been ups and downs but nothing really out of the ordinary. We're not here for long, so please make the most of every moment. This fact is very often forgotten, and we get caught up in our own individual missions and desires.

We think we have forever and a day and in one way, we may be correct—for are we not eternal spirits, temporarily residing in some finite physical form? I thank God for my life, my family and my friends.

As you grow up, you'll have your heart broken more than once and it's harder each time. You'll break hearts too, so remember how it felt. You'll disagree with your best friend. You'll cry because time is passing too fast, and you'll eventually lose someone you really love.

And so, take lots of pictures, laugh too much and love like you've never been hurt, because for every 60 seconds you spend upset, is a minute of happiness you will never, ever get back. Remember, one day you'll wake up and there's no more time to do the things you always wanted to do—do it now! Time is like a river; you cannot touch the water twice because the flow that has passed will never pass again. Enjoy every moment of your life.

Chapter Thirty
Philosophy for Old Age

Losing Trisha was a truly dreadful experience and one that has made me reflect and realise what the true meaning of life really is. I've been very fortunate so far not only with my health, relatively speaking, but also with my finances. I have some fantastic family members and friends. What follows is a list of observations, values and principles that I believe everyone should embrace:

1. Do you realise that the only time in our lives when we like to get old is when we're kids? If you're less than 10 years old you think in fractions.
   'How old are you?'
   'I'm four and a half.'
   You're four and a half, going on five…that's the key.
2. You get to your teens, now they can't hold you back. You jump to the next number or even higher.
   'How old are you?'
   'I'm gonna be 16!' You could be 13 but you're gonna be 16.
3. And then the greatest day of your life…you become 21.
   Even the words sound like a ceremony. You become 21…Yes!
4. But then you turn 30, Oh!
   What's happened then, it makes you sound like bad milk.
   'He has *turned*; may as well throw him out. There's no fun now, you're just a sour dumpling. What's wrong, what's changed?'
5. You *become* 21, You *turn* 30, and then you're *pushing* 40…whoa. Put the brakes on, it's all slipping away.
6. Before you know it, you *reach* the age of 50 and your dreams have gone.
7. But wait, you *make* it to 60, you didn't think you would.

8. And so, you *become* 21, *turn* 30, *push* 40, *reach* 50 and *make* 60. You've built up so much speed that you *hit* 70, after that, it's a day-by-day thing.
9. You get into your 80s and every day is a complete cycle…you *hit* lunch, you *turn* 4:30 and you *reach* bedtime.
10. And it doesn't end there, into the 90s you start going backwards; I *was* just 92.
11. And then, a strange thing happens. If you make it to 100, you become like a kid again. 'I'm 100 and a half.'
12. And to finish with:

The Train

At birth, we boarded the train and met our parents, and we believed that they would always be with us. As time goes by, other people will board the train and their presence will be significant, for example, siblings, friends, children and even the love of your life.

However, at some stations, our parents will step down from the train, leaving us on this journey alone. Others will step down over time and leave a permanent vacuum, some however, will go unnoticed and we don't notice that they have vacated their seats. This train ride will be full of joy, sorrow, fantasy, expectations, hellos, goodbyes and farewells.

Success consists of having a good relationship with all passengers requiring that we give the best of ourselves.

The mystery to everyone is, that we do not know at which station we ourselves will step down, and so, we must live in the best way we can, love, forgive and offer the best of who we are.

It is important to do this because when the time comes for us to step down and leave our seats empty; we should leave behind beautiful memories for those who will continue to travel on the train of life.

"I wish you all a joyful journey."